Second Language Learning:
Theoretical Foundations

APPLIED LINGUISTICS AND LANGUAGE STUDY

General Editor
Professor Christopher N. Candlin, Macquarie University

For a complete list of books in this series see pages xxiii–xxiv.

Second Language Learning:
Theoretical Foundations

Michael Sharwood Smith

Longman
London and New York

Longman Group UK Limited,
Longman House, Burnt Mill,
Harlow, Essex CM20 2JE, England
and Associated Companies throughout the world.

Published in the United States of America
by Longman Publishing, New York

© Longman Group UK Limited 1994

First published 1994

ISBN 0 582 218861 PPR

British Library Cataloguing-in-Publication Data

A catalogue record for this book is
available from the British Library

Library of Congress Cataloging-in-Publication Data

Sharwood Smith, Michael, 1942–
    Second language learning : theoretical foundations / M.A. Sharwood
Smith.
        p.   cm. — (Applied linguistics and language study)
    Includes bibliographical references and index.
    ISBN 0–582–21886–1
    1. Second language acquisition.   2. Interlanguage (Language
learning)   I. Title.   II. Series.
P118.2.S55   1994
418—dc20   93–33640
                                                                CIP

Set by 8 in 10 on 12pt Ehrhardt
Produced through Longman Malaysia, TCP

To Kirsty and Ania

Contents

92905

General Editor's Preface

Twenty-five years (or thereabouts) since the beginnings of a field of academic study might be a good moment to take stock, to explore boundaries, objectives and achievements, to assess positioning in relation to epistemological questions of disciplinary identity and to chart fresh research directions, explore engagements with theory and assess potential for applications. This latest contribution to the *Applied Linguistics and Language Study* series from Michael Sharwood Smith can serve as such a stocktaking, though as readers will readily see, its value is not at all only historical. The book is no mere critical archive. Nor is the book only directed at its chosen subject-matter, *second language acquisition* (SLA); much more than that, it argues a case for identity and identification in any new subject-matter – here the acquisition of a second language – where natural disciplinary allies, here principally linguistics, psychology, sociology and pedagogy, pose natural threats to such identity while at the same time providing the wherewithall for the sourcing of the new subject-matter's disciplinary self-sufficiency. After all, if one posed the question (as the author does) '*how on earth do people learn new languages?*' and offered a research fund for its solving, many scholars in those contributory disciplines would believe it their appropriate and even exclusive right to apply. In this charting of the identity and substance of a particular field of inquiry this book has thus much more general scholarly relevance. This is especially so in its engagement with the often contentious relationship between theory and practice, and the issue of which theory to choose among contenders in the field. From a reading of this book, historians of social science could do worse than to choose the disciplinary emergence of second language acquisition as a criterial case for their inquiries.

How then can one capture the central themes addressed here by Dr Sharwood Smith? One might recall some of the issues that had a vibrancy twenty-five years ago and which, clearly form this book, continue to engage the field. There are perhaps three such central issues: that of *directionality*, that of *directness*, and that of *direction*.

Directionality goes to the heart of the question of identity and identification. It asks of some new intellectual endeavour the extent to which its authors see their task as primarily drawing on the existing knowledge encapsulated in other disciplines or whether, more dynamically, they see their innovation as making some reflexive contribution to current disciplinary knowledge. Corder (who many with justice identify as the founding father of SLA) devoted much time to that issue in relationship to the discipline of applied linguistics as a whole (to which, though nowadays much more contentiously than then, some SLA researchers have a weakening allegience), asking whether applied linguistics was characteristically linguistics applied or whether its relationship to its 'parent' was more mutually engaging and influential. Michael Sharwood Smith makes a convincing case that such a question is to be answered not in terms of asserting some article of faith but against the experience of history. Directionality is a construct whose nature it is to evolve. As principles are adopted and applied they are necessarily revalued, especially against novel data, and if the communciations are right, the influences work back.. Readers of this book will clearly see this process identified, and not, of course, merely in relation to linguistics. What they will also notice, however, is that such mutuality is neither to be taken for granted nor is its existence or its pervasiveness uniform. One would have to ask, for example, to what extent *does* SLA research figure as a contributing discipline to curricula and research agenda in psychology, linguistics, education? After twenty-five years we are only at the beginning of such mutuality. Territoriality and interdirectionality appear to make the best cocktail. Perhaps the issue here is in part the identification by these other disciplines of what SLA is. Reading this book will greatly assist them in such identification, and yet, although there *is* considerable consensus about the research agendas of SLA, there is still considerable variation in the ways SLA researchers theorize and practice. Take for example the key constructs of any theory: its principles, its objectives, its admissible evidence, the relationship between such evidence and the formulation of principle, the matter of methodology. As Dr Sharwood Smith's book makes clear, all these key concerns are still in debate. Indeed, it is often more personalized; *whose* SLA obscures for many the prior identifying question: *what* SLA?

Our second issue, that of *directness*, addresses one of the author's central concerns in this book, the relationship between theory and practice. In his *Introducing Applied Linguistics* Corder spoke of levels or *orders* of directness in such a relationship. It was foolish, he implied, for practitioners (and at that time there was really only one sort of practitioner as far as SLA was concerned, namely the language educator) to assume that research results could be chalked up on some Monday's blackboard (though some of them were) and, equally (though he was too polite to say it) researchers in SLA ought to turn to guard against seeking credibility (or notoriety) for their theorizing by promising instant applicability. Given the worldwide investment in language teaching, a discipline which identifies the successful language acquisition of the second language learner as its main objective and the processes of such acquisition as its main theoretical justification, it was in hindsight too sanguine to have expected that Corder's sensible injunction would have prevented some language teachers from homing in on SLA as the theoretical answer to their practical prayers. Indeed, at worst presuming the support of theory and at best hoping against hope for it, a good deal of language teaching has shown itself in the recent past all too ready to assume some direct linkage between the theoretical speculations and the laboratory experiments of SLA and its own legitimate practical concerns. At the same time, there is plenty of evidence that teachers who understandably seek some external rationalization of their own informal theories, have been prey to snake oil salespersons with a theory to grind. This is especially the case where in some documented instances, whole school systems have declared themselves for a particular under-researched theory, rather like some latterday Reformation zealots. Indeed, in some unfortunate cases mass baptisms have been followed, quite typically, by personal ideological vendettas. Against this Sharwood Smith's book is an important antidote. It is refreshingly clear about directness. Although perhaps too categorically for some, he draws clear boundaries between theory and practice and within SLA the distinctions between research which is theory-focused and that which is application-focused. As elsewhere, perspective and purpose are the key concerns that matter. The structure of the book helps to reinforce this discrimination. From a critical and evaluative survey – the *quick round tour* – of Part One, the book addresses key SLA constructs of learner systems, creative construction and interlanguage analysis. Here, for many readers, the discussion can be usefully linked to other recent publications in the *Applied Linguistics and Language Study* series, namely the book by Larsen-Freeman and Long and that by Selinker. In Part Two we see how the issue of *directionality* is itself indirectly affected by that of *directness*. The author shows how the matter of variability in SLA was itself influenced quite explicitly by sociolinguistic studies of variation in linguistics and discourse analysis and how the outcomes of such studies of variability in product began to impact on cognitive questions of variability in process and the relationship between knowledge and control. It is at this point that the book takes an original turn in that rather than focus unprofitably on matters of applicability to practice, it explores in considerable but clear detail how SLA data can be used to evaluate competing theoretical explanations of the acquisition process and its outcomes. Here directness, in terms of the explanatory or understanding value of documentation, is given importance *within* theory and not only externally in terms of applicability to practice. Epistemologically, the debate here and especially in Part Three (Sharwood Smith's *'Coming of Age'* of SLA) surrounds the issue of absolutism versus relativism within theory. One might even say, to paraphrase Hockett, the god's truth SLA versus the hocus-pocus. A careful reading of the highly significant Part Three shows how the author eschews the extremes, avoiding the emptiness of relativism and the dogmatism of a theoretical singlemindedness. If one could ask for anything here one might wish for a larger dash of another contributing discipline to SLA, one, however, which has not had until late as much of an influence as it might. The debates charted here are, as we have indicated earlier, not limited to SLA. They are characteristic within the philosophy of science and philosophy *tout court*. Discussion within SLA of debates within philosophy concerning method, in particular debates informed by the introduction of documented research practice, would, I am convinced, elevate the status of the hermeneutics inherent in much current scientific inquiry to a greater place. It would also direct us away from an obsession with causality and point out the necessary transitoriness of theory. Such a focus might do much to obviate the wish for some simple directness of relationship between theory and practice, emphasizing the important reflexivity of research and application, whether or not one went further (and it would be further than the objectives of this book) towards the social theoretical implications of praxis.

What then of our third issue, that of *direction*? Again, we may speak theoretically and practically. In practical terms, I have earlier alluded to the probably unhelpful convergence of SLA with language pedagogy. There are many other disciplines eligible for such a relationship, notably first language acquisition, and the study of communication disorders. As others have done, Dr Sharwood Smith rightly emphasizes the links between SLA and bilingualism and draws on both sociological and cognitive research in this field in his exploration of the construct of *strategy*. More closely linked to pedagogy is that of language testing and assessment; useful connections are beginning between SLA research into fluent behaviour and its evaluation. After all, *fluency* as a construct is extensively drawn upon by language testers but quite typically as some undefined given. More excitingly, combinations of disciplines offer themselves as productive links with SLA. Research into the cognitive aspects of bilingualism, focusing especially on the acquisition of second, third and fourth languages, and within particular sociolinguistic and sociological milieux, and for particular populations both ordered and disordered, offers great potential, not only in its own descriptive right but as a source for explanatory evidence for acquisition *per se*. That there will then be diagnostic rewards from such an interdisciplinary direction to study is entirely likely, though *indirectly*, as Corder made very clear. More than new directions in practice, however, this book argues for new directions in theory and in theory building. Current debates on theorizing in SLA may need some diversion if, as some have detected, they are pointing towards absolutism. This book is an important corrective to the path of the exclusive brethren. In saying this I declare a personal preference: Luther has always (though not in all his works) seemed a more congenial model to me than Calvin. Leaping at this point several disciplinary gates, readers of this book could do worse than to read carefully on this point Michael Sharwood Smith's final chapter on *Implications and Applications*. Having done that, if they don't then go to bed like Mr Macmillan to solve the problems of the interrelationship of theory and practice with a good Trollope they might at least try Spinoza or, if they were really daring, Bourdieu.

On reading this important book we may claim to have arrived at a time, then, for some more mature reflection within SLA. A time, perhaps, when the bases of its theoretical claims can be more closely examined in its historical and contemporary context and its epistemology explored. A time to weigh up what we mean by 'application' anyway and to assert (if we needed to) that not only does a sound theory need no practical sauce but if it does have application, its range of potential applicability and the effect of that in turn on theory, cannot be predicted. We might agree we need a book which argues a case, one which while retaining a certain scepticism about its still volatile subject-matter, sees its role as offering an informed, impartial yet critical account, providing evidence where this is available, and not being shy to own up to speculation where no evidence is to hand and, above all, to be honestly personal about directions in the disciplinary field. In my view, Michael Sharwood Smith, in authoring *Second Language Learning: Theoretical Foundations*, has produced just such a book.

Professor Christopher N. Candlin
General Editor
Macquarie University, Sydney

Author's Preface

How on earth do people learn new languages? Even today, the way in which language learners gain knowledge and skill in a language that is not their mother tongue is still very much of a mystery. What research in the last decade or so has shown is that even the early stages must be accomplished with the help of subconscious psychological processes of great subtlety. Second language acquisition can be seen as a real cognitive feat on the part of the learner. Second language knowledge or 'competence' is gained via many processes which we are only just beginning to understand. A study of the language performance of any kind of second language learner can lead to insights about the external and internal mechanisms that drive and inhibit language development.

This area of investigation may be referred to as 'second language research' but it is also known, in various teaching institutions across the world, by various other terms such as 'SLA' (second language acquisition), 'psycholinguistics' and 'interlanguage studies'. From one point of view, it should be seen as most immediately related to *first* language acquisition studies looking at the psychological processes underlying mother tongue development. Indeed, child language bears some resemblance to non-native learner language or 'interlanguage'. At the same time, second language research, in that linguistic development takes place in given social contexts, also involves sociolinguistic concerns. The cognitive feat, once accomplished, implies new social resources and new behaviour. And it is also about second language users that have ceased developing and may even be 'losing' their language. Here, second language research merges with research into what is normally called 'bilingualism'.

Over the last decade there has been an explosion of literature on this new subject. This book is aimed at providing the reader (teachers, students and full-time researchers) with a reasonably up-to-date survey and analysis of second learning theory without covering all aspects of the field exhaustively. We still await separate accounts of second language lexical theory or second language phonological theory, for example. This book will focus on that part of the literature that has tried to guide the psychological analysis of learner language in general and will attempt to demonstrate the development of ideas in the subject and give an idea of the state of things in the 1990s. Inevitably it is an account that is tinted by my personal vision of second language research past, present and future.

This book is divided into three parts. To see how different perspectives on acquisition and performance have been expressed by different models and different metaphors, a historical analysis of research carried out in various parts of the world in the 1970s and 1980s is provided: this begins with the pioneering proposals of Corder, Nemser and Selinker. This is something which might usually be passed over cursorily as simply 'historical context' but which is used here as a way of illustrating the way in which people's thought processes develop as they consider the facts of second language behaviour more and more carefully. Readers are invited, so to speak, to develop their own understanding of second language theory by following the history of the subject. This is meant to be as a precursor to later chapters which comprise an account of the most recent trends and various implications are drawn both for future second language research itself and for people wishing to apply this research to other areas of activity. An interim section (the second part) comprises a discussion of theoretical problems arising from early approaches and touches on a number of alternative approaches that were tried.

This book also provides some study questions and activities as well as practical guidelines on the use of available research resources. The aim is that the discussion should act as a stimulus to further critical reading in specialist areas within the field for those who wish to do research in this area. It should also provide useful information for students in other related disciplines such as bilingualism, first language acquisition, and various branches of applied linguistics. Fairly extensive use is made of graphical illustrations (diagrams of models) which may help some readers more than others. For the selective reader, the first three chapters should provide a brief overview of the essential concepts and controversies in modern second language research.

Various research frameworks are dealt with. This means that the book will not involve detailed descriptions of empirical studies that have taken place over the last fifteen years. These can be studied at source, in the literature or gleaned from other books which provide more detail of this kind. Such studies will be employed here first and foremost as examples of attempts to treat second language learning in a truly scientific fashion. The topics to be discussed will include the role of mother tongue influence, the contribution of conscious processes in learning, and the differences and similarities between second or foreign learner language and child language development. If this introduction to the field has a bias, it is in its focus on theory-building, on the development of ideas, hence the importance of following up any leads by consulting the sources mentioned in the text and in the section on research tools.

It should be noted that second language is a very broad area, not just syntax and morphology, and this includes such aspects as phonology, pragmatics and the lexicon: however, despite some interesting recent work in these fields, grammar has occupied the centre of the theoretical stage and inevitably receives the lion's share of attention in this book. Also, the theorising about non-native grammar has inspired theoretical thinking in pragmatics, phonology and lexis. In other words, a more grammar-related discussion can also serve as a partial introduction to these other aspects of non-native language acquisition as well.

To help those readers who wish to use this book as a course book, either as students or instructors, a number of supplementary aids are provided in addition to the research tools section and the questions and discussion topic section, namely two glossaries, a short preliminary one in section 1.2 and a longer one at the end. The reader may adopt various strategies in reading this book. The (relative) beginner, and the reader more interested in practical applications, might skip the sixth and seventh chapters.

Acknowledgements are due, in particular, to: Lydia White, Peter Skehan, Bill Rutherford, Eric Kellerman, Paul van Buren, Bonnie Schwartz and James Pankhurst and, of course, a number of anonymous reviewers who have commented on earlier versions of this book as well as colleagues at Utrecht, notably Wolfgang Herrlitz and Gerard Westhoff who took the trouble to read and comment on a more recent version and, finally my perspicacious editor Chris Candlin. Apologies are due to those many friends and colleagues not cited here, or not cited enough, but who have nonetheless contributed in one way or another to the formation of ideas discussed in the various chapters that follow.

Michael Sharwood Smith, 1993

Acknowledgements

The publishers are grateful to the following for permission to reproduce copyright material:

Cambridge University Press for Figure 1.1 from article by M.A. Sharwood Smith 'Input enhancement in instructed SLA' in *Studies in Second Language Acquisition* 15: p. 168. 1993; Georgetown University Press, Washington D.C., U.S.A. for our Figure 3.2, being Figure 2 on page 225 from Heidi C. Dulay and Marina K. Burt, 'Strategies of Child Second Language Acquisition' in Dato, Daniel P., *Developmental Psycholinguistics: Theory and Applications [Georgetown University Round Table on Languages and Linguistics 1975]*

PART I:
Towards Theory

1   A quick round tour

1.0   Introduction

To know only one language is abnormal. At least this is what the statistics say. The majority of people on this globe can call themselves speakers of at least two languages even if their mastery of each language is not identical. Pure monolingualism is a result either of physical isolation from speakers of other languages or it is the result of cultural isolation. The latter type means that, in an area where more than one language is spoken, the dominant group of language speakers insists that its mother tongue is the standard way of communicating. For them, mastering any other language spoken in the area in question is thus rendered unnecessary.

Some people even believe that learning a second language can be harmful, at least in the case of young children. Might not children end up being non-native in any language, having no language to call their own? All the false ideas spread about the ill effects of bilingualism seem to stem from a fear of loss of identity and/or a loss of domination in a particular community. People actually living in established multilingual communities do not necessarily have this problem. Research does not show that bilingualism is a disadvantage unless, of course, bilinguals are discriminated against. It can even be an advantage.

This book, despite the above remarks, is not about the joys or woes of being bilingual. It is about the processes of becoming bilingual. More particularly it is about the psychological mechanisms that enable us to accomplish this feat even if we do not become indistinguishable from native speakers of the target language.

The notion of bilingualism (or multilingualism) as used in this book is a *relative* concept ranging from a hesitant command of a fledgling system to a fluent and sophisticated command of a second or other language. There have been many attempts to throw light on these mechanisms and the intention here is to give some idea of the various options that have been considered so far. This chapter introduces some important concepts in second language research together with the basic terminology. The aim is to give the reader a feel for the subject and the basic thinking that underlies it. All the

3

concepts introduced in this chapter will be elaborated on in later chapters. A more numerous and detailed list of terms is provided in the glossary at the end of the book.

1.1   Pure and applied studies

Where does the study of second language learning best fit in? Is it an arm of the language teaching enterprise or is it part of some much more theoretical field? One key concept in second language research, which dates back to the late 1960s when the field of second language acquisition (SLA) was in its infancy, provides the best introduction to this issue. The most widely known term for this concept is 'interlanguage' (IL). It most generally refers to *systematic non-native linguistic behaviour*. Learners, i.e. non-native speakers, are seen to be in possession of their own language system. They are not viewed as simply having a cocktail of errors and non-errors. Put another way, their systematic performance shows them to be speakers of a sort of dialect of the language (an IL). Interlanguage may be contrasted with native language (NL).

In its attitude to learner behaviour, second language research parts company with the field of language-teaching methodology. Language teachers, like many language learners, typically focus on ways of bringing the learners' *current state of knowledge* into line with the knowledge of a native speaker: we might call their approach to learner behaviour 'target oriented'. Whatever learners know and do is related directly to the native target, i.e. to what they ought to know and do if they were native speakers. Deviance from the standard norms of the language is seen simply as the making of errors. The making of errors tells the teacher and learner what still has to be learned. Their errors are, for teacher and learner, not interesting phenomena in themselves. They just say where the learner 'goes wrong'.

The new area of second language research, on the other hand, is not target oriented. It focuses on the nature of a particular current state of knowledge in a given learner or group of learners. In other words, what the learner knows and does at a given stage in his or her learning career *is interesting as a phenomenon in its own right*. Hence, strictly speaking, the term 'error' is misleading since it both calls our attention to the difference between the learner's own system and the system of the native speaker and makes a negative value judgement about it. It is a target-oriented term. It is really more convenient to think of a learner as a native speaker of his or her own special dialect (Corder 1981).

The original impetus behind the study of learner language (interlanguage) might have been to provide a better base for language *teaching* strategies. The more we know about learning, the more, you might suppose, we should be able actively to influence learning. However, interlanguage studies, as an area which highlights language *learning* strategies, is more properly associated in the first instance with theoretical or experimental fields which purport to investigate the human language faculty. In a broader sense, it is part of cognitive science. That is to say, it is part of the general investigation into the workings of the human mind.

It should be added that although psychological and linguistic concerns have been uppermost in the field, second language research also has its place in sociology. Second language learning and use take place in a social context. The social behaviour of interlanguage users is, therefore, also to be viewed as an area of investigation within the broader framework of the social sciences. Conventionally, the social patterns exhibited by IL users are part of 'bilingual studies' rather than acquisition studies *per se.*

Ideally, second language researchers should, first and foremost, pursue their investigations without paying attention to the concerns of teachers. In practice, as was suggested above, IL research has often been done with reference to possible pedagogical applications. This has been because such studies were born as part of 'applied linguistics' and had the applied, i.e. practical, aim of facilitating *guided* language learning. It is not clear whether second language research or practical language teaching benefits from such a direct connection between pure and applied concerns. This is especially true at this rather early stage in the history of the field since researchers may become too eager (or feel too much pressure) to apply research prematurely to teaching and testing methodology.

Suppose someone found that, under certain conditions and with respect to certain limited grammatical constructions, drawing the learners' attention to the rules of grammar had absolutely no effect at all, no matter what technique was used. It would be only too easy to jump from this finding to a much more general claim that 'giving learners rules is a waste of time'. Actually, this is a fundamental tenet of some current language teaching methods. Such a research finding, incorrectly generalised, would seem to offer attractive scientific backing to people wishing to promote such methods to the exclusion of all others.

Research findings can be too rapidly applied to practical areas. Furthermore, there is the danger of a neglect of possible, interesting connections with other *non*-applied fields of research. If the primary goal is to advance our understanding of the processes of second language acquisition *irrespective of its relevance to teaching*, then second language acquisition research can profit from much closer links with first language research, psychology, linguistics and sociology.

It is useful, then, to accept the distinction in SLA studies between *pure* and *applied* research. The point is an important one given a general over-eagerness to make connections between second language research and more practical areas of activity. However, looking at matters from the opposite perspective, one can observe an equally warped view. There is no need to seal off second language research and let it live on in splendid isolation. In other words, non-applied research is frequently relevant to, for example, language teaching, to speech therapy, to the phenomenon of language awareness (among monolinguals and bilinguals), and any other problems experienced by bilingual communities. The plea is more for a certain *indirectness* in the relationship between what second language researchers' main concerns should be and the urgent and very specific needs of a given type of language practitioner. In view of the relative youth of second language research, this book will, then, focus on the non-applied domain although applied matters will receive some attention in the concluding chapter.

1.2   Basic terminology

Some terminology in this book will need to be interpreted within different theoretical perspectives. However, for ease of reading, some working definitions are first necessary. Various standard abbreviations also need to be mentioned: for example, 'interlanguage', which, as mentioned above, may be defined as referring to the *systematic linguistic behaviour of second language learners* (see below for the definition of 'second') will be used interchangeably with the abbreviation 'IL'. Readers more familiar with the psychological literature on the subjects covered will appreciate that specific theoretical assumptions are simply made here and not discussed. Any discussions that are necessary will be held over to later chapters. The annotated glossary will also serve as a foretaste of the interesting theoretical issues that a careful definition of terms gives rise to. A more extensive glossary is provided at the end of the book.

1.2.1 Second language (SL, TL, L2, L3)

'Second' language will normally stand as a cover term for *any language other than the first language learned by a given learner or group of learners a) irrespective of the type of learning environment and b) irrespective of the number of other non-native languages possessed by the learner.* This includes both 'foreign' languages (for example, French as a foreign language for Austrians) and languages which are not one's mother tongue but are nevertheless spoken regularly in one's own community (for example, French for English-speaking Canadians). 'Second' seems better than definitions such as 'secondary' or 'non-native' which imply lower status. 'Second language' is often abbreviated to 'L2' (as opposed to 'L1' – the mother tongue). An L2, then, means, unless otherwise specified, a particular 'non-native language under discussion', that is, the so-called 'target' language (TL). In certain circumstances, the more literal terms L3, L4, etc., may be also used as in 'the influence of a learner's L2 German upon her L3 Dutch'. Second language research is to be interpreted as covering a large area, including psychological, neurological, pragmatic and sociological aspects of L2 development and L2 use.

1.2.2 Interlanguage (IL)

IL most generally refers to *the systematic linguistic behaviour of learners of a second or other language*; in other words, learners of *non*-native languages. It calls our attention to the possibility of viewing learner language such as 'the Finnish of English learners of Finnish', for example, as possessing systematic features which can be studied in their own right. The idea is that they are not merely imperfect reflections of some norm – in this particular case that norm would be 'educated native speaker Finnish'.

The 'language' part of the term 'interlanguage' suggests this idea of an autonomous linguistic system while the 'inter' of 'interlanguage' reminds us that this version of Finnish is supposed to be a half-way house, an intermediate stage in the user's linguistic development. In using the term 'interlanguage' as a noun, it is best to keep to the behavioural definition. Essentially this means the language events that you can actually observe and record. It is not the invisible language *system*: this must exist somewhere in the mind of the user but we cannot perceive it directly. Interlanguage is, as it were, the bees and beehives we can see, touch, hear and smell and not the principles that dictate their shape and determine all the fascinating activities that we can observe. In this way we can talk about given samples of 'interlanguage' and speculate about the 'interlanguage system' that underlies it.

The terms 'interlanguage' and 'learner language' will be used interchangeably in this book. Without denying their sociological value, it can be said that interlanguage studies typically focus on the linguistic and psychological aspects of second language research. For the linguistic and mental systems underlying interlanguage, terms such as 'interlanguage system' or 'interlanguage grammar' or 'interlanguage lexicon' will be employed.

1.2.3 Input and intake

Another term which is widely used is 'input', taken from information processing. The most normal meaning in language acquisition research circles is *language data (utterances, texts) which the learner is exposed to:* that is, the learner's experience *of the target language in all its various manifestations.* Hence, 'input studies' are studies of the 'language bath', i.e. the actual language that the learner is exposed to. It does not include explanations and rules concerning language (see section 1.2.4) but just samples of language conveying messages.

'Input', taken literally, is a misleading term. Since we cannot know from observation alone exactly what is processed by the learner at a given moment in time, many utterances to which the learner is exposed to may contain elements which the learner does not register at all. In other words, the input 'data' may be registered on the researcher's tape recorder as having been *available* to the learner at a given time. The utterances or written texts, and the structures they contain, may be registered very clearly in the *teacher's* memory, where formal learning is concerned. However, whether they have been registered consciously or subconsciously by the *learner* is another matter. So, I will use 'input', unless otherwise specified, in the sense of *potentially processible language data made available to the learner.* That part of input which has actually been processed by the learner and turned into knowledge of some kind has been called *intake* (Corder 1981). Input is, as it were, the goods that are presented to the customer, including the articles that the customer picks up to look at.

Intake is what is actually bought and taken away from the shop, i.e. what passes into the ownership of the customer.

When interpreting and producing utterances, the learner makes use of non-linguistic input. Knowledge of the world together with a whole host of contextual cues may be used to enrich the information coming from the linguistic signal. By pointing at a car or making an appropriate noise, for example, the language user can convey the idea of a jet plane more clearly, especially when there is uncertainty about whether the 'jet plane' is the correct expression or is one which the listener will immediately be able to understand. However, when unspecified, input is conventionally assumed to be that part of the flow of information that is specifically linguistic. Non-linguistic information is, of course, vital for learning. Once the learner has linked the (linguistic) input 'jet plane' with the gesture and thus interpreted the message, then the possibility exists for a new word or set of words to enter the learner's developing lexicon.

It is important also to recognise that language proficiency either develops as a response to input or it fails to grow *despite* that input. Incoming signals may be processed for meaning alone. That means that learners may be exposed to target forms that could in principle force them to reorganise their interlanguage system but in fact do not bring about any change. Their interlanguage system may have them forming negative statements like 'I *no must* do it'. Being exposed to 'I *must not* do it' may not necessarily bring about a change in that system. They may have processed the utterance simply for meaning and not noticed and stored the different structure manifest in the input: their 'Language Acquisition Device' has not received the input. It has not become intake. Two examples are given in Figure 1.1 (using the star/asterisk: '*' to indicate 'non-native' forms).

From the output in Figure 1.1 we see that part of the relevant input has become intake. The learner can form negative statements and can use the verb 'run' with past meaning. However, what has been ignored is the position of 'not' in the first example and the irregular past form of 'run'. The learner has processed this part of

Input	Understood?	Learned?	Ouput
'I must not do it'	yes	no	*'I no must do it'
'I ran there'	yes	no	*'I runned there'

FIGURE 1.1   Input: learning versus only understanding.

the input according to his or her own IL system. Nevertheless, he or she has probably achieved 100 per cent comprehension of such messages despite the fact that the system has not been adjusted to produce exactly what was heard.

1.2.4   Metalanguage

In most normal everyday language use, we are not especially aware that we are following rules. We even select many of the words unthinkingly. When saying 'he was kissed' we do not consciously refer to a passive rule for constructing this passive sentence. We are more concerned with expressing our thoughts and understanding what people are saying. In other words, producing more or less correct utterances is not done in the same way that most of us solve a mathematical problem, where we consciously juggle with numbers. It is possible, however, to shift our attention to the sounds, letters, words and constructions we are using. If, for example, someone suddenly asks a question such as:

'What is the *word* for an animal you keep at home?'
'What *words* did she actually use when she refused?'
'What is another *way of saying* "I don't mind if I do"?'

then the listener's conscious attention is directed suddenly to the language itself and not just to meaning and messages. We could call this going into the *meta* mode.

'Metalanguage' (literally 'language about something') and its associated adjective 'metalinguistic' here refer to *ways in which language and particularly the language system is seen and exploited as an object of conscious attention*. Hence, a linguist or language teacher when drawing attention to the formal properties of a language (or interlanguage) will employ metalanguage – a set of terms to talk about language, for example:

'These *verbs* all take the *preposition* "of"'

Hence language awareness, here called 'metalinguistic awareness', is the awareness of language as an object. Such awareness may appear spontaneously in children who try to exploit it for their amusement by creating rhymes, and linguistic jokes (puns, word play). This is 'meta' because it involves inspecting the form of words and not only their meaning even though children, in the meta mode, do not have any technical vocabulary to talk about language beyond the simple terms such as 'word' or 'way of saying'.

Metalinguistic awareness may be deliberately nurtured during formal education and refined by means of analytic activities such as parsing sentences and finding synonyms for words, and so on. In the latter case, a descriptive terminology, a metalanguage, has to be developed by the teacher/linguist ('synonym' being one example) and these terms may be used to create formulae, i.e. rules or principles for formally expressing the observed regularities of the language system. Such formalisations of metalinguistic awareness, we may call 'metalinguistic knowledge'. So pre-school children may be metalinguistically *aware* when they make a play on words but they need metalinguistic *knowledge* to be able to explain why it is a joke. This kind of knowledge they get during formal education from the moment they learn to count the number of syllables there are in a particular word.

It is still an open question as to how much conscious awareness of the formal properties of language, and hence instruction based on inducing this awareness, actually helps the development of spontaneous language use (see Sharwood Smith 1980, Rutherford and Sharwood Smith 1988, Rutherford 1987a, Sharwood Smith 1991). In any case, it is useful to talk of metalinguistic ability as something which involves a scale. The scale ranges from the fairly primitive ability that very young children have, most easily captured by the term 'awareness', to what the literary scholar and especially the creative writer has, or, indeed, the highly sophisticated technical knowledge possessed by descriptive and theoretical linguists when they talk about language structure.

1.2.5   Acquisition, learning and development

Unless otherwise specified, the three terms listed in this title are virtually all synonyms of each other. 'Acquisition' is often associated with informal modes of learning (Lambert 1966, Krashen 1976) but, as far as this book is concerned, the three terms will be used interchangeably unless the context makes it clear that some special theoretical definitions are in force. The only differences are in where the emphasis lies.

'Development' is the best term as it focuses on the process itself, i.e. as something that 'happens' inside the learner or acquirer. The other two terms call attention to the locus of development, i.e. the person or persons in which language development is taking place. Accordingly, they mix in extra notions such as the conscious intention to learn. The language learner is presented not only as 'someone in the process of learning' but also, by implication, as someone who intends to learn and, a further implication, who is somehow controlling at least part of the activity we call learning. Since we do not yet know the actual effect of wanting to learn, or wanting to control the manner of learning, it is better to look for more neutral terms that exclude these extra notions.

Unfortunately, there is no suitable neutral term like 'developer' or 'developee' which clearly indicates that the learner is 'a place where development is taking place', so 'learner' and 'acquirer' have to be used. In any case, it is assumed that language proficiency is the result of a process most aptly called development but often called learning and/or acquisition. The most important thing is to keep learning/ acquisition/development separate from 'teaching', which is the attempt (usually by others) to make the learner's task *easier*, etc.).

1.2.6   Strategy

'Strategy' is a word which invokes the idea of general or business executives planning their next move. The term is used in a variety of ways and its precise meanings are sometimes difficult to ascertain. Learners are often said to adopt strategies to cope with the business of handling non-native languages, for example 'learning strategies' or 'communicative strategies'. Strategies have to do with 'how to learn X' or 'how to communicate X' and the term 'strategy', as used in the literature, should be understood as a systematic approach to a task:

(a) whether or not the language user is actually consciously *aware* of applying the strategy in a given context;
(b) whether that strategy is part of a *stable* repertoire of problem-solving techniques or whether it is a sudden ad-hoc invention which the learner, pressed for time, say, devises on the spur of the moment;
(c) whether the idea behind the strategy is to facilitate *acquisition*, i.e. further the development of the learner's knowledge and proficiency in L2, or whether it is purely and simply designed to facilitate *communication* at a given moment in time.

To take a couple of examples, a subconscious learning strategy would be when the learner, without thinking, uses mother tongue knowledge to create forms in another language (for example, automatically adopting mother tongue word order in L2 questions). A conscious communicative strategy would be when a learner resorts to a gesture or invents a word on the spot which he or she knows to be incorrect but which serves to convey the intended meaning.

1.2.7 Crosslinguistic influence/language transfer

The term 'transfer', especially as used in the 1960s and 1970s, refers to the influence of the mother tongue (L1) on the learner's performance in and/or development of a given target language. This is a more limited use of the term than is common in general psychology since it refers only to the effects of transferring elements of one linguistic system to another. It is actually even more limited than this: the direction of transfer is usually understood to be from the mother tongue to the L2. In actual fact, the direction of transfer may be the reverse; that is, the term may also be used in studies of language loss where a previously learned language (e.g. the L1) is changing under the influence of new language learning. The meaning does, however, cover *the influence of any 'other tongue' known to the learner on that target language*. For example, a German learner of Italian might be affected by his or her previous knowledge of Spanish.

The favoured term for this concept of language influence in this book will be *crosslinguistic* influence (CLI) but the older term (transfer) will also be used to aid the study of other, and especially earlier, books and articles on this topic. CLI covers all kinds of external linguistic influence including situations where learners fight shy of making connections between different languages they know because they feel such links to be unlikely. This other form of crosslinguistic influence is where the learner actually *avoids* carrying over, say, some sound, word or grammatical pattern from the other language because the target language is perceived to be different. In such cases, similarities between systems are not expected (see, for example, Kellerman 1985). The learner may not expect that borrowing a particular plural ending (like '-es') from the mother tongue, or a particular idiomatic expression (like 'kick the bucket'), will result in a perfectly acceptable target language form. Avoidance of transfer is hardly transfer, but it can be considered as a form of crosslinguistic influence. Notice that crosslinguistic influence does not refer directly to languages influencing one another in the outside world: it refers to what happens in a language user's head (mind).

1.2.8   Knowledge

What do we really mean when we say of someone 'she knows Ukrainian'? In point of fact, 'knowing' a language takes on a number of different meanings. The handiest way of capturing the psychological idea of knowledge is to see it as a type of mental organisation. Since someone knows Ukrainian, there must be something in her head that corresponds to her obvious possession of some Ukrainian. Even though we are quite unaware of exactly which parts of her physical brain handle that knowledge, we do know that at least some of the language system we call Ukrainian is 'represented' in her complete mental system. In the same way, if you post a letter and hear later that it has reached its destination in the Ukraine, you can safely assume there must be a functioning postal system even though you have little idea of what it actually looks like. It is best to think of linguistic knowledge as *a systematised body of mental representations underlying the learner's language use, irrespective of whether those mental representations coincide with those of a mature native speaker of the language.* And just to underscore the separation of that mental system and the physical manifestation of that system (in the physical brain), one could add 'and irrespective of where and how the mental representations are actually located in the head'.

The essential insight here is the fact that knowledge is a system that the language learner builds up on the basis of exposure to the language; where that exposure (input), limited as it may be, leads to the formation of some systematised beliefs about the language, some of which may deviate from the native-speaker norms, we can talk of interlanguage 'knowledge'.

'Knowing' does not, then, necessarily involve 'knowing the native-speaker norms'. So, if a learner regularly produces 'goed' where native speakers produce 'went', we take this as evidence of learner knowledge that happens to deviate from native-speaker knowledge. We do not classify it as a *lack* of knowledge (cf. Davies 1991).

The above liberal or technical use of the term 'knowledge' should help us get away from the notion of a language learner's linguistic behaviour as being simply composed of a combination of two things, errors and non-errors, where 'errors' means deviations from the native-speaker norms. Knowing Ukrainian is not necessarily knowing native-speaker Ukrainian. It is simply possessing a Ukrainian system of some sort, something that people recognise as a type of Ukrainian however they might disapprove of it. Indeed, the liberal use of the term precludes the notion of knowledge as somehow existing in the ether just waiting to be sucked up from outside. This misconception is, it is argued here, encouraged by the use of terms like 'internalise' as in 'the learner internalised rules', illustrated in Figure 1.2 (see second example in section 1.2.3 above).

The truth of the matter is that the learners do not take in the rule. They take in *examples* of the rule which they use to 'crack the code'. So they in fact create or recreate rule systems for themselves. The only thing that is internalised is raw data (input), which, as the term 'raw' indicates, has to be processed by the learner and turned into mental representations, i.e. 'knowledge' of some sort. Saying that systematic learner behaviour reflects an internalised rule is as unhelpful as saying that the patterns on a cabbage leaf are internalised sunshine or internalised rain. Sunshine and water were certainly needed to make the plant grow like that but the internal *structure* of that plant is not determined by the sunshine. This is determined biologically, long before the cabbage gets its first welcome drop of rain or ray of sunshine. Language input may seem more complex but it is powerless without a pre-existing mental organisation or 'programme' to make sense of it. Input combines with mental mechanisms to create knowledge or skill.

1.2.9 (Processing) Control and mental library

You may know something but not be very good at showing your new knowledge in actual language use, especially when under pressure. The term 'control' (which stands for processing control) will be used in this book to refer to *the productive and receptive control possessed by the language user over the knowledge he or she has of various aspects of the linguistic system.* Associated terms, perhaps more familiar to the reader, would be 'skill' (as opposed to 'knowledge'), 'degrees of fluency' and 'automaticity'. Hence, hesitant linguistic behaviour may be attributed to a lack of relevant knowledge but it also might be

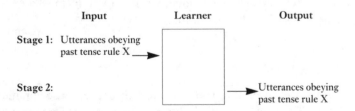

FIGURE 1.2   Internalising rules: a misconception.

attributed to the actual possession of the relevant knowledge without fluent *control* over that knowledge (see also 1.2.8, above). I may know how to say 'Look out, there's a car coming!' but I may not have sufficient control over that knowledge to shout it out suddenly and spontaneously.

Controlling means getting hold of and assembling the relevant information, i.e. processing it for various different purposes. *Low* control over knowledge means that knowledge is available but can be accessed only under optimal conditions – that is, the accessing process requires more-than-average time or freedom from distraction. The notion of processing control allows us to separate out those factors of language ability that we want to call 'knowledge' and those factors that have to do with the more or less skilful deployment of knowledge in actual performance millisecond by millisecond. The degree of control that a learner has over available knowledge will depend on the demands of the task involved. Two learners having identical knowledge in some area may not be as skilled in showing that knowledge when, for example, answering an unexpected phone call in an emergency. One learner may have a higher level of control than the other. The other learner may fall back on other knowledge that is more easily accessed or, of course, simply fail to convey the message.

As suggested above, control refers both to performance involving 'reception' (listening and reading) and performance involving 'production' (speaking and writing) . However, since control is always control of something, in terms of actual performance, control comes closest to the everyday use of the term 'proficiency'. Fluency, proficiency or 'skill' in a language includes the idea of being able to control *efficiently* what you know. Someone who knows something but cannot control it efficiently in, say, normal conversation, would not, in this everyday sense, be thought of as being proficient in that language. The *everyday* use of the term 'competence' (competence as skill or proficiency), unlike Chomsky's use of it (competence-as-knowledge), also has this implication.

1.2.10   Variability

Language varies according to the context of use and also for more strictly psychological reasons. A different word or structure may be more or less appropriate in a given situation: for example, formal words like 'request' (for 'ask') are not used, by definition, in informal conversational contexts. Again, technical terms will be used when two experts are talking about a technical topic. Also, a word or structure may be more or less likely to occur depending on the speaker's, or writer's frame of mind at the time. Haste or fatigue, for example, may result in the use of more common words, or an emotional state may lead to more emotional language.

Interlanguage reflects the same kind of variation as native-speaker language although the results may be different. In addition, the language learner may have different degrees of control (see 1.2.9) over given words or structures according to their status in their current interlanguage, whether they are in the process of being acquired or exchanged for something new. This will also cause variation in what is done at a given moment, depending on the nature of the task involved.

Since the learner is in possession of more than one language system, variability in performance may have different outcomes than would be the case in a monolingual situation. One language system may intrude upon the other in interesting ways. A word from one language may be borrowed and used in another, either deliberately or without the learner being aware of it. A possible parallel for this in native-speaker usage would be a learner switching between items and constructions that belong in different varieties, styles or dialects of the L1. Indeed, there may be a close parallel since a given native speaker may not be truly 'native' in one or other of these subsystems of his or her mother tongue. Studying interlanguage variability provides the researcher with a rich area of investigation posing many challenging theoretical questions.

1.2.11 Modularity

The treatment that will be favoured in this book will be one which views language learner behaviour not as reflecting a single albeit complex system but as a *complex of quite different systems each obeying different principles*. Just as learning how to drive a car engages quite separate systems – sound, vision, motor skills, knowledge of traffic rules, etc. – learning how to assemble complex *syntactic* structures is driven by one system, and learning how to match words from available resources to particular situations, i.e. speaking *appropriately* as well as accurately, is driven by quite another system. Treating the language user as a complex of, sometimes, quite independent subsystems (modules) may be dubbed the 'modular mind' approach (see Fodor 1983 for a classic example). Any theory has, of course, to explain how the modules interact, whether their operation is entirely independent or whether the operation of one module cannot be completed before the output of another module has been made available. For example, the intonation system in language clearly needs to await the pragmatic module before, say, the assignment of stress can be completed.

One important idea to keep in mind is the possibility that, although there may be evidence in all kinds of different spheres of activity that there are general learning principles, we can at least expect in some subsystems that there will be very specific learning principles that are irrelevant to other areas. Acquiring knowledge of the world of, say, sounds or vision may need explanations quite separate from learning how to pass a geography test. There may be different requirements to guarantee successful learning. For instance, learners may need correction of their errors in one domain of the L2 while, in another, their learning may proceed simply by exposure to the language. If this is so, then, clearly, special learning theories are needed to account for these different areas. One set of learning principles may not be enough.

Another example of thinking of knowledge and skill as being composed of different subsystems is when considering the possibility of native-like L2 ability. It may be possible for many people to achieve native levels in some subsystems but not in others. So the question of whether one can become a native speaker, and how likely that may be, can be addressed separately for each of those modules, e.g. pragmatic ability, stress and intonation, lexicon, etc. This idea of modularity will be considered later, starting with the discussion on experimentation in Chapter 4.

1.2.12   LAD

LAD stands for Language Acquisition Device and is a term that was widely used in the 1970s (see Chomsky 1965). It is a cover term for a battery of mechanisms in the mind that are supposed to be responsible for creating a highly complex grammar from the language experience that a learner – notably the very young, immature (pre-school) L1 learner – undergoes. Since these mechanisms are not, according to the theoretical position adopted by the users of this term, like those which drive the learning of other types of knowledge and skill, the theoretical implication is a modular one (see 1.2.11., above). LAD is supposed to be 'special', i.e. it is specifically designed to create linguistic knowledge. It is what the young, cognitively immature child crucially relies on. That child is not able consciously to analyse and work out the complex grammatical system of its mother tongue on the basis of what it hears without help, and is not even able to profit from systematic professional instruction, were it provided.

Using the term LAD also has the advantage of focusing on the process of language development without involving the idea that the learner is consciously and intentionally controlling every aspect of learning. With LAD, a great deal of learning just 'happens'. The cracking of the L1 code takes places at a more or less intuitive level leaving only the simpler lexical aspects open to conscious reflection. Children do talk about words and sounds but they certainly do not mull over the finer points of grammar. As suggested above, it does not require any serious conscious analysis or instruction. One big question is: Does the L2 learner have a subconscious LAD of this kind or are second languages learned in a quite different way?

1.2.13 Elicitation

If a teacher or a learner wishes to find out how close the learner's knowledge and skill are to that of a comparable native speaker of the language in question, then it becomes necessary to run a series of tests on the learner. 'Language testing' is a field in applied linguistics where research is carried out into various forms of tests with the aim of refining the instruments used to measure a learner's language proficiency.

Clearly, many language-testing techniques may also be used when the focus is not so much on the target norms as on the interlanguage system of the learner – that is, simply on what its properties are irrespective of its native-like or non-native-like character. However, probing deeply into the properties of the learner's current linguistic system involves many more specialised instruments than are usually used in language testing. It is, for example, enough for a teacher to know that such and such a structure is not yet 'mastered' so the presence of a language error is a sufficient signal to say that more time and perhaps more teaching is needed. The interlanguage researcher is immediately interested in more information about that so-called 'error'. Really, for the researcher at least, it is not so much an error but a possibly interesting fact about the learner's current system. It may be a stable feature of that system or a 'slip'. If it is a stable feature, then it is important to find out how it fits in with other features there. It is also necessary to see if it can be explained by some particular theory. It is quite a different operation to see in straightforward terms how close or how far it is from what the native-speaker equivalent would be. If a learner of English produces 'I love the nature', we can, as language teachers, note that the article 'the' is used where a native speaker would omit it. We can also establish from the context, and perhaps by asking the learner what he or she meant, if the use of 'nature' is non-English and if another term like 'countryside' or 'scenery' would have been chosen by a native speaker. This gives the teacher a sense of what has still to be learned. It says nothing about such 'irrelevant' matters as to whether some theory would have satisfactorily explained the reason for the error and how it fitted in to that leaner's current L2 system (see discussion in Bley-Vroman 1983).

In principle, the teacher might also like to know more about the learner's current system but, in practice, the combination of time, interest and specialist knowledge are seldom available to profit from this. The term 'elicitation' is reserved for the *non-applied probing of learner knowledge and learner skill*. Applied researchers experimenting with language testing techniques, that is, with a view to refining, say, classroom tests, might well make use of elicitation tests as defined above. The extent to which classroom tests come closer and closer to elicitation techniques used by second language researchers is presumably a sign of ever more fruitful contacts between the two different worlds.

1.3   Myths and prejudices

1.3.1   Overview

A short review of some common-sense views of 'the person in the street' is necessary to disentangle what needs to be denied immediately and what is interesting enough to merit further investigation. People are ready to stand in awe of the feat accomplished by children learning their first language without instruction. They are less ready to appreciate the achievements of second language acquirers. This is because so much effort seems to go into it; learners are older and wiser and ought to manage better, and success seems to elude a large number of people despite all their efforts.

1.3.2   Is second language learning doomed to failure?

Depending very much on where people come from, the answer may be 'yes' or 'no'. If you live in a large community which dominates other cultures enough to make the language spoken there useful all over the world, then you might view foreign language learning as very problematic. If you come from a small multilingual community you will have seen many people become highly skilled users of more than one language. You may even be multilingual yourself. You are therefore more prepared to see second language acquisition as something that can, in principle, be achieved up to native-speaker levels. Successful second language acquisition is, then, a worthy topic for investigation (see also discussion in 1.2.11).

1.3.3   Does instruction help?

Most people assume second language learning to be similar to many other kinds of learning. This means that the value of language instruction is seen as being self-evident. Nothing could be further from the truth. (Unbiased) research to date has not revealed a golden language-teaching technique that absolutely guarantees successful acquisition. And this is after centuries of systematic language teaching. It shows people learning despite instruction, without instruction, and in ways that differ from the goals of a particular instructional programme. The value of instruction is by no means undermined in principle. Its value has simply been called into question. This is why more research on the way in which learners are exposed to a new language and its effect needs an enormous amount of investigation before we can point to any golden method. Second language acquisition research is, logically speaking, a crucial prerequisite to course design. However, we have a centuries-old tradition of looking elsewhere for guidance in language teaching. The field of SLA has only been around for a couple of decades, more or less, and it is not surprising that course designers are not aware of it and have no access to its findings. In any case, at the moment, it only has a modicum of insights and cautionary remarks to offer that we can really be confident about.

2 Learner systems

2.0 Overview

This chapter, like the one that follows, will provide a survey of the field as it developed during the 1970s. Here the focus will be on the notion of interlanguage. This will not just be a historical survey but will also introduce some fundamental theoretical issues and methodological problems: for this reason detailed discussion of the empirical studies will, on the whole, be avoided so that the more essential problems may be highlighted.

2.1 Early perspectives

The field of second language research may be (very broadly) divided into three stages of development, roughly equatable with, respectively, the 1960s, the 1970s and the 1980s.

The first period, which will not be discussed in any detail, is characterised by an attempt to relate behaviourist 'habit-formation' psychology and (pre-Chomskyan) structural linguistics to the problems of foreign language learning in order to provide a scientific backing for teaching techniques and teaching materials (see Lado 1967). In other words, it was 'applied linguistics' in its most commonly accepted sense. The basic idea was that the linguist provided a list of linguistic similarities and differences with respect to a particular L1 and a particular L2, and the applied linguist used the list of differences as the main predictor of learning difficulty in trying to work out ways of facilitating language teaching. Both the linguistic and the psycholinguistic models employed have been abandoned. Although no one would deny that language learning involves the acquisition of new habits, the processes underlying that acquisition are now seen to be vastly more complex than any simple habit-formation theory would suggest. Learners produce utterances to which they have never been exposed, and, given that they do not yet 'know' the native-speaker rules, those utterances seem to follow a plausible rule system. More specifically, they use structures that are not used in the input (systematic 'errors'). Finally, their errors cannot be wholly explained by the mechanical, negative effects of their mother tongue.

The second period, which will be discussed in some detail, saw the abandonment of the psychological and linguistic frameworks just mentioned and a beginning of the rift between the applied and theoretical aims of researchers in this area. It saw the learner as an autonomous creator of language systems. The terms 'interlanguage' and 'creative construction' might have be chosen to label this period. Rightly or wrongly, the latter concept made a greater impact at the time, initially at least, both in the research literature and, as it transpired, in the teaching world (see next chapter). This is undoubtedly because its claims were more precise and more radical.

The third period saw an attempt to refine current models of language learning and to seek closer links between second language research and other theoretical disciplines, especially linguistics.

Second language studies really began at the close of the first period and were initially characterised by some fairly simple empirical investigations and a great deal of fruitful speculation. Preliminary models were proposed incorporating suggestions as to how best to begin the study of second language learning. The assumption now was that learning was not straightforward habit-formation but rather had to involve complex mental organisation of the input.

2.1.1 Corder

The history of IL studies is short but eventful (see Selinker 1992 for a detailed account of the early period). Perhaps things really got under way at an influential centre at Edinburgh University, in Scotland, where a group of applied linguists, including visiting scholars, were working on a more systematic way of studying language learning and language teaching. In 1967, the then head of the Department of Applied Linguistics, Pit Corder, published the field's first seminal article, called 'The significance of learner's errors' (see the collection of papers in Corder 1981). In it, he argued that second language research should follow the example of first language research and view the learner's development as a development of underlying linguistic competence (in a Chomskyan sense: Chomsky 1965). That is to say, the learner is a creator of rules and these rules are the outcome of a process of hypothesising.

Systematic errors (such as the incorrect placement of the adverbial before the modal auxiliary 'will' in 'I quietly will go', 'I carefully will walk', etc., as well as completely native-like phenomena observed in learner behaviour may be taken by the researcher as evidence of a learner's current transitional competence (or transitional 'dialect'). This was Corder's term for the learners' current mental rule-system or 'grammar'. In other words, they reflect the learners' attempts to make sense of the input in their own particular ways, that is, trying to organise the information provided by the language to which they are exposed.

Corder further argued that the L2 learner may well have a 'built-in syllabus' (cf. Corder 1981:9 and Mager 1961), i.e. an internally programmed sequence for learning various aspects of the target grammar which may or may not coincide with the syllabus imposed on him or her by the teacher. Hence, learners will follow a sequence of development (the in-built syllabus) because of, or in spite of, the sequence imposed on them from outside.

The teacher, not knowing what the hidden psychological learning programme is, may introduce examples of a rule – say the addition of third person singular -s ending, as in 'he runs' – at a particular time but, according to this view, that learner will not actually be able to learn this rule properly unless he or she is ready for it. 'Ready' here means specifically 'at the appropriate point in the predetermined in-built learning programme'. Early teaching of a late-learned form would seem to be a waste of time. The learner might appear to be stupid or stubborn. In fact, the learner is not responsible for the failure to acquire the target form in question. Neither is the teacher, except in the sense of asking the impossible from the learner and hence creating an illusion of failure. This, at least, was the idea behind the inbuilt syllabus.

As mentioned earlier (see the glossary in Chapter 1) we may, as Corder pointed out, distinguish between *input*, what the learner is presented with, and *intake*, what the learner is actually ready to process, i.e. actually takes in (Corder 1981). Intake is determined by the supposed internal programme, the exact nature of which is the object of the researcher's investigations. Hence, at any given time, the learner, like it or not, is ignoring certain aspects of the input which ought in principle to inform him or her about the target grammar but for which the learner is not yet mentally prepared.

With regard to what learners actually do with their current L2 resources, Corder pointed out that correct (native-like) behaviour cannot necessarily be interpreted as a genuine attainment of the native-speaker norm. For example, learners in a formal classroom environment may be induced to produce superficially correct behaviour via some teaching technique; for example, the teacher may require the repetition of some memorised utterance from a standard textbook dialogue such as :

'Mr Brown leaves for the office in the morning.'

Learners may, even at a later date, be able to produce this utterance verbatim without really having the relevant rules and vocabulary to generate it spontaneously. Also, they may indeed have a non-native-speaker intention underlying some utterance which at first glance seems appropriate and native-like: Corder's example was:

'I want to know the English.'

This may not be used to refer to the English as a people but rather refers to 'the English language'. In other words, it exemplifies what a teacher would call the 'misuse' of the definite article. So, not only should (systematic) errors be regarded as something other than unwelcome deviations, but what looks like 'correct' performance should be regarded as potentially non-native (see definition of 'knowledge' in Chapter 1).

In fact, Corder made a distinction between 'errors' and 'mistakes', the latter being what in Chomsky's perspective had become known as performance phenomena, slips of the tongue and so on. Hence, the conveniently understandable term 'error' (highlighting the non-standard character of a form) was retained even though the force of Corder's argument was to see transitional competence as a system in its own right and not just as systematic deviance from a norm. 'Transitional form' might have been a more objective substitute for 'error'.

The essence of Corder's proposals is presented diagrammatically in Figure 2.1, which shows how learning is seen as an operation whereby the learning device (or LAD, see Chapter 1) builds a system using the language to which the learner is exposed (input) and creating out of that input a particular transitional system. This transitional system is then modified when new input encountered by the learner is seen to conflict with the rules of that system: the learning device's 'hypotheses' are disconfirmed (see feedback loop on the left). The learning device thus functions as a little linguist in the head. For example, it hears 'she runs', 'it goes', etc., hypothesises a rule adding -s and permits the learners to produce 'goes' as well as (perhaps) the non-native 'he cans go'. The learner later will have to modify that rule so that some but not all verbs allow the -s.

When using his or her transitional system, the learner produces systematic utterances (apart from the normal slips and mistakes), some of which may conform to the native-speaker norms and others

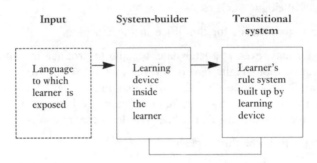

(Hypotheses tested against new input)

FIGURE 2.1   The creation of transitional systems: a partial model.

which will not. The non-conforming features are what the teacher would call (systematic) 'errors'. To take another, classic example – irregular verbs – the learner is exposed to forms like 'walked', 'pulled', etc. (regular past forms) and irregular past forms like 'ran'. This would go into the INPUT area in Figure 2.1. Acting on this input, the SYSTEM-BUILDER would create a regular system which always applied the past morpheme. This rule would then be part of the TRANSITIONAL SYSTEM. The output of this system would be forms like 'walked' but also forms like *'runned', conforming to the learner rule. At some point, the SYSTEM-BUILDER would compare forms like 'runned' against the input, which, of course, consistently contains 'ran': an exception would be created in the TRANSITIONAL SYSTEM to bring it further into line with the input (and bring the TRANSITIONAL SYSTEM closer to the native system). The learner's performance would then involve the use of native forms like 'ran', and 'runned' would disappear (but see Rutherford 1989 and also Bowerman 1983).

Figure 2.1 is actually incomplete: it needs some refinement (see Figure 2.2.). In fact, three additional main points need to be made to complete the picture underlying Corder's proposals.

If we first take the notion of input and output, there are, in fact, two possible outputs. The first is the product of the system-builder, i.e. the transitional system itself. The learner's system-builder notices, say, particular word-order patterns in the input and devises a word-order rule for the transitional system. That word-order rule is the output (product) of the system-builder's operation. In this way, learner rules are the output of the knowledge-building process.

The second output of the system is the actual behaviour that the learner's current transitional system generates, i.e. learner performance. This second type of output concerns the production and comprehension of actual utterances on a given occasion. The first type of output concerns the knowledge that the learner (alias the system-builder) develops gradually over a period of time. The second type is the outcome of the learner's use of the set of rules they have developed.

It is important to stress that both receiving and producing messages are included here. One result could be an error of interpretation where the learner, due to non-native aspects of his or her transitional system, misinterprets some native-speaker utterance and assigns it a different meaning to the one that would be assigned by a native speaker. If the learner hears:

'the boy was hit by the man'

and interprets this as a statement about a boy hitting a man, then he or she is using a rule which interprets post-verbal nouns as objects and pre-verbal nouns as subjects, and this IL interpretative (rather than productive) behaviour is also a product or output of the transitional system.

It is necessary to insist on these details of model illustration not only to avoid the casual use of such diagrams but also because it is easy to fall into the error of thinking of learner behaviour as production alone. For practical reasons, much of the research has concentrated on production and our understanding of receptive performance lags far behind (see papers in Brown 1986). Figure 2.2 fills out the picture according to the above amendments.

Output 1 is the output of the process of building new knowledge, i.e. from the system-building device. Output 2 is the output of

Output 1	Output 2
The result of development over a period of time: the transitional (or interlanguage) system	The result of using the transitional system (= Output 1) to produce or interpret messages in L2 at a given time

FIGURE 2.2 Two kinds of 'output': the result of development and the result of performance.

another process, namely, the process of activating available knowledge (see Output 1) – in other words, using the current results of learning in order to produce and understand L2 at a given moment in time.

2.1.2   Transitional competence building

Three further, important aspects of transitional competence concern:

1) the role of the mother tongue
2) the status of the term 'learner hypothesis'
3) the unique character of learner systems vis-à-vis 'normal' languages or dialects.

The first addition to the picture presented in Figures 2.1 and 2.2 should be the role of the L1. Corder accorded the learner's L1 an important role in the building of transitional systems. The learner, in some sense at least, has the job of restructuring the L1 system. The system-builder has, so to speak, to ask whether the system (or set of systems) of the new language is the same as, or different from, that of the learner's (L1) (Corder 1981: 12). This means that hypotheses are formed not simply on the basis of the input but also with reference to the native (L1) system. The role of the mother tongue learner is recreating the L2 as it were from scratch, and not restructuring it using L1 as a basis.

The second point is that the process of hypothesising should be seen as being largely intuitive. It is not literally meant to be the kind of conscious hypothesising that a linguist in the jungle might use in order to unravel the system of an exotic language. The little linguist in the head is not the conscious analyst that the 'big' linguist is. That is to say, the learner does not spend his or her time actually thinking about the learning process: much of it takes place 'underground', i.e. below the level of conscious awareness. At the same time, there are some important parallels to be drawn with the scientist's hypothesising. Wherever the ideas come from, and whatever the degree of awareness is, these beliefs may be subjected to testing and are altered as a result of experience that disconfirms the beliefs, or rather hypotheses, as we choose to call them.

Learner 'hypotheses' should then be seen in this special, metaphorical sense. We may imagine the language learner or the learning mechanism inside him or her saying: 'I believe the L2 to possess a tense system of such and such a type or to have a rule whereby all obstruents are devoiced in word-final position unless followed by a voiced sound', or ' I now see that my belief that the tense system was a simple one is not true and that I have to incorporate two more tenses...', etc.

As was mentioned earlier, to get away from automatically assuming that the learner is consciously involved in this kind of mental activity, it is useful to adopt the notion of a 'language acquisition device' (LAD) as a cover term for that part of the mind which is responsible for building new mental (linguistic) representations and ensuring their storage in long-term memory for use in actual language performance. LAD is a useful term, then, even for those who do not subscribe to particular theoretical characterisations of what LAD entails.

The third and final point is the fact that the personal transitional system possessed by an individual learner is different from a language or dialect in the normal sense of those terms since it is possessed by one individual only: for this reason Corder (1981) refers to it as an 'idiolect'. It may, of course, be very like other idiolects possessed by the same kind of learner at the same stage of development learning the same language and having the same mother tongue. A group of learners in a class, for example, may to all intents and purposes have a common transitional system, so perhaps on occasions one could talk of a mini-dialect for that group. This is a matter for researchers to investigate.

It should be noted here that the way we group learners, for example in a school, may eventually obscure differences in development between individual learners in that group. That is to say, taken over time, learners of a given L2 may all have the same internal syllabus but one learner may still travel through this 'route' faster than the others so that, in the same class, different learners may nevertheless be at slightly different stages of development, i.e. at different points along a common route (their internal syllabus): this point will be further discussed in later sections of the book.

2.1.3 Nemser and Selinker

After Corder (1967), two other pioneering researchers published similar proposals concerning learner systems. In 1971, William Nemser, who had been working on an English–Hungarian contrastive linguistic project, proposed that second language development should be seen as a succession of evolving systems that took the learner nearer and nearer the target system and further and further from the source system. The source system was defined as that language which is creating the interference (usually the L1, i.e. the native language). The idea was that learners were not exposed to the complete target system in one 'blinding flash'. Rather, they processed the input in smaller digestible doses and, on the basis of this (limited) input, could be said to create their own systems to account for what had been processed to date. More properly, they create a series of systems that, ideally, get closer and closer to the target, i.e. the native-speaker norms. These learner-based systems Nemser called 'approximative' systems. In 1972, Selinker, whose term 'interlanguage' was eventually adopted by most people when talking about approximative systems (Corder used the adjective 'transitional'; Corder 1967) proposed an approach similar to that of Nemser's (see also Selinker 1969, 1992).

In this way, at approximately the same time, three people proposed that second language errors were to be viewed in quite a different way from the negative manner in which teachers (and indeed most learners) traditionally perceive them. All three proposals had three essential features in common. They assumed:

(1) the existence of a complex, creative learning device;
(2) internal coherence in the learner's language system;
(3) the independent character of the learner's system.

In other words, all three views were anti-behaviourist. Learners were not simply in the grip of mechanical mother-tongue habits interfering with their performance or, if they were lucky, allowing them to get it right almost from the start. The three accounts involved the idea of complex mental processing whereby the linguistic input was organised into interlanguage systems. Learning was no longer viewed as the outcome of simple learning mechanisms that allowed the individual learner's personal experience of the language to be the single major role in shaping his or her linguistic behaviour. The learner (as a language acquisition device) could be viewed as a creative selector and organiser of input, filtering the information from the environment by largely subconscious and very complex methods in order to build up a linguistic system in ways that suggested a great deal of commonality with other learners whose experience might in many respects be different.

There are, in fact, two kinds of creativity to be found in the language learner's achievement: 'developmental' creativity and 'structural' creativity. The language acquisition device inside the learner is developmentally creative in the sense that it uses the evidence it has available to create new forms and new rules for which evidence is not available, or at least not yet available to the learner. Hence, on the basis of certain evidence such as 'I may do it' and 'I may have done it' where auxiliaries co-occur, the language acquisition device may construct a rule which chains modal auxiliaries in such a way as to sanction such (perfectly interpretable) IL English utterances as 'I may can do it': such structures are not permissible in (standard) native-speaker English – modal auxiliaries cannot co-occur. We cannot say that the learner grammar is based completely on the evidence provided by the learner's experience of the language as spoken and written by native speakers.

It should also be said that the developmental creativity of the learning mechanisms which lead to the production of novel forms and original non-native rules also leads to the development of a human linguistic system which is creative in a second sense, the Chomskyan sense (Chomsky 1965). The grammar allows the speaker to produce (and interpret) millions of sentences that he or she has, hitherto, never personally encountered but which nevertheless accord with the norms followed by other adult native speakers of the language. This structural creativity means that learners, like native speakers, can use their system to produce thousands of sentences they have never encountered. In other words, developmental creativity means the forming of original rules that may actually defy the evidence of language encountered by the learner. Structural creativity means that the learners can produce entirely original systematic utterances, that is, whether or not they are native-like.

There is, indeed, a wealth of evidence in both first and second language acquisition that learners 'go their own way' and create novel forms which are reflections of some personal grammar of the language. Figure 2.3 shows how the building of these intermediate linguistic systems may be viewed as a series of ILs growing over time as the learner's beliefs interact with the evidence supplied by his or

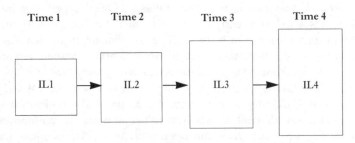

FIGURE 2.3 Building linguistic systems: a complex mental process.

her experience of the L2, experience which is not absorbed in toto but some of which is actually taken in and used as a basis for forming further hypotheses about L2 structure.

The three proposals concerning the nature of learner language systems also assumed that learner systems could be seen as being to some degree different in kind from mature native-speaker systems. One might then conceptualise learner systems as dialects of a given target language (cf. Corder 1981), i.e. as whole jigsaw puzzles, perhaps with fewer pieces than mature systems but certainly with some different pieces. The notion of an IL as a complete, internally coherent system is, it should be stressed, an idealisation: one may assume, at least in the case of an IL that is still developing, that it is unstable and not completely consistent but the idea of an autonomous learner system is a useful, insightful one at the very least because it forces us away from the teacher's perspective – the flawed, incomplete jigsaw puzzle with missing pieces, as it were (see Figure 2.3). Corder's terminology focused on the dynamic, developmental nature of the learner system; Nemser's highlighted the notion of a journey with a destination (the target norms); and Selinker's emphasised the autonomy of the system as a 'language' in its own right and its more static aspects. Some have preferred to see IL growth not in terms of jumps from one stage to the next, as is suggested in Figure 2.3, but in terms of a gradual progression; that is to say, IL growth is a continuum in which some new rule slowly spreads and acquires a greater coverage within the grammar or, alternatively, becomes progressively more limited in scope (see Corder 1981; Dickerson 1975).

Finally, the ideas of systematicity and common patterns of development allow a way of distinguishing those aspects of development which fall within the scope of the term 'interlanguage' and those that fall outside it. The acquisition of L1 or L2 lexical material, for example, is going to depend very much on the individual learner's chance exposure to the language. One learner may learn 'shock absorber' very early (as a result of a car breakdown) while another might learn it very late, and yet another might not learn it at all. However the systematic way in which learners assemble words (e.g. 'unwrap' from 'wrap') and indeed invent entirely new words (not in the input, e.g. 'unappear' from 'appear': see discussion in Bowerman 1982) should fall within the scope of IL studies. Hence we cannot say that all things lexical fall outside IL studies, and essentially the same goes for pragmatic or indeed phonetic and phonological development.

2.1.4   Interlanguage and child language

Selinker's position, as expressed in his 1972 paper, differed from Corder's in that, while reference was made to similarities between first and second language acquisition, the thrust of Selinker's arguments was in the direction of a qualitative difference between the two types of learning. The relevant debate here centres round the interpretation of Lenneberg's Critical Period Hypothesis (Lenneberg 1972). Lenneberg pointed to the difficulty experienced by people with language disorders in relearning their language when the brain damage had been sustained after puberty. He also made a passing reference to the difficulty in learning a second language by (normal) adults. He advanced the hypothesis that there was a critical period for learning language: the mind is programmed to receive and act efficiently on linguistic input only for a limited time, after which there is a loss of plasticity and learning becomes problematic.

Lenneberg associated this loss of plasticity with the lateralisation of brain function (see discussion in Lesser and Milroy 1993). That is to say, when language becomes a specialised function of one particular side (hemisphere), full recovery of language ability after brain injury is no longer assured. If one accepts the evidence of children deprived of linguistic input prior to this critical point, as far as normal people are concerned, exposure to language input after lateralisation will not automatically assure full language acquisition in the way it does before that time. Simply put, if you do not get exposed to a language before this period is over, you have missed your chance of ever becoming a native speaker. Selinker accordingly proposed that the psychological basis (and also, presumably, the neurological basis: see Selinker and Lamendella 1978) for acquiring a second language was qualitatively different from that which was involved in first language acquisition. Different mechanisms had to be engaged since the original mechanisms had, it was claimed, atrophied.

The possibility that normal language acquisition prior to the critical period might guarantee both first and subsequent second language acquisition by the relevant mechanisms was not considered. This was in view of the apparently indisputable fact that second language acquisition was seldom successful. Selinker guessed that about 95 per cent of second language learners failed to attain a state of nativeness (Selinker 1972). The process whereby development ceased despite continuous exposure and practice was termed *fossilization* by Selinker. In other words, 95 per cent of learners remain at some IL stage, what Nemser (1971) called a 'stable intermediate system'.

It follows from Selinker's argumentation that interlanguage and child language should be treated differently despite any similarities that might strike the eye. IL, which was the result of learning a language after the critical period, was therefore to be seen as the result of a different and less successful learning process. However, this simple picture was disturbed by observations of pre-pubertal children in Canada who, it turned out, were producing typical IL (rather than child L1) forms based on transfer from the mother tongue. Accordingly, Selinker had to modify his claim. In a paper co-authored by Selinker (Selinker *et al.* 1975), what was now called the 'Interlanguage Hypothesis' was extended to pre-pubertal children learning a second language in certain circumstances, namely sequentially (i.e. not simultaneously with their first language), and in the absence of fellow native-speaking peers, (i.e., among learners like themselves. This seems to imply that only bilingual children learning two languages simultaneously, L1a and L1b, would produce 'child language' and not 'interlanguage', that is, provided they were only exposed to mature speakers of each language and not to other young learners like themselves. This would be because (a) the original learning mechanisms had not yet atrophied in combination with (b) the fact that they were receiving sufficient linguistic input from an appropriate source. In actual fact, as parents will testify, such bilingual children do produce language reminiscent of the IL of the former type of learner. Their L1 and L2 input may also sometimes be combined to produce mixed forms. This is one indication that even the extended IL hypothesis still leaves something to be explained.

Much of the focus of Selinker's attention is on the final, fossilised IL system. Fossilisation or 'partial attainment' poses a major challenge to second language theorists: you must, logically speaking, make one of two claims. You either claim that first and second language acquisition are driven by different mechanisms, hence explaining fossilisation in one blow, or you say that they are driven by the same basic mechanisms but that the process is 'disturbed' by some external factor or cluster of factors such as inadequate input, lack of motivation or indeed interference from the mother tongue. These factors – to foreshadow the discussion in the next chapter – have been subsumed under the general term 'filter' (Dulay *et al.* 1982). Selinker, as we have seen, took the position that quite different acquisitional mechanisms were at work: 'LAD' was not the same as the IL-creating system. This point of view still has strong supporters today (see discussion in Bley-Vroman 1986, 1988,

Schachter 1988, 1990, Eubank 1991). In fact, the basic controversies described in this chapter and the next are still live issues in the 1990s even though the theoretical climate has changed.

As suggested above, not everyone maintains that the second language learner's brain has changed sufficiently to make L2 acquisition inevitably less successful than L1 learning. A more differentiated approach to neurological limitations on L2 learning is taken by other people (for example, Seliger 1978) who suggest that 'complete' acquisition may be possible in some areas and not in others. For example, the broad mass of second language learners, may find native-like control of target language phonology to be impossible, whereas grammatical aspects of the language may be mastered (given the right input and motivation) up to native-speaker level. Hence loss of (neurolinguistic) plasticity in older learners may be expected to bring development to a halt in some domains and not in others.

This idea of different subsystems being affected in different ways accords with the principle of modularity introduced in Chapter 1 (see 1.2.11). Clearly, lexical development, in the simple sense of adding new words to the lexical repertoire, is not particularly hampered in L2 acquisition whereas a large proportion of learners appear to find perfect accent beyond their grasp (but see Neufeld 1980).

Finally, it should also be pointed out that the (adult) attainment of convincingly native-like L2 performance is not in itself proof of the continued operation of the child's LAD. The older and wiser adult may be able to use resources that are simply not available to the cognitively immature L1 learner (see, for example, Bley-Vroman 1986). In this way, native-like behaviour in some area of the language might, indeed, be the result of different processes – for example, what the child can grasp best intuitively may be attainable by the adult but in a very conscious way. And the use of that knowledge at a given moment in time might be achieved efficiently either subconsciously by the younger learner and very deliberately and consciously by the adult. A case in point would be the written language where the adult might easily do better than the young child.

2.1.5 IL product and IL processes

There is an equivocation in the term 'interlanguage', as used in the literature, as to whether it refers to the product, i.e. the actual observable linguistic performance of language learners, or to the various underlying process(es) that must have led to that product. As has been made clear in many treatments of the subject, the product/ process distinction is absolutely crucial to an understanding of what goes on in the creating and use of second language systems (ILs). The term 'IL' actually suggests the former (product) interpretation: a 'language' is generally considered to be an object in the outside world possessed by many people and open to our inspection. By observing the behaviour of language users and registering the utterances that are produced in speech or writing, we are dealing directly with language as a product, something that can be observed and measured. On the basis of investigations into the IL product, the investigator draws inferences about the processes, call them 'IL processes', that underlie it (the observable product).

Once behaviourist explanations of learner behaviour were abandoned, the learner was assumed to possess a complex set of learning mechanisms and this meant that a variety of possible processes might underlie one particular product. If a deviant pattern in IL like 'I may can do it' appeared, it could no longer be assumed to be an L1 habit at work. Just as arrival at a given part of town may be achieved by following one or other of two quite different routes, so, too, a given piece of IL knowledge, as manifested in IL behaviour, may have alternative explanations as regards the processes that brought it about.

To help explain the patterns in learner language (IL), Selinker posited a number of 'central processes' (see Selinker 1972). As was mentioned above, one of these processes, language transfer, had been the one single process in the behaviourist explanation. In transferring the associations appropriate to the use of the mother tongue to the use of the target language, the learner was either aided (where the two systems were the same) or hindered (where the two systems differed). In this perspective, most or all errors produced by a person in the process of learning a second language could be attributed to interference from the mother tongue.

In Selinker's model, language transfer was not a question of an automatic transferring of habits. It formed one of a set of options for organising linguistic input. The idea of complex mental organisation, and of a mind that is highly selective in what it registers, was of course quite opposed to the behaviourist idea of simple associations between stimulus and response. Nonetheless, transfer did play a major role in Selinker's model. It was not, however, the only central process. For example, the learner might also 'overgeneralise' some rule or principle of the target language without reference to the L1 system, a process that Nemser called 'internal interference' (Nemser

1971). This type of systematic error had been found in the interlanguage of learners of English in studies of written performance (see Dušková 1969, Arabski 1971). It had been a crucial reason for abandoning the first habit-formation model of learning where almost everything could be explained by transfer. It had also been a reason for these early researchers to draw parallels between first and second language performance, an approach that was to underlie the third model, to be discussed in the next chapter. One example of overgeneralisation would be to make regular use of the present progressive not only where a native speaker of British or American English (for example) would use it:

'I am reading the answer'

but also where the non-progressive form would normally be inappropriate:

'I am knowing the answer' (instead of 'I know the answer').

Another example would be the chaining of modal auxiliaries mentioned earlier.

Again, another explanation for a given systematic IL form might, according to Selinker, be transfer of training. Here some special feature in the input intentionally or unintentionally created by the teacher or textbook leads to acquisition with a non-native result. Overemphasis of a structure thought to be difficult for the learner (such as the English progressive forms) might lead to a non-native degree of frequency of occurrence in the learner's IL and this would be the consequence of an artificial bias in the input.

Figure 2.4. shows three IL central processes that account for aspects of the learner's IL system according to Selinker. It should be pointed out that there is a fourth type of IL rule (not mentioned in the diagram) which would be identical to some rule possessed by the native speaker. It is important to remember that IL is not simply a system of deviant rules for producing 'errors'. Also, time T (in the diagram), which here is shown as a transitional stage in the learner's development, could also be the final stage – that is, it could be the ultimate result of the process of fossilisation whereby repeated practice and exposure to the language does not lead to any further development. Selinker also speaks of the phenomenon of *backsliding*, which is a process by which the learner temporarily reverts to a previous IL stage – in other words, produces (or 'receives') an utterance in a manner in which he or she used to do, systematically, at an earlier stage of development. In this way, IL performance at time T may also contain, in addition to non-native behaviour:

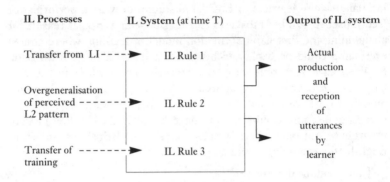

FIGURE 2.4   Three IL rules derived via three different IL processes (Selinker 1972).

(1) behaviour which is identical to that of a native speaker following native-speaker norms (following the fourth type of IL rule);
(2) behaviour which is no longer characteristic but used to be at an earlier stage of development ('backsliding': Selinker 1972).

It should already be clear that there is no longer any one-to-one relationship between deviance in learner performance and inter- ference from a competing system (the L1). In other words, from the form of a learner's utterance, choice of the -ing, we cannot automatically determine the psychological process that led to a particular product.

One concrete example of the difficulty of interpreting IL behaviour would be the non-native use of the present progressive form in English, as in the following sentence:

'I *was admiring* him for many years but eventually came to despise him.'

Here a native-speaker would have said:

'I *admired* him for many years...', etc.

Is the progressive form of the verb in the non-native version the outcome of language transfer? Or is it some sort of overgeneralisation from instances where the progressive form is used by native speakers? Let us suppose that the speaker was a native speaker of a Slavic language such as Polish. These languages have so-called perfective and imperfective forms of verbs. Imperfective is used with verbs when describing states and events that last (have duration or are incomplete). It would be the right choice for the 'admiring-for-many-years' situation depicted above. In English, however, actions and events that have a narrative function – that is, move the story on one step (see Sharwood Smith 1987, reprint) – must take the simple past, i.e. the non-progressive form 'admired'. This is not the case in Polish. You could say 'I was admiring him when she came in', here a continuing event (state), 'was admiring', is juxtaposed with a completed event, 'came in'. But, in a text in which 'admiring' is followed by a new step in the narrative 'despising', English forces the progressive, as it were, off the stage. The Polish learner's use of progressive might perhaps be influenced by assumption, subconscious or otherwise, that the trigger for 'admiring' is what would be a trigger for the imperfective version of the verb in Polish. In fact, three separate arguments could be built up to support three separate claims about the underlying psychological process at issue:

1 Argument 1 (process of language transfer): (as above).
2 Argument 2 (process of overgeneralisation): 'I was admiring her' is an overgeneralised use of the progressive form. The learner has acquired native-like use of this form in other contexts (as in 'I was admiring her when she suddenly turned and looked at me') but has not yet established the native restrictions on the form. Possibly, the learner is trying to regularise the IL system by making the progressive form the only one, obligatory in all contexts and, by so doing, avoiding 'simple' forms (e.g. 'I admired, I admire', etc.) altogether. This kind of phenomenon is a familiar one and can even achieve a status of acceptability, as appears to be the case in Indian English.
3 Argument 3 (process of transfer of training): 'I was admiring her' is the result of transfer of training. The learner uses textbooks which overemphasise the use of the English progressive form, thought by the textbook-writer to be problematic, i.e. requiring extra practice. The learner is misled by the teacher's, or the textbook's, emphasis on the progressive form into thinking that it is more widespread in standard English than it actually is (cf. George 1972, Lightbown 1983).

Finally one could argue that the form is the product of two or more of these processes interacting: it is a 'conspiracy' of factors (cf. Sharwood Smith 1983a; see also Anderson 1978, Hakuta 1974) that has led to this one form being used in this context, which gives us four more options (i.e. seven arguments in all):

4 Argument 4: process 1+2+3.
5 Argument 5: process 1+2.
6 Argument 6: process 1+3.
7 Argument 7: process 2+3.

To cap it all, we can add an infinite range of arguments if one takes into account the relative contribution claimed to obtain for each process in the last four arguments. Is it, for example, more transfer than overgeneralisation, or vice-versa? This conspiracy problem, based on the ambiguity of learner utterances as to what process or processes should be posited to account for them, should convince anyone interested in non-simplistic models of learner behaviour to look for a well-argued theoretical framework for conducting research into interlanguage.

2.1.6   Interlanguage strategies

Selinker believed that interlanguage behaviour was that language which was produced when the language learner was performing spontaneously. This ruled out systematic utterances that were closely controlled by some teaching technique, i.e. in a drill or exercise, the repetition drill being the most obvious example of this (cf. elicited imitation, which is different; 4.2.4.3). However, there was a role in his IL theory for the learner's deliberate attempts to solve particular problems during the course of his or her development. These he called 'strategies' and they provide us with the other two types of IL central process.

The first type of strategy had to do with solving problems in communication (following a suggestion by Coulter 1968). Communicative strategies were resorted to when learners were performing in the L2, but especially when they were having difficulty in expressing their meaning given their current IL resources. Later, people adopted the term 'compensatory strategies' to denote attempts to get round deficits allowing a broader use of the term 'communicative strategies' which can then include attempts to facilitate communication where the language user does have sufficient means to do so (Poulisse *et al.* 1984).

The second type, learning strategies, involved, for example, deliberate attempts on the part of the learner to commit aspects of the L2 to memory. Rote repetition is the prime example of this. Imagine a learner with a word or structure that he or she finds particularly important and which has not yet been learned. The learner may resort to repeating that item again and again in an attempt to 'force' it into memory. Another example would be the use of 'mnemonics', i.e. little tricks to help him or her to remember something difficult.

Selinker also allowed for 'internal strategies' of the sort suggested by Corder's inbuilt-syllabus idea. He names *simplification* as one of these, for example, reducing two present tenses (as English has) to one, or making all verbs regular or transitive or missing out grammatical formatives like articles and verb inflections. In other words, learning strategies may be conscious or unconscious.

2.1.7 Some conceptual problems concerning IL strategies

It is not very clear why internal strategies like simplification are not central processes or why transfer and overgeneralisation are not also called learning strategies. In any case, Selinker appeared to accord to transfer and overgeneralisation some special status by calling them 'central processes'. In other words, strategies or processes like simplification were not central and therefore had a lower status in the theory. In fact, Selinker was not at the time advancing a complete theory and these passing observations can be taken more as speculations than anything else.

Another problem, recognised by Selinker, was to decide which of the two types of strategy was involved in some observed learner behaviour. Simplification, as described above, could equally well be a communication strategy enabling learners to speak more smoothly and not irritate their interlocutors with their slow and hesitant speech. A further example might serve to illustrate this problem of ambiguity. Suppose a learner does not know how to order a theatre ticket and stands close to other people in order to catch the words and phrases they use and memorise them. Is this a communication strategy designed to solve the immediate problem of getting a ticket? Or is it a learning strategy designed to commit the appropriate words and structure to memory? The operations seem identical and the classification seems to hinge on whether the learner intends to remember the words and structure for use on a later occasion (see also Littlewood 1984: 27ff).

There has been much controversy surrounding the classification and explanation of strategies since Selinker's 1972 proposals. Some prefer to see strategies as having a special status in interlanguage theory while others see them more simply as a reflection of general human problem-solving behaviour and nothing specific to L2 behaviour (see Bialystok 1990). Even, as far as language is concerned, people using their mother tongue may experience sudden difficulty in finding the right words to express some concept. In this case they may find some other method of expression, or may simply abandon the attempt just as a second language user would (see Bialystok and Kellerman 1987). Some language teachers would like communicative strategies taught to L2 learners to help them keep a conversation going while others regard this as a waste of time, since, as just pointed out, learners already possess 'strategic' ability before embarking on L1 learning.

2.2 Summary

The 1970s really represent the formative years of second language acquisition research in Europe and then, especially from 1972 onwards, in North America where the early ideas advanced by Corder, Selinker and Nemser fell on fertile ground. This period saw the identification of all the fundamental issues that are still a matter of lively debate today. Even in the early part of the decade, researchers in this newly emerging field of study were beginning to accept that:

(1) second language acquisition is not easily understood; it is a complex process;

(2) second language acquisition is not a random process. It shows a great deal of systematicity;

(3) there are some theoretically interesting links to be made with mother tongue development despite the different circumstances in which learning takes place;

(4) learners have a great deal of control over their own development but, unfortunately, not conscious control;

(5) learners, often quite intuitively, approach the learning task strategically, forming hypotheses and testing them out, simplifying their task in systematic ways and often ignoring both the evidence of native-speaker input and the demands of their teachers;

(6) a major goal for research was to determine how and where fossilisation takes place.

3 Creative construction

3.0 Introduction

This chapter proceeds further with the examination of the major models of second language acquisition that were established in the 1970s. As was seen from the last chapter, a realisation grew up in the early years of that decade that attention in language research should be directed towards the mental processes that underlie learner performance. The initial interest of such people as Corder, Nemser and Selinker was in the mixture of processes that lay behind the systematic performance of non-native speakers. This chapter looks at a school of thought that researchers in Los Angeles developed in the early 1970s as an alternative to the interlanguage approach.

The 'creative construction' model was more radical than the IL model, and was to have an even greater impact on the field at the time. The term 'model' is employed here somewhat loosely. A model is a way of representing the various aspects of a theory so that the way that theory hangs together to form a coherent explanation is made clear. The theories and models with which we are dealing are really preliminary sketches of theories and should be judged accordingly. Again, the model to be represented in this chapter will be considered as an example of theoretical thinking about second language acquisition and various extra possibilities within the model will be considered that were not the focus of research at the time.

The reader should treat the discussion as an illustration of ways of looking at second language acquisition as though development were fully or partially preprogrammed such that learners, irrespective of their background, follow the same basic route, learning native L2 rules (principles, constructions) as though guided by an inner, subconscious teacher. To what extent this idea has been vindicated by research findings is controversial but the idea itself is an interesting one and enough has been discovered not to dismiss it as fantasy.

3.1 Links with first language acquisition

Whatever theoretical position one wants to take concerning the difference and similarities between first (mother tongue) and second (non-native) language acquisition, observation and common sense alone tell us a number of things, for instance:

1. The L1 acquirer knows considerably less about the world and hence has only fairly basic things about the here-and-now (ongoing experiences and feelings) to communicate. L2 learners have more complicated ideas they may want to communicate even when their L2 resources are inadequate for the job.
2. The L1 acquirer has little fear of making 'mistakes'.
3. L1 acquirers are highly motivated to communicate in their L1. L2 learners may have very different levels of motivation in this respect.
4. L1 learners, as Klein has pointed out, for instance, spend considerable time acquiring their mother tongue (about 9000 hours in the first five years, he estimates: Klein 1986).
5. The L1 acquirer will acquire native-speaker status in the normal course of events.
6. L1 acquirers do not normally undergo grammatical instruction. Some L2 acquirers do.

3.1.1   Short overview of research

In the 1960s and early 1970s, there were two types of research into child language which are reflected in L2 research. The first trend was to look at children's utterances as reflecting some sort of grammar (see Ingram 1989: 263ff). Martin Braine proposed that, once children started to produce two-word utterances, they followed what he called a 'pivot grammar' (Braine 1963). Briefly, he argued that words fell into two classes: *pivot* and *open*. Open items were less frequent but they formed a large class, e.g.:

cookie, dry, mama, shirt

Pivot items were frequent but formed a smaller class, e.g.:

all, more, there, no.

Moreover, pivot items occurred neither alone nor with other pivot items. Also, they were either initially occurring or finally occurring, e.g.:

more cookie
cookie *there*.

At some point, open items might occur together and they might also occur alone, e.g.:

cookie
cookie dry.

L1 researchers have debated about whether the child grammar starts out as a semantic system with its categories based solely on meaning like 'Agent' (the one who performs an action) or 'Action' and then later develops into purely syntactic categories where semantic notions such as action will be expressible by different syntactic categories. For example, a semantically based system might say the first position is always filled by the agent, the performer of some action, whereas a syntactically based system makes no such reference to meaning but simply says: 'In this language, the first position in the sentence is filled by the subject of the sentence.'

In a syntactically based account of basic sentence word order, then, the subject position may be filled by an agent or it may not. Compare the following two sentences where, in the first case, the agent (John) is the subject and, in the second – its passive counterpart – where the agent (John) is not the subject but the object, i.e. occupies another position in the sentence, after the verb:

John (*agent as well as subject*) stroked the chimp
The chimp (*not agent but subject*) was stroked by John (*agent but not subject*).

Indeed, children were found to interpret such passive sentences as active ones precisely because they assumed first position always to signify agent. So, in 'the chimp was stroked by John', they tended to think that the chimpanzee was doing the stroking, not John. It looked as though subject position, for them, was determined by meaning, the meaning of agent. David McNeill tried to work Braine's pivot grammar into a theory about an emerging transformational generative grammar (McNeill 1970) with the pivot class forming the basis for the nominal and verbal categories in the syntactically based adult grammar.

More recently Pinker has developed an approach involving 'semantic bootstrapping' whereby children first come to know about semantic notions like 'change of state' and, once learned, these notions immediately trigger given syntactic categories like 'verb' (see Grimshaw 1979, Pinker 1984) and the grammar is 'born'. These syntactic categories do not develop out of the semantic notions as in the earlier account but are available (in a mental waiting room as it were) from the beginning. However, they do not actually play any role until the appropriate semantic development has taken place. They need the child to provide the semantic notions first. The semantic notions provide the necessary basis for already available syntactic categories to be 'bootstrapped' on to them.

By way of contrast, Brown's classic 1973 study, in which he traces the early language development of Adam, Eve and Sarah, provides an example of a more thoroughly semantically based account of early grammars. Here the position of words is related directly to their meaning as described above in the example with John and the chimp: the position of words is dictated by their meaning (agent, patient, etc.). Semantics, of course, does not necessarily involve pragmatic or discourse meaning: this has been the focus of others, particularly Halliday (1975), looking at how child language develops in terms of their conversational ability (see also Lewis 1936/51 and discussion in Ingram 1989: 219ff).

3.1.2   L1 and L2 acquisition

It can be seen from the above that mother tongue learners start out as cognitively immature beings with relatively simple language systems. Following one theory, at last, they seem to have to learn concepts such as agent and action before any development can take place in their grammar. Older learners have this conceptual development behind them. They do not need to wait for syntactic categories to have something to slot into. Their first language has a rich array of syntactic and semantic terms ready and waiting. In this way, if any bootstrapping is going to take place, it is more likely to be between the L1 system and the L2 system – that is, in the form of crosslinguistic influence (transfer). This makes it possible for them to start with fairly complicated utterances once they have a few lexical items in their interlanguage repertoire. They also possess conversational skills which, in principle, they can use or adapt to gain maximum benefit of a small linguistic repertoire.

In certain respects, then, the difference between the course of early child language development and early (L2) interlanguage is striking. We cannot speak of conceptual development or conversational immaturity delaying the onset of acquisition and we cannot speak of one-word or two-word stages in the language of more mature learners. L2 learners already have:

(1) a mature (L1) semantic, pragmatic and syntactic system available;
(2) have a great deal of world knowledge and hence much to talk about;

(3) have the option of using some or all of their L1 system as a starting point for building the L2 grammar.

Even if they do not build up new grammatical knowledge on the basis of old L1 knowledge, L2 learners can still, when actually trying to communicate in the L2:

(4) form utterances using the few L2 words they know and cunningly recruiting the L1 grammar as a skeleton for those L2 words.

With regard to (4), learners may not literally assume that the L2 grammar is identical to their native grammar. Still, they can build up complicated messages at an early stage by 'stealing' from their L1 system and slotting L2 words into an L1 sentence frame, as in the following example where native L2 norms would require sub-ject–object–verb order (as in 'Mary the apples ate') but an L1 subject–verb–object order is used instead:

X (L2 subject noun) Y (L2 verb) Z (L2 object noun).

The lexical items, X, Y and Z, are not L1 items but the word order is identical to what it would be if it were a sentence in L1.

The availability of the L1 system gives L2 users a headstart over L1 acquirers in terms of sheer communicative ability at the outset of learning. At the same time, it may also lead them into delays or other complications with regard to actual grammatical development in L2 if that useful L1 prop becomes a hindrance. That is to say, they may come to rely too heavily on the L1.

Despite the acknowledgement of the striking difference between L1 and L2 learners, the IL model does involve what can be seen as links between interlanguage systems and the early and more primitive grammars of children in the sense that researchers wanted to see developmental systems as grammars in their own right. Also, Selinker's process of overgeneralisation is directly relatable to the regularised forms produced by children. This had already been pointed out by, for example, Dušková (1968) in Czechoslovakia when she analysed her students' written errors and found more than half of them difficult to ascribe to influence from Czech. Rather, they appeared to be based on an L2-rule, the constraints on which the learners had not yet fully grasped.

Where the creative construction position is concerned, the most salient proof of the close relationship between L1 and L2 acquisition was, initially at least, the *sequence* of development rather than this building of 'interlanguages' or intermediate systems. Roger Brown's pioneering work on Adam, Eve and Sarah (see Brown 1973) made a great deal of data available for theories about intermediate L1 systems, but it also provided the crucial notion of a fixed sequence of development. That is to say, Adam, Eve and Sarah developed control over 14 morphemes of English (like progressive-*ing*, plural-*s*, third person singular-*s*) in a strikingly similar fashion. Differences in the rate of development through the stages were not accompanied by changes in the sequence. The order seems to remain predictable. It was this finding that prompted Corder to advance the idea of an internal syllabus for L2 learners as well, and it was also this finding that lay at the heart of the 'creative construction' theory that came to dominate L2 research in the 1970s.

3.2   Creative construction theory

It was the 'creative construction' theorists that really drew most attention to the product/process problem mentioned at the close of the last chapter. They did this by questioning both the contrastivist approach and, at the same time, the current IL model as proposed by Selinker (see papers by Carroll and others in Alatis 1968 for early criticisms of the habit-formation view; see also Dušková 1968, Arabski 1971). Marina Burt and Heidi Dulay drew attention to the fact that many errors that superficially represented constructions in the L1, and hence might be assumed to be L1 transfer errors, could also be interpreted as overgeneralisations, as was illustrated in the previous section. This was especially compelling where those constructions also appeared in data from children learning the same language as an L1. One example they used was:

'he no wanna go'

This was a typical construction produced by a Spanish child learning English: the pre-verbal placement of the negator *no* mirrors that of Spanish but also appears in data collected by Klima and Bellugi and characterised by them as Stage II in the L1 English development of negation, clearly nothing to do with Spanish (Klima and Bellugi 1966, Dulay and Burt 1974).

The thrust of Dulay and Burt's argument was to support an 'L2 acquisition = L1 acquisition' hypothesis and to try to explain away as many of what they called 'interference-like goofs' as they could so that the source was either acquisition processes that occurred during L1 acquisition or, at the very least, ambiguous and therefore open in principle to an L1-oriented explanation. By removing or downgrading the role of the L1, they provided the field with a simpler, more elegant account of L2 acquisition.

The equation between L1 and L2 acquisition made by Dulay and Burt meant that the notion of IL was also downgraded: although learners did, in some cases, systematically produce deviant forms – as indicated by the research into the stage-by-stage development of negation and question forms – these forms were usually reminiscent of L1 acquisition and therefore the term 'interlanguage', which seemed to suggest that transitional forms had to be transitions between L1 and L2 constructions, was apparently seen as misleading. L1 did not provide the database for L2 acquisition. L2 input did.

In addition, the creative construction approach avoided the IL idea of there being some interim grammar, that is, as a system in its own right. In this way, they came close to the degree of target-orientedness typical of everyday language learners and language teachers (see section 2.1). In general, the research tended to focus on when and in what order the *native* forms came to appear regularly in learners' utterances. The learning model was basically *target-oriented* and *incremental*. Learners proceeded up separate ladders from one transitional form to another until they acquired the native form. Sometimes the ladder had several rungs (as was the case in negation and interrogation where learners had to go through a series of transitional stages) but, in this case, the learner was not seen as having an integrated language system, i.e. an interlanguage in Selinker's sense. Sometimes the ladder had only one rung worth mentioning: either you supplied the article in 90 per cent of obligatory contexts or you did not supply it at that level and therefore had not officially acquired it (according to the definition). Once a native form was acquired, it was not lost again. This idea is illustrated in Figure 3.1.

In the case of the morpheme orders, learners simply added on

FIGURE 3.1 An incremental and target-oriented view of development.

target forms in a predetermined order, hence filling out the gaps in their L2. To take the jigsaw puzzle idea mentioned earlier, the target language represented the complete jigsaw and any stage prior to that represented an incomplete version of that *same* jigsaw. The pieces were simply put in the right place in a fixed order, the nature of which was to be established by researchers. This, at least, is the abiding impression given by the creative construction theorising and experimental research as reported in the literature.

3.2.1   The main tenets

Creative construction theory received its fullest and most coherent expression in a book that finally appeared in 1982, *Language Two* (Dulay *et al.* 1982), but essentially brings together an approach that characterises the dominant trends of the 1970s (cf. McLaughlin 1987). It dominated for a number of reasons: it was a more radical point of view than that put forward by Selinker, and it provided a link-up with another, more established, research field (see Hatch 1978), namely the study of child language. 'Creative' in the sense used by this school of researchers refers to the way in which the learner creates an L2 system (or indeed a mother tongue system) on the basis of the data provided by the environment. This is in contrast to the behaviouristic view of what happens to language learners, i.e. that they were 'conditioned' by their experience: their new language habits were dictated primarily by what they individually experienced. According to the creative construction theorists, language develop-ment is not dictated by the environment but rather the learner subconsciously selects from all the information flowing in from outside only certain bits at a time. That selection process is part of an internal programme which is, they claim, essentially the same programme that drives mother tongue acquisition. This approach may be summed up as follows:

1. Second language acquisition is driven by essentially the same set of processes that are active in first language acquisition.
2. L2 structures are developed *in a particular 'pre-programmed' sequence* irrespective of the L1 background of the acquirer. The sequence is similar (but not necessarily identical) to that of an equivalent L1 acquirer (see Figure 3.2 for a sequence collapsed into four basic stages).
3. Within the sequence in which target forms are acquired, there are

sometimes regularly appearing sequences of 'developmental', non-native forms. In other words, a given target is not necessarily acquired in one stage, from 'no pattern' directly to the target native-speaker pattern: there may be a mini-sequence of intermediate forms leading up to that particular target (see Figure 3.3).

4. Acquisition takes place via exposure to the language not by means of any conscious analysis of the linguistic but by *analysis at a subconscious level*. It is thus not directly amenable to deliberate control by either learner or teacher.

5. For development to take place, language input must be *comprehensible to the learner* and must contain samples of the next construction on the list in the developmental sequence (see 2 above), i.e. the next target form or the next non-native form which characteristically leads to the next target form.

Expressed in these global terms, it has to be said that this is very much a preliminary model since the evidence to support it comes mainly from a very restricted part of the morphological and syntactic system of English as a second language.

Secondly, the theory as originally set out in the early 1970s, provides no *explanation* for the sequence as a whole (see Hatch 1979), i.e. why this particular sequence and not some other one? If the contributions by Selinker and particularly Corder were more theoretical in nature, those researchers following the creative construction line of thinking were less concerned with elaborating theory and more with testing out very limited hypotheses. The serious theorising was, it appeared, to be postponed to a later date. This allowed the field as whole to develop a battery of experimental techniques with a minimum of theoretical grounding. Later developments in creative construction research were to involve the elaboration of a preliminary theoretical framework on the basis of the morpheme studies (see points 1–5 above).

3.2.2 Developmental patterns

It should be emphasised that acquisition is being viewed here as being highly pre-programmed. The language input data act as triggers but development unfolds according to Corder's in-built syllabus and not according to the sequence in which structures are manifested in the input. This means that a certain form, for instance, third person singular -s in English, can turn up regularly from the very beginning in the input but still not be acquired by the learner (appear in their production) until much later.

The equation (or fairly high degree of similarity) between L1 and L2 acquisition respectively might suggest that interlanguage and child (L1) language will look alike: in fact, much of the research intended to demonstrate the creative construction model focused on this type of similarity in the product. Linguistic patterns studied in L1 were used as a basis for L2 theorising.

Figures 3.2 and 3.3 show the morpho-syntactic patterns of development that formed the bulk of research supporting the creative construction position (see Brown 1973, Klima and Bellugi 1966). Figure 3.2 shows the much discussed morpheme order. Here the target (native) forms are not actually listed in a straightforward order but are grouped together into three basic stages. This allows for some learner variation in which targets are acquired, and in which order, *within* the different stages. The idea is that within each stage the forms are developed almost at the same time. We could equate the targets with cities such as Toronto, Montreal, Stuttgart, Berlin, Beijing, and Shanghai and the stages with, say, Canada, Germany and China. So all learners, as it were, get to Germany at the same time but may not go to the two German cities in the same order.

The patterns are not related linguistically in any obvious way except trivially, as they are all options in the morphological repertoire of English. However, this lack of coherence is not true for the developmental sequence in Figure 3.3 which shows transitional stages in the acquisition of a *particular* structural area, namely negation.

The classical picture is, then, of learners of all types and background, moving through the same stages. Here, the target system is native-speaker English but the theory holds that this principle is true of all target languages, that is, all 'L2s'.

3.2.3   Rate and route of development

It is instructive to consider the logical possibilities left open by the basic claims put forward. Despite the classical creative construction argument, one might nevertheless predict highly *dissimilar* deviations among learners with different language backgrounds while maintaining that the attainment of the 'target', i.e. the native-like norm with respect to a given structural area of the language, would still follow the *same* basic sequence.

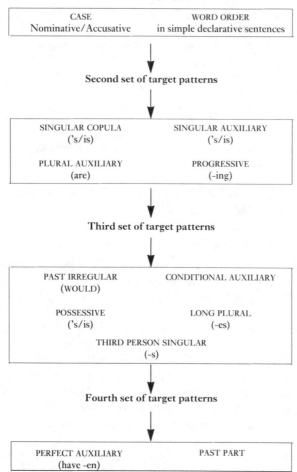

First set of target patterns

CASE	WORD ORDER
Nominative/Accusative	in simple declarative sentences

Second set of target patterns

SINGULAR COPULA ('s/is)	SINGULAR AUXILIARY ('s/is)
PLURAL AUXILIARY (are)	PROGRESSIVE (-ing)

Third set of target patterns

PAST IRREGULAR (WOULD)	CONDITIONAL AUXILIARY
POSSESSIVE ('s/is)	LONG PLURAL (-es)
THIRD PERSON SINGULAR (-s)	

Fourth set of target patterns

PERFECT AUXILIARY (have -en)	PAST PART

FIGURE 3.2 The development sequence (from Dulay and Burt 1975; see also Dulay *et al.* 1982: 218 for details).

After all, the main point was that learners without any conscious planning followed a fixed programme by which they attained specific L2 targets, say, the definite article, such that one target was always acquired after or at the same time as, but never before, another. In other words, given the *same* sequence of targets 1, 2 (see Figure 3.2) which might be manifested in L1 and L2 acquisition of a given language, the routes up to 1 and 2 respectively might still be

---

Step 1:   Negator in external position:
NEG I sit/I sit NEG

Step 2:   Negator in internal position before verb (no auxiliaries):
I NEG sit

Step 3:   Negator correctly placed in post-auxiliary position:
I can NEG sit, I have NEG sat, I do NEG sit, etc.

TARGET ATTAINED!

FIGURE 3.3   Mini-developmental sequence (after Klima and Bellugi 1966; see also Dulay *et al.* 1982: 123ff).

different. This is illustrated in the first pair of hypothetical learning scenarios presented in Figure 3.4.

3.2.3.1   Variation in the route

Let us imagine that, in a given language, researchers have noted and numbered a whole range of developmental (i.e. non-native) patterns produced by various types of learner and leading up to particular target constructions – that is, before learners regularly produced the native pattern, they produced their own variants of the target. It is as if all learners were, to use an earlier analogy, 'programmed' to go along a certain route, e.g. Toronto, Montreal, Stuttgart, Berlin, etc., but that different learners follow a different route between those destinations, some going from Toronto to Montreal over Ottawa, others following a quite different path but still ending up in Montreal. These individual paths between destinations are, so to speak, their developmental patterns.

To abstract away, for a moment, from actual recorded examples, including the particular L2 (typically English), and focus on the idea of developmental variation itself, let us mark the various observed non-native variants which lead up to a particular target (say a plural marker) as 'Dpat' (developmental pattern) plus a letter, e.g. stages P, Q, R or rather Dpat P, DPat Q, DPat R, etc. By this method we can see the various ways in which the acquisition of some targets (a given aspect of the target language system) by different types of learners – e.g. L1 versus L2 learners of that language, or L2 learners with differing L1s – might be studied and compared. Let us assume that native targets are numbered 1, 2, 3, etc., in the order they are always supposed to develop, while the non-native patterns are marked, as shown above, with letters.

A simple, concrete example of a non-native DPat (developmental pattern) sequence (adapted slightly from real, observed sequences in the acquisition of English) might be the development of negation (see Figure 3.4.). Native-like use of negation would then be the 'target'. Here DPat P, say, happens to be the result of a rule placing the negator in initial position (e.g. 'NOT taxi will come'), DPat Q is the negator in pre-auxiliary position ('taxi NOT will come'), DPat R, an alternative stage, is negator in sentence-final position ('taxi will come NOT') and the final non-deviant stage (TARGET 1) would then be the negator in the post-auxiliary position ('taxi will NOT come'). Note that similar examples could be made up for any area of interlanguage, for example in the development of the spelling of a particular lexical item, its pronunciation or its semantics and pragmatics although the overall course of development, in each case, would probably be quite different.

In our hypothetical example shown in Figure 3.4, the route to TARGET 1, for example, is marked by two transitions in both cases but the first stages in L1 and L2 acquisition respectively differ in that young monolingual children produce DPat R whereas L2 acquirers of that same language produce DPat P. However, they both progress to a similar stage, namely DPat Q, before producing the native form TARGET 1.

At least in this first case, there is partial overlap between the L1 and L2 learning scenarios. This situation may be compared with the route to TARGET 2. Here, L1 acquirers go through one developmental stage (Z) whereas L2 acquirers go through two (different) stages (Y, Z). Here, L1 and L2 differ both quantitatively and qualitatively as regards the developmental stage leading up to the target but still share the same TARGET 1, TARGET 2 sequence.

3.2.3.2 *Developmental patterns and L1 influence*

In the L2 acquisition sequence above, one might imagine that the different deviant patterns that regularly appear in L2 performance

---

Same developmental sequence: different in between routes

L1 acq: DPat R - ->DPat Q - ->TARGET 1 - ->DPat Z - ->TARGET 2

L2 acq: DPat P - ->DPat Q - - >TARGET 1 - ->DPat Y - ->DPat Z - ->TARGET

FIGURE 3.4 Different routes in L1 and L2 acquisition: a hypothetical example for target patterns A and B.

prior to the acquisition of TARGET 1 *and* TARGET 2 might be transfer forms from the learner's L1 (for example). For instance, German post-verbal negation (as in 'Ich liebe ihn NICHT': 'I love him NOT') or Spanish pre-verbal negation (as in 'NO es verdad': 'NOT is true') might be the source for a similar construction in the IL of German or Spanish learners, respectively. In this case, the actual DPat that appears will be one thing for learners who are native speakers of a particular language but perhaps another thing for native speakers of some other language where the system of negation is quite different.

Those maintaining the creative construction view in its strongest form would claim that *language transfer is not involved in the creation of new grammars and only manifests itself as a performance phenomenon*: the learner falls back on the separate L1 system in moments of crisis, i.e. when L2 resources fail to meet the demands being placed on it. Hence IL, in the creative construction view, may contain developmental patterns ('transitional forms': Dulay *et al.* 1982) but, in the strongest version of the theory, these will be *stable across learners with different L1s*.   Some have questioned the apparently complete denial of a role for L1 in IL development. In the light of their research results, they have strongly suggested, for example, that where a standard (universal/common) transitional stage (for any type of learner) in the development of a given area of IL (say, negation, for example) matches a standard structure in the L1 of a given learner, that learner will experience fossilisation or prolonged delays in that stage: the 'crucial similarity' (cf. Wode 1978; see also Ravem 1974, Schumann 1978, Zobl 1978 for the idea of a delay) functions as a kind of trap or distraction. In this way, although the same 1-then-2 sequence is observed for all learners, the L1 may cause longer periods in the transitional stages prior to TARGETS 1 or 2. In other words, when we compare the two developmental scenarios, there is a difference in *timing* in the attainment of a given target. Although the route is the same, the **rate** of acquisition is different. Recently, for example, Tang studied Chinese learners of English learning interrogative structures and noted that although they followed the same universal pattern observed in many different L1 and L2 studies, there were delays in the acquisition at those points where a feature of their L1 (involving non-inversion in questions) had a very close counterpart in an L2 developmental pattern (Tang 1990; see also below).

The supposition that learners of different types might have

different delays *en route* gives us the following logical possibilities for IL development (in particular those illustrated in Figure 3.5):

(i) Same developmental sequence, same routes, same rate.
(ii) Same developmental sequence, same routes, different rate.
(iii) Same developmental sequence, different routes.

All these alternatives are compatible with the basic creative construction approach, which focuses on the identity of the sequence rather than the rate aspects. The reader is encouraged to read the creative construction literature for actual illustrations of these various logical possibilities (see, for example, contributions to Hatch 1978, Andersen 1981a and discussions in Dulay *et al.* 1982).

Various studies on the development of question (interrogative) structures, as suggested above, provide illustrations of this model. In 1966, Klima and Bellugi characterised L1 acquisition in this area as a three-stage development starting with intonation questions in very simple phrases ('Ball go?'), intonation in more complex phrases ('ball can't go?') and only in the third stage, subject–verb inversion in yes–no–questions ('can ball go?'). Development is only complete when inversion spreads to wh-questions ('where can ball go?'). Embedded questions ('I don't know where the ball goes') come later if only by virtue of their structural and/or semantic complexity.

People have also looked at the order in which particular wh-words (what, where, why, how, when) emerge and have found 'what' and 'where' to be typically early (Brown 1973, Tyack and Ingram 1977, Wode 1976, Felix 1981). The frequency of these forms and their usefulness in conversation seem to play an important role in determining the order.

```
(i)    (All L2 learners): DPat R ---->DPat Q --->TARGET 1
(ii)   L2 learner with L1 Japanese:
                    DPat R ---->DPat Q---->TARGET 1
       L2 learner with L1 Spanish:
                    DPat R ---->DPat Q--->TARGET 1
(iii)  L2 learner with L1 Chinese:
                    DPat P --->DPat R --->TARGET 1
       L2 learner with L1 Polish:
                    DPat R --->DPat S ---->TARGET 1
```

FIGURE 3.5 Relative delays and varying routes in the L2 acquisition of target pattern '1': hypothetical possibilities.

The general pattern of inversion before inversion seems characteristic of most L1 and L2 studies. However, Ravem reports the early appearance of inversion in Norwegian English so that a separate, prior intonation stage is hard to establish. He ascribes this to the availability of inversion in L1 Norwegian. Compare this with Tang's findings, mentioned above, where non-inversion not only occurs but seems to have a prolonged life in the development of questions in Chinese learners, the explanation being the same as in the case of Ravem's subject, namely that the nature of the L1 system influenced the shape of L2 development up to attainment of the native target.

3.2.4   Differences in emphasis

Although, in later statements of the creative construction model, more attention was paid to developmental forms in the L2 learner's repertoire, as mentioned earlier, the focus was never really on interlanguage as conceived of by Selinker. It was more on when, and in what order, learners attained particular target forms or constructions (such as our hypothetical TARGETS 1 and 2 above). The effect of acquiring one form on the rest of the developing system was not considered. This was looked into later, a notable example being the study of the acquisition of a new present tense form in English (the continuous or progressive form as in 'I am running'). Adopting the new form did not simply mean adopting native usage of that form but rather destabilised the use of the one (present simple) form in use (e.g. 'I run'). The net effect was a new non-native present tense system (see Lightbown 1983, 1985).

This relative lack of interest in the systematic transitional (IL) patterns that learners go through allowed us to characterise creative construction theory as target oriented but not in quite the same way as was indicated in the first chapter. Rather, to reiterate a point made earlier, it implies an *incremental* view of learning such that different parts of the native-speaker system, pieces of the jigsaw puzzle, as it were, are acquired in a particular order. Learners do not, in this view, radically restructure their intuitions about the target system (cf. White 1982); they just acquire it bit by bit in a predictable order.

3.3   Summary

In this chapter, an attempt has been made to capture the essential messages that were coming from the international literature on second language acquisition in the 1970s. The other aim was to distil from that debate a number of important issues that arise once one has abandoned the idea of a learner following a programme of learning imposed from outside. These issues – the relationship between first and second language learning, the impact of conscious learning, and the status of mental learner grammars – have to be faced in any theory of language acquisition. The following chapters will deal with the way in which the development of ideas in the field has coped with these problems. Part II continues with the first attempts to enrich the rather simplistic picture of second language theory presented in Part I.

4 Analysing interlanguage

4.0 Introduction

The first chapter provided an introduction to the way in which people began to rethink common attitudes to second language learning. Another way of getting a realistic feel for the kind of thinking that guides second language research is to look at methods and techniques used in actual investigations. The discussion here will deal with some of the practical and theoretical problems that arise when actually collecting and analysing IL data. General questions of experimental design and statistics should be gleaned from appropriate books (e.g. Hatch and Farhady 1982, Butler 1985, Seliger and Shohamy 1989, Hatch and Lazaraton 1991).

Section 4.1 will deal with how to tackle the practical aspects of research and there will be a moral to this particular tale, namely that *a*-theoretical (blind) data-collection should be kept within strict limits.

Section 4.2 will review some central aspects of theoretically inspired studies, that is, where investigations are set up to test particular hypotheses for which the researcher provides good arguments or with regard to studies which are derived from theoretical claims discussed in the literature.

4.1 Heuristics

Faced with the task of setting up some investigation into interlanguage, the novice will be somewhat overawed by the methodological problems involved. Without any previous training, it is easy to fall into the trap of adopting a purely target-oriented approach (recall the discussion in 1.2). That is to say, you can look at the problem not from a more objective, research angle but from the point of view of a teacher or learner with practical considerations in mind. For example, one might have recourse to data-gathering techniques that are based on simply discovering the extent to which a learner has 'achieved' a level of nativeness in the L2 under consideration. Such techniques may well obscure interesting facts about the learner's intermediate beliefs about the L2.

As will have become very clear by now, this is not the main aim of second language research: it is not target oriented to this extent. It does not ask the question: 'How far along the path to perfection has the learner come?' Putting aside complex notions of wanting to be similar to or different from native speakers, wanting to avoid the embarrassment of making errors and so on, the 'target' of the language acquisition device (1.2.12) does have the same basic sense as it has for the conscious learner: it is to make the learner's system compatible with the L2 input. Once that has been stated, it is important to stress that the notion of target and of aiming towards some distant goal is not so straightforward. We cannot assume, for instance, that when the learner has the conscious intention to get closer to the native-speaker norm, his or her learning mechanisms will automatically co-operate and, indeed, continue to operate. Nor can we assume that when the learner has decided that his or her L2 proficiency is more or less adequate for the job in hand, the learning mechanisms dutifully shut down operations. With such considerations in mind, it is just as interesting to look in detail at what the learner's state of knowledge actually is, and how it works for that learner at a given moment in time *irrespective of whether such and such a target norm is violated.* Close analysis of the learner's performance will inform us most directly about what the current learner system is. That is, indeed, the main focus of interest in IL research. It does not involve a simple shopping list of 'target norms' to be attained.

One way a beginner might tackle L2 research is, then, to draw up a checklist of native-speaker targets, e.g. the 'passive', 'asking questions', a specific area of vocabulary, etc. Another educationally inspired technique would be to 'gather errors' to see 'what has gone wrong' or where there is 'room for improvement'. Again, although somewhat nearer the mark, gathering errors can still be a disguised way of finding out simply how *non*-native a learner is. Interlanguage is neither those parts of the learner's performance that conform to the native norms nor those parts that deviate. Nevertheless, provided that point is accepted, it should be added that results from proficiency tests and error collections do constitute a useful heuristic for selecting promising linguistic areas for further research.

In view of all that has been said to date about the ambiguity of errors, the data that have been collected will not be very informative beyond their signalling potential areas where the IL of the learner is noticeably different from the native-speaker norms. A better heuristic is:

(1) reading the literature to find out what has been done in a given area of the languages, what techniques have been used and to what extent they proved to be useful;
(2) selecting an area and methods from a respectable study that has actually been carried out.

This would seem to be matter of common sense and hardly worth mentioning here. Nevertheless, experience as a journal editor has shown that many people still set out to test hypotheses they have formulated on their own initiative without checking the more recent international literature properly. Leafing through the titles and abstracts of the last five or ten years of *Language Learning, Second Language Research, Applied Linguistics* or *Studies in Second Language Acquisition* can save embarrassment at a later date.

4.1.1   Gathering spontaneous data

Language data can be taken from more or less spontaneous learner performance. Complete spontaneity can be assured if the learner is completely unaware that he or she is unobserved, i.e. where the method is clandestine. Some countries place legal restrictions on this 'candid camera' approach and most researchers for this and other practical reasons resort to some degree of control. Hence spontaneous data (or, more accurately, 'semi-spontaneous data') has come to mean to most people data that are produced when the subject is supposedly relaxed and not focused on producing language to satisfy the investigator. The subject's attention is therefore focused on conveying meaning in the language and not especially on the form in which that meaning is expressed, at least no more than would occur in a completely spontaneous speech situation. Completely spontaneous data rarely figure in the research literature. There are a number of possible reasons for this: one might be the time and effort required to amass a corpus large enough to draw some useful conclusions. However, there are also some theoretical considerations, which will be mentioned below.

The most obvious candidate for spontaneous data of a more controlled type is oral (conversational) data where subjects are asked to describe a picture, or talk about their experiences in a relaxed, informal atmosphere or even retell a story which has just been related to them. In the latter case, the idea is that the subject is too involved in trying to remember the details of the story to become self-conscious about formal correctness.

An obvious example of the picture description technique may be found as part of the Bilingual Syntax Measure (Burt *et al.* 1975). Picture description enables the researcher to elicit certain structures without appearing to be interested in anything except perhaps whether the subject knows the words. If the investigator is wise enough, he or she will ensure that the vocabulary is already known by the subject. Alternatively, if vocabulary is the area of investigation, then the subject's knowledge of syntax should be perfectly adequate for the task in hand.

The investigator also has to consider (particularly when investigating vocabulary) the effect of pronunciation difficulty: the subject may well avoid words that are difficult to pronounce. Hence, even with 'spontaneous' data collection, there are quite a number of factors to consider as far as (subtly) controlling the learner's performance is concerned. If learners encounter serious problems in expressing meaning in the target language, they may become too aware of the conditions under which they are performing and hence cease to be spontaneous. William Labov referred to this problem as the Observer's Paradox (Labov 1970; Tarone 1979). The observer wishes to observe spontaneous language behaviour, yet the very presence of an observer has the effect of preventing spontaneity in the subject being investigated.

As was mentioned above, certain relaxations have to be made to the notion of 'spontaneous' and the investigator has to provide as good a simulation of unobserved language performance as possible. The closest researchers get to true, uncontrolled language performance using a method which is not clandestine is when radio-microphones are attached to subjects and they are allowed to interact among themselves in some natural situation. For example, children playing in the school playground have been investigated in this manner (see, for example, Pienemann 1984 and, for first language research, Wells 1985).

Where the collection of *written* data and spontaneous composition (e.g. letters, informal essays, etc.) is concerned, the observing investigator is conveniently absent during the subject's performance of the task. However, this advantage is offset by the fact that writing is generally less spontaneous in character. Actually seeing one's own performance manifested in written texts may itself provoke some degree of attention to form that is supposed to be the hallmark of non-spontaneous production. Again, investigators may have to create a special definition of 'spontaneous writing' for the purposes of investigation, perhaps introducing some degree of control by, say, encouraging the writer to write quickly, or to write long texts without regard for errors, or otherwise satisfy themselves that the writer is not focusing on form but only on the content of the written message (see Krashen *et al.* 1978).

It should be noted that no rationale for collecting or experimentally eliciting spontaneous data has yet been mentioned, apart from the heuristic one. One possible reason for collecting *only* spontaneous data would be that one should only collect data which *directly reflects natural language use* because all other data are artificial and hence suspect or even automatically invalid. One might dub this the 'naive naturalistic' approach or perhaps the 'dirty data' approach. Few people take this extreme line seriously. Spontaneous data can be so ambiguous and confusing that some 'cleaning up' is necessary. That is, collection has to be focused on particular types of data and this means ignoring or suppressing those phenomena that are irrelevant and will obscure the answers to the questions being asked. In the same way, a doctor has to ignore many aspects of a patient's spontaneous behaviour in order to find the answers to particular questions he or she has about that patient's condition. The main point is not that it is of little value if people (patients, learners) are encouraged to act spontaneously, but rather that elicitation of information from patients or learners has to be carried out in ways that encourage the production of *relevant* information.

The creative construction approach to be described later does provide a rationale (rather than a naive belief) for collecting only spontaneous data, namely the argument that subconsciously acquired knowledge, i.e. gleaned without any formal learning, is most transparently reflected in spontaneous language behaviour. Any elicitation device which allows learners to reflect on what they are doing, also allows them to alter their behaviour according to what has here been termed 'metalinguistic knowledge'. Their responses become, in this view, artificial and untrustworthy if we want to discover their real intuitions about the nature of the target system. These 'gut feelings', in this particular approach, are the only true reflections of the learner's developing L2 system so that any deliberate manipulation of structure in the learner's head serves to complicate and confuse the picture given by the test. In a sense the tester is (here) supposed to be like the Freudian psychoanalyst trying to tease out the patient's real subconscious thoughts and feelings and get past the smokescreen created by the patient's conscious censor which automatically works to manipulate and conceal the 'truth' from both the psychoanalyst and the patient. Given time to reflect, the argument goes, the learner may provide data which have been altered to fit consciously held preconceptions about what ought or ought not be the case in the L2, preconceptions that have no time to work in really spontaneous performance.

Despite the supposed unreliability of data which do not spring spontaneously from the language learner in the heat of the moment, there may be special theoretical reasons for wanting to try a less direct approach to elicitation. Indeed, the Chomskyan argument has been raised against the informativeness of spontaneous data (see Sharwood Smith 1986) claiming that such behaviour is itself an unfaithful reflection of underlying linguistic knowledge, i.e. competence. This is because only *well-controlled* competence shines through. Knowledge that is only partially controlled is left untapped. It tells us more about what the learner knows and *can use unhesitatingly* than about what the learner knows and *would have used in less demanding situations*. Secondly, there is the problem of conflicting rule systems within the language. We would be getting samples of different styles and varieties of the language, which may have different underlying rules. It might not be so easy to tell from performance alone when the learner was style-shifting. To treat performance as reflecting some homogeneous language system would be folly, as most linguists would quickly corroborate.

In addition – as will become clear in the discussion on the creative construction approach to transfer – pressure to perform can induce learners to borrow from their well-controlled competence in another language, notably the mother tongue (L1). This means producing behaviour that we would not want to ascribe to their developing *second language* (L2) knowledge. And, finally, a Chomskyan approach would entail finding out about the learner's knowledge (beliefs, assumptions) about ambiguity and ungrammaticality. This information about the nature of the learner's (or indeed native speaker's) subconscious 'competence ' (Chomsky 1965) could never emerge clearly and reliably from spontaneous performance data.

From what was said above, spontaneous behaviour would seem to reflect a mixture of well-controlled IL competence and well-controlled (back-up) L1 competence as well as a combination of styles matching the language to various speaker needs and social situations. For instance, unless we see marks of hesitation or other signs of difficulty, we must assume that the learner is using the competence from either language system that he or she controls effortlessly. This provides an example of how crucial theory is to the elicitation and interpretation of IL data. True, the outside world provides the data but, in effect, the theory determines what is relevant for the researcher, and not vice-versa. At the same time, one should never underestimate the thorny problems inherent in a 'clean data' approach to IL methodology. Once you try to manipulate the learner, you have even greater need of a theory to guide you in how you do it and how you interpret the results. You need a theory about what constitutes knowledge of a language. You need a theory of language variation. You need a theory of on-line language processing to inform you about access and integration of knowledge as the milliseconds tick away in live performance. Nothing, it transpires, is easy for the hapless researcher.

4.1.2   Counting types of tokens

Given a minimal theoretical framework and a corresponding lack of precise research questions, the would-be interlanguage investigator may well decide, after collecting some learner data, to do some counting. The data collected would be counted to establish some gross observable characteristics which might suggest some avenue of investigation. If no nice well-worked out theory is available, one has, after all, to begin somewhere. Here are some obvious types or clusters of data types for which tokens may be sought. You might look at:

   I. Native forms versus non-native forms.
  II. Morpho-syntactic structures used.
 III. Lexical items used.
 IV. (where relevant) Phonological (sound-related) structures used.
  V. (where relevant) Graphological (writing-related) structures used.
 VI. Pragmatic and sociolinguistic structures used.

  Sample tokens of the above data types:

   I. '*I cause that he went' versus 'I caused him to go'
  II. 'I walked', 'I *runned' (regular past tense rule)
 III. know, see, come, go, house, money (simple vocabulary only, say).
 IV. [bet] for 'bat'; [bet] also for 'bat' (spoken forms)
  V. <tend> for <tent>, <ruff> for <rough> (written forms)
 VI. Mixing up 'this' and 'that' when referring to something said earlier or something about to be said; using 'in my opinion' to express modesty in formal written English where the unintended effect on native readers is pomposity.

As far as Category I (native versus non-native forms) is concerned, the investigator may be able to get some gross measure of the learner's IL stage and some intuitive notion of possible psycholinguistic processes that may be operative at this level: 'native' here means 'in accordance with native-speaker norms' rather than 'signifying native-speaker rule in the learner's grammar', the first meaning being purely descriptive, the second theoretical (and explanatory).

Counts looking at the other categories will provide some insight into the complexity of the learner's productive IL repertoire, what syntactic structures are used (or *avoided* cf. Schachter 1976), what lexical items, what speech sounds, what systematic spelling patterns and what pragmatic functions. In addition to these *linguistic* labels, the researcher may care to add *psycholinguistic* categories such as 'L1 influence' where the data reveal a pattern which accords with a pattern in the learner's L1 and 'overgeneralisation of a correct L2 rule'. This means that the researcher must make a guess about the process for each piece of data. The use of the word 'potential' as in the label, 'potential L1 influence', may help to emphasise the tentative nature of these categories. They are, after all, guesses which simply point at *possible* psycholinguistic processes and in no way constitute a well-worked-out theoretical claim about the data.

Of course, it is impossible to collect the data completely blindly. The researcher will, however, already have a low-level theoretical decision to make: he or she must decide whether or not to use this category only for *deviant* (i.e. non-native) patterns in the data. What happens, for example, when the L1 structure, if carried over to the learner's IL, would produce a perfectly good native utterance? Suppose that we encounter that utterance in the learner's production. The Dutch learner of English produces the question form Verb–Subject–Object: 'Is it good?' Is that to be categorised as 'lucky L1 influence' (from the identical Dutch question construction, as in: 'Is het goed?'). Or, can we say that, because it happens to be native-like English, because it has been evidenced in the input, the learner has simply learned that little bit of the target system? Is there real knowledge of English, in other words?

It is relevant to note at this juncture the *amount* of data that are necessary before certain sequences manifest themselves as *patterns*: in some cases very large stretches of spoken or written text are required. The subjunctive does not occur too often in informal spoken French so that hours of transcript may be required to gather a decent collection of contexts in which we might expect a native speaker to use that construction. In this sort of situation, the investigator may have to reconsider the value of the chosen heuristic (rough and ready data-gathering) given such a large investment of time and other resources. It may be wiser to resort to manipulating the learner in order to get more tokens of the structure in which he or she is interested.

If all one is to end up with is a gross categorisation of data and a set of numbers without explanation, it is extremely doubtful whether such rough-and-ready data collection is worth while. In any case, especially where making use of database software (see 9.4.1), the researcher would be well advised to reserve space for a large number of categories (for the structure of the corpus) in advance, since experience usually suggests all kinds of new and potentially relevant features of the corpus that should be noted down for later use: these will minimally include *linguistic* categories, probably using some widely accepted modern descriptive grammar of the L2, and *psycholinguistic* categories suggesting potential L1 influence, use of metalanguage, etc. (drawing on some broadly accepted psycholinguistic terminology). (See, for example, Van der Sande and Opstal 1987 for an account of a system for storing coded Dutch–English IL data using Dbase III, and Pienemann 1987b, 1992, for a Macintosh-based system.) If such provisions are made when the investigator *does* have precise theoretical questions, there is a greater chance that the corpus of IL data will yield something of interest.

4.2   Theory-driven techniques

Data collection without any real theoretical perspective is only worth while provided that it claims minimal resources and generates some interesting ideas that can be worked out before large-scale data collection is undertaken. This means that one is then left with two options regarding the other approach, i.e. *theory-driven* data collection. The first option is to have a set of theoretical questions that have been carefully considered and which share a common framework, i.e. they are posed in order to test a more general theoretical position which itself has been properly argued, or, secondly, one can collect data which can be used for a number of different specified purposes. To do this one has to have in mind what those purposes might be: for example, one might elicit oral data from a set of learners with a view to looking at lexical development as well as syntactic development. However, to do this one would still need to know, via a consideration of previous research reported in the literature, the interesting aspects of both types of development in order to build this into the elicitation instrument, otherwise one would be back in the situation mentioned earlier which, when taken to extremes, might be unkindly characterised as superficial botanising. Classifying and labelling may give you a feeling of being 'scientific' but this is no substitute for looking for *explanations* of phenomena.

What, in fact, would be a useful way of distinguishing the two more or less 'multipurpose' methods of gathering data is to refer to the heuristic type as 'collection' or 'gathering' and to refer to the second type as a particular kind of 'elicitation'. 'Elicitation' may thus be defined as *principled data collection*.

4.2.1 Naturalistic data

In view of the discussion thus far, it seems that confining research to the observation of learners' performances 'in their natural habitat', so to speak, is only of heuristic value; that is, its value is limited as far as psycholinguistic research is concerned. This may not hold for sociologically oriented investigations with other research methodologies. Here spontaneous data may yield more immediate insights. However, such naturalistic data are too rich and confused to offer any immediate explanation of the psychological processes that shape the interlanguage product. A considerable amount of more controlled elicitation may be needed to achieve a coherent interpretation of what is going on in the language users' heads.

The opaqueness of naturalistic data, where unsupported by further research, holds even for those aspects of interlanguage that bear on the uses to which IL knowledge is put in different types of situation and in different types of speaker intention: *pragmatic* issues, in other words. You really have to know for sure what the coughs and hesitations mean, what the speaker had in mind when using a particular word, and so on. You can only progress so far by guessing what lies behind the pragmatic performance captured on recordings of one type or another. The problem of interpretation without further investigation even occurs at the stage where recorded data have to be transcribed. And the opaqueness or ambiguity also bedevils those aspects of IL that obtain, irrespective of pragmatic functions. This view, casting doubt on the inherent value of naturalistic data, runs directly counter to the view propounded by the creative constructionists of the 1970s who, as mentioned above, accorded a privileged status to spontaneous data and to elicitation devices that got as close as possible to it. Clearly, research needs input from both types of data. If the situation is such that one just has to rely on one type rather than the other, then the preference should go to elicited data. The researcher's own personal experience of the learners in question will then have to function as a substitute for spontaneous data specially collected for the occasion.

To provide a graphic illustration of the above point, let us consider the following annotated informal oral exchange between a native speaker (NS) and an IL speaker (ILS) producing such behaviour.

NS: What do you think of Mary's behaviour in the film?
ILS.   I think ... (speaker pauses here) ... it's not very friendly.

COMMENTS:

1. Does the IL contain no neg-raising (moving the 'not' up to the main clause): 'I think that it is *not* friendly' in IL English rather than, in native-speaker English: 'I do *not* think that...' where 'not' is indeed raised up to the main clause, or is this a wrong assumption? Is it actually the case that the pause after 'think' indicates a real break, and what follows is the start of a new sentence? How do we analyse this IL utterance?

2. Would this same ILS when faced with the sentence 'I think it is not friendly' be able to identify it as non-native and, furthermore, be able to give the native version? In other words, assuming for a moment that this is really a single sentence with no neg-raising, is it purely a fluency (control) phenomenon or does it reflect a rule in the speaker's IL system such that the ILS really *believes* it to be an acceptable sentence in L2?

3. Would the ILS regularly produce non-neg-raising constructions in *casual* speech while producing the native version in other contexts of use, for instance, *formal writing*, thus assuming that neg-raising is an *optional* rule in the *grammar* but that a pragmatic rule restricts neg-raising to formal writing styles? In this case we would have a partial overlap between IL and native grammar accounted for via pragmatic considerations.

In this way, an apparently innocent pause in this simple dialogue has many important theoretical implications for the researcher.

4.2.2   Subject selection

The selection of subjects for an IL investigation should, in principle, be decided or at least constrained by the theoretical questions being asked. Often, practical limitations play a role since most IL investigators have limited access to subjects: there may not be enough of them to do an effective group study. They may be the wrong age or at the wrong level, or they may not be available for the length of time needed for the experiment.

Some of the variables associated with experimental subjects may be different to control, others not: age, sex, IQ and motivation all have to be considered as possible factors interfering with the results and appropriate experimental design techniques have to be adapted where the theory adopted suggests that a given factor is relevant. If, for example, the researcher has good reason to discount age as a relevant variable, then mixed age groups will not be a problem, and vice-versa: for example, if, out of a lack of confidence in their intuitions, young secondary school learners yield unreliable results in standard acceptability judgement tests, then, clearly, such tests have to be adapted or ruled out. In fact, the researcher should always check whether the subjects have experience of the particular technique to be used and this should be mentioned in the report of the experiment.

Intelligence is often discounted as a relevant factor in language acquisition, an assumption dangerous to make in a modular approach (1.2.11) – but even where it does not play any direct role, it may, for example, affect the way subjects understand the test instructions. Motivation may also play a part here. Subjects with low motivation may not take the tests seriously. These are the types of question that textbooks on statistics raise but do not answer. IL theory must provide the appropriate guidance. Where it does not, the investigator must play safe and follow the general rules suggested by the statisticians (see Robson 1973 for an introduction; see also Butler 1985: Ch. 6, Nunan 1992).

4.2.3 Linguistic variables

As mentioned previously, modularity applied to IL research requires that many different areas of IL under investigation could potentially require a different type of theoretical approach. This might be true even *within* areas such as syntax. Hence, previous research might, to take a hypothetical example, have shown that metalinguistic know-ledge played no facilitating role in the syntactic development of conditional clauses. As a result, a new investigation into some other area of IL, say word order in subordinate clauses, might be set up without any test of the subject's metalinguistic knowledge. This decision would be unwarranted, at least for the reason stated. It might be that some learners actually spend some time explicitly focusing on the problem of word order and trying to create L2 utterances for themselves following some explicit rule like 'place verb in final position'; it might also be that this conscious concern with word order makes them especially sensitive to the absence of non-final verbs in the L2 input and that this leads them to develop in a native-like manner more quickly. It may also be that the concern for word-order distracts them from other kinds of relevant evidence in the input causing delays in development towards the norm. Indeed, delays might occur in word order development if metalinguistic awareness played a distracting role in IL development. If there are no clearly stated arguments to the contrary, it is, therefore, always safer, until one knows better, to provide tests which tap conscious awareness of the area in question as well as those which tap the learner's intuitions.

The fruitful incorporation of linguistic theoretical concepts into IL studies may introduce many new linguistic variables to account for. One particular example of a linguistic theoretical concept being applied in an acquisition setting is provided by some proposals made recently by Radford concerning L1 acquisition. Radford attempts to show that an early stage of child syntax – roughly that prior to the appearance of *wh*-phrases in questions and auxiliary constructions as reported by child language researchers (Klima and Bellugi 1966, Bloom 1970) may be characterised as a 'small-clause' stage (see Radford 1990).

Without going too deeply into the technical aspects, small-clauses in adult English may be viewed as *verbless* clauses or clauses without an inflected verb: compare 'to be' with 'is', with its inflection marking it as present tense and third person singular, for example. Examples of small clauses are provided by the following:

'her to be clever' (as opposed to 'she is clever')
'it a good idea' (as opposed to 'it is a good idea')
'him nice' (as opposed 'he is nice').

These clauses are introduced by constructions containing verbs such 'consider' and 'find' as in:

'I consider [her to be clever]'.

Radford finds the various syntactic characteristics which we can find in adult small clauses – for instance, no possibility of making *wh*-

phrases with them or of including auxiliaries – and the early English utterances of children learning their mother tongue similar in many ways. Moreover, he has explanations for the few ways in which they do diverge (e.g. word order).

In the L2 literature on naturalistic L2 acquisition, similar kinds of construction as illustrated above may be found. It would, therefore, be of interest to apply the same ideas in child language to early IL utterances. Moreover, one might speculate, there are enough aspects of small clauses which are reminiscent of pidgin languages, which suggests a link up with the ideas proposed by Schumann (Schumann 1978, also Andersen 1981a: pidgins are characterised by use of pre-verbal negators, typically 'no' rather than 'not', no question inversion, lack of auxiliary, etc.).

The above examples provide only a few of the myriad possibilities that may stimulate interlanguage research. At the same time, whatever linguistically based question is the focus of a given investigation, it may happen that the theory may obscure certain very *practical* concerns. One example has to do with the linguistic level of the subject(s). It is a common experience of investigators into IL that a particular linguistic construction is selected for investigators with certain experimental subjects in mind and it then turns out that the learners had hardly any relevant competence at all: in teacher's terms, it was far too 'difficult' for them. The investigators misjudged the subjects' linguistic level in the area concerned and, hence, were unable to complete the test and much time and effort were lost. This can also happen the other way round: a ceiling effect can manifest itself such that most of the learners produce the *native* form thus providing little of interest to the IL researcher. It therefore pays to do a pre-test with a few subjects to check, among other things, if the larger group will produce interesting and analysable results. Only then will it become clear if the selected linguistic variable is relevant.

An associated problem (briefly mentioned earlier) is testing for some grammatical construction and then discovering that the subjects were distracted from the main task because of vocabulary they did not understand. By the same token, a test of lexical knowledge would have to involve only grammatical structures that were easy to handle in order to avoid the same problem.

4.2.4   Controlled elicitation techniques

Listed in the following sections are a number of techniques which are used in IL research; the reader is, however, advised to treat this as a sample list for an idea of the sorts of techniques used, and read the available literature in the journals for more information – particularly in the case of research into phonological, lexical and pragmatic patterns in IL, not forgetting investigation into IL spelling patterns (see Luelsdorff 1987).

As was made clear above, it is possible that the would-be IL investigator wishes to use a given technique demonstrated in the literature but within a different theoretical framework. In this case, the interpretation of the results will be quite different. For example, a test originally aimed at tapping grammatical competence, say, translation or oral picture description, might be used as a test focusing on the ability of the subjects to control their current grammatical knowledge under conditions of stress. The researcher will decide to use (old or new) techniques and will explain in advance in what way they are designed to serve the theoretical questions being asked. It is sometimes possible and useful simply to review the results of an investigation reported in the literature and interpret them in a new way according to a new theoretical viewpoint. You can take findings that were originally interpreted as proof of transfer from the mother tongue and, by using an alternative explanation, try to show that they can also support a quite different interpretation, namely that the mother tongue patterns were in fact overgeneralisations of an L2 rule (see Dulay and Burt 1974). In this case, you are pointing out an alternative interpretation missed by the original researcher and are making a contribution to the field without actually having carried out an experiment yourself. Of course, you can also do a critique of the methods used in the experiment and try to argue that the findings were unreasonably biased precisely because such and such an elicitation technique was used. In this case, you would be undermining the conclusions. The theory may still be valid but another approach would be required to provide support for it.

Inevitably, more work has been done on tests of production than on tests of reception (or 'comprehension'). People working with some version of the knowledge/control distinction (see 1.2.8 and 1.2.9) often recommend the use of a production test to tap levels of control and more receptively oriented tests to tap IL intuitions (levels of knowledge; see, for example, Kohn 1986). The idea, here, is that, although reception still involves controlling available knowledge, the degree of control necessary is less than that required for actually producing language. Hence, if we wish to find out how a learner feels about a given word or construction, we will get a relatively clearer idea by *not* forcing them to produce it. It should be noted here that comprehension tests, focusing on the ability of learners to comprehend L2 speech and writing, are different from other tests involving mainly reception which seek to tap the learners' intuitions about the L2 system (see 8.2 and 4.2.4.6, below). Learners may comprehend a great deal of a given text using intuitions (interlanguage knowledge) backed up by much educated guesswork. If we want to know how they actually feel about the acceptability of some word of construction, we do not want them to employ guesswork.

4.2.4.1 Guided speech

Relatively free speech can be elicited by using visual aids such as objects to be described, or a picture or a sequence of pictures; where greater control is required, the investigator's questions can be preplanned to elicit particular target structures, like negatives, for example, or past time statements. Subjects can also be asked to listen to a short story, specially designed to contain a high frequency of given target structures, and then be asked to retell it in their own words (see also the rationale for elicited imitation in 4.2.4.3 below). This is called a *story recall* test.

4.2.4.2 Guided writing

There are many forms of guided writing. One of them, translation, is very controversial in that translation is generally thought to be a special skill not directly linked to L2 proficiency level. It may be a question of training, whereby people accustomed to translating may be good subjects for translation tests: this is suggested in a small study by Lococo where subjects showed less L1 influence than in other tests (Lococo 1976). This was thought to be surprising since people have often suspected that translation tasks artificially provoked L1 influence by virtue of the fact that many people tend to translate literally, i.e. they are fixated on the surface form of the L1 original and are reluctant or unable to seek different structural ways of expressing the meaning of the source test. Lococo explained the result as the effect of their training: translation was the only activity where correctness was insisted upon; hence, they were especially careful when faced with the translation elicitation device and tended to avoid L1 transfer as a result. This in itself might be unsettling news since a technique should not provoke special test-taking strategies on the part of the subjects, particularly a strategy that might confuse the interpretation of the results.

The convenience of translation is that the investigator can control the meaning of the IL utterances he or she is trying to elicit. When the effect of translation on the subject is a cause for concern, other tests should also be used to see if those artificial effects are being created.

Other writing techniques used in IL research include *cloze* tests. These are blank-filling texts with blanks removed at regular intervals (say, every seventh word, regardless of whether it is an easy or a difficult item), and proper names and dates are left out of the calculation. Cloze tests were originally used to test comprehensibility of texts and have been used by applied linguists as a measure of general language proficiency. They may then be used to check that the level of the subjects is, broadly speaking, the same so that they can be grouped together for experimental purposes (see 5.2.2). There is also *story recall* – which is simply a written version of the same technique described in the previous section (see Van Baalen 1983 for an example) – and more straightforward *blank-filling* tests where the investigator chooses the items to be removed. A more controlled version of this is to provide *multiple-choice* items in the blanks. The question then is how to choose the distractors: an obvious ploy would be to take IL forms that have already emerged in other tests or in corpora of spontaneous speech and writing. Note that 'blanks' need not be of single word length: phrases, clauses, whole sentences or larger discourse units may be involved.

4.2.4.3   Elicited imitation

Elicited imitation requires subjects to repeat rather long utterances. The idea is that they should rely solely on their IL system when producing these utterances while at the same time exerting a very close control on what they produce. This is accomplished by getting them to imitate sentences which are short enough to be reproducible by the subjects in some form or other but too long for them to imitate in parrot fashion without understanding what they are saying (Sachs 1967). In other words, by making the stimulus sentences too long for rote repetition, they are also too long for the subjects to retain them in short-term memory. The capacity of the short-term memory store is supposed to be highly restricted. If any of the message is to be retained, the precise details of the string of sounds carrying the message have to be discarded in favour of a more abstract representation of their meaning. This meaning then forms the basis of the subjects' repetition: they re-express the meaning (rather than literally what they heard) using their own IL grammar (see Naiman 1974 and Flynn 1986 for a discussion of this technique).

If the subjects are unable to process the stimulus sentence and cannot generate any useful response, then at least, the investigator knows that the construction involved is quite out of reach of the subjects' competence. The receptive control of the subjects is limited: they may be able to understand the speech when it is spoken much slower and clearer, but not under normal everyday conditions. The other possibility is that the subjects' current knowledge of the language does not allow them to make sense of the utterance, and that is why they cannot reproduce it. Normally, however, they are able to reproduce a bit of what they hear and the question is: What does that bit tell the researcher about their current state of L2 (IL) knowledge?

In a sense, then, elicited imitation is as much a test of reception or comprehension as it is a test of production. However, since the subject is placed under conditions of mild stress, there have to be production (as well as reception) performance factors at work. The learner may be able to process the original test utterance in a native-like manner but still have problems in reproducing it at speed because he or she lacks the appropriate fluency. We might, therefore, want to adopt additional, more relaxed techniques to check that the subject's competence is not being seriously under-represented because of immature control over newly acquired native structures. As in many tests, if syntax or morphology is in focus, the investigator should only use familiar, properly mastered words and sounds.

4.2.4.4 Act-out

In act-out tests, subjects are asked to manipulate objects (for example, miniature furniture, dolls and bricks of various shapes, sizes and colours). A similar task is provided by a choice of pictures which differ only in one crucial respect. The idea is to see if a particular target structure, like the passive, has been acquired. Children asked to act-out (or choose appropriate pictures for) 'the dog bit the rat' and 'the dog was bitten by the rat' might, in both cases, have the first-named participant (the dog) doing the biting. This would show that they had not processed the passive construction in 'was bitten by'. Act-out tests are useful substitutes for, or additions to, acceptability judgement tests, especially where judgement tests are seen to be problematic for the particular type of experimental subject involved in the investigation.

A typical danger that most researchers take into account in this kind of test arises when subjects are able to guess the meaning from the context or from their knowledge of the world. In 'the postman was bitten by the dog' for example, the probability that the postman was doing the biting is small enough to make the child respond according to this fact rather than opt for the first-named constituent. Their knowledge about the likelihood of a postman plunging his teeth into the hide of a fierce dog should cause them to reject the interpretation they might otherwise prefer on the basis of their knowledge of the world. Hence, researchers have to design their act-out experiments with this kind of danger in mind.

4.2.4.5   Acceptability judgements

Perhaps the most important test of linguistic intuitions used with native speakers and with learners is the acceptability judgement task: subjects are provided with samples of language and asked to judge them as 'acceptable' or 'unacceptable'. For statistical reasons, a third choice of 'don't know' is usually recommended, that is to say, a *ranking scale* is preferred over categorical judgement (right or wrong). It is also possible to have two scales, a scale of acceptability and a scale of confidence in each judgement: in this way one is able to tease that status of a supposed rule in the learner's IL system (Sorace 1985; see also Sorace 1992 for an interesting study on the use of magnitude scaling). Such tests are usually in the form of a list of sample sentences but could in principle be running texts, i.e. subjects could be given a sort of 'error detection test'.

This highly convenient way of tapping competence has its dangers. Although, normally speaking, not much performance stress is involved, the subjects' focus on the target form or structure in the test items may be hindered by a number of factors. For example, they may be overawed by the 'tyranny of the printed word' and be biased towards accepting utterances simply because they are presented in print. Less linguistically sophisticated learners – particularly younger learners – may be particularly susceptible to this. In this case, the test technique must be abandoned in favour of, for example, an act-out experiment, or made more effective in some way (perhaps by having the stimulus sentences hand-written, for example). Also, it has to be said, some subjects may simply prefer to accept items because of a general lack of confidence in their intuitions.

Subjects may also make their judgements for *stylistic* reasons: they may reject what they would in principle accept because they have been taught that the form or construction in question is non-standard or stigmatised. The instructions have to make clear to the learners exactly what 'acceptable' means with respect to the task in hand.

Again, performance factors may be introduced deliberately to a test of high control – as is the case with lexical-decision tests when items are flashed on to a screen and the subject's judgement is timed.

Another problem involves the precise focus of the judgement required of the subject. To avoid any metalinguistic factors intruding upon the experiment – such as stylistic judgements (see above) or applying a rule of thumb instead of using intuition (see 4.1.5) – the investigator may attempt to disguise the real target forms or constructions: this may be done by introducing distractor items containing material irrelevant for the test. Another advantage of this is that there is more variety: a long list of passive constructions or conditional clauses can be either boring or tiring, or both. However, if the subject's judgement is spread over a large range of forms and construction, there is no guarantee that with certain items the focus of the assessment will be on a relevant form or structural feature. If the learner's attention is on some irrelevant feature, then this would allow an unacceptable target form or structure to slip through unnoticed when it might otherwise have been rejected.

Finally, there is choice of control: the native speaker whose own performance is supposed to be the norm against which the experimental subject's performance is matched. Native speakers may not match the non-native speakers: one might be comparing highly literate people with much less literate people, for example. This would be a bad idea where more sophisticated areas of the language were being tested. Furthermore, native speakers can vary in their judgements to quite an extent. It is a mistake to assume that their response to any language test will always be uniform. In fact, the moment one tries to define exactly what native norms are one runs into a whole host of difficulties that suggest that the idea of a 'native speaker' may be a convenient fiction, useful as long as it is not defined too explicitly. It may, in fact, escape clear definition (see Davies 1991 and Sharwood Smith 1992 on this topic).

In general, care has to be take not to overtax the subjects' attentional capacities and their motivation (see techniques reported in Van Buren and Sharwood Smith 1985, for more general discussion of judgement tasks see, for example, Schacter *et al.* 1976, Chaudron 1983, Greenbaum and Quirk 1970, Greenbaum 1977, Sorace 1985, 1989, 1992, Kohn 1986, Birdsong 1989, Bley-Vroman and Masterson 1991, Ellis 1991, Hedgecock 1993).

4.2.4.6   *Explicit metalinguistic judgements*

In the present framework, explicit metalinguistic judgements are distinguished from tests of linguistic intuition (see 4.2.4.5) as follows: intuitional judgements simply ask whether something is acceptable or not. They do not require any conscious reflection about the structure of the test item. Such tests of intuition are admittedly metalinguistic in the minimal sense that they ask the subjects to treat a word or utterance as an object: they are implicitly metalinguistic. But the focus here is not on analysing that object but on tapping intuition, i.e. 'gut-feeling'. However, if the subject starts to think too analytically about the structure of the target utterances, then, arguably, the judgements cease to be wholly or even partly intuitional. They become more explicitly metalinguistic. Depending on one's theory about possible differences between intuitive knowledge and explicit metalinguistic knowledge, this could be seen as an experimental confound. It would make straightforward interpretation of test results impossible. What are here specifically called 'metalinguistic' judgements, then, require the subjects actually to reflect on their judgement: this implies that they have some analytical ability. This comes out, for example, when they are asked to identify errors in a text. It often demands some kind of technical knowledge as well, and a repertoire of technical terms, i.e. a metalanguage, even if this repertoire is fairly primitive (just using such terms as, for example, 'sentence', 'word order', 'verb', 'noun', 'question' and 'statement'.

In teachers' terms, we might distinguish between error-*detection* tests where subjects are simply required to identify errors, and error-*explanation* tests, where subjects are required to explain why an error is wrong and perhaps why they think they made the error. So, a metalinguistic judgement is a test which draws on subjects' metalinguistic knowledge rather than their intuitions (see sections in 4.3). It also includes what might be called 'meta-psycholinguistic' responses, namely, reasons why subjects feel they did something or avoided doing something. These introspective techniques are quite useful for establishing the conscious strategies that were used by the learners. The investigator can draw up protocols whereby the learners listen to their production and explain what was in their heads as they were taking part in the particular act of speech or writing involved.

Clearly the learners cannot talk about subconscious processes, and when they try to they may produce an entirely false impression of what really happened. When asked to account for their behaviour, people sometimes appear to invent (without necessarily realising it) a reply to satisfy the investigator. One case in point is a learner who told me that a given error had been caused by L1 transfer and then corrected herself with an embarrassed laugh when she realised that this strategy would have produced a native-like form; learners may be much more reliable when it comes to compensatory strategies where they have consciously tried to make up for some perceived deficiency in the resources, e.g. tried a paraphrase when they could not find the correct word, or when they did not know the right spelling or pronunciation of the preferred word (see Poulisse *et al.* 1984 for a useful review of research on compensatory strategies).

4.3 Summary

From the preceding discussion, it should be clear that the IL researcher needs a whole range of techniques to ascertain different facets of competence (of whatever kind) and different facets of control. These range from indirect approaches to the learner, gathering samples of more or less spontaneous data, to highly controlled elicitation tests probing some very specific aspects of the learner's linguistic or communicative ability in the second language. It is not enough to select a number of tests in the hope that the combined results will present a clear picture, however. This strategy is a good one provided there is a good argument for supposing that the various tests used are in fact tapping the same thing. One needs a theory to determine this. At the same time, there are already a large variety of elicitation techniques available and, with the advance of computer technology, many of these may be made more effective and easier to administer. What theory that might be is the topic of the various chapters that follow.

PART II:
Revisions and Alternatives

5 Early refinements

5.0 The big three

It is not appropriate to treat the three models of second language learning that were most fully discussed in the international literature of the early 1970s as 'theories' in anything but informal terms. They are best thought of as competing hypotheses. One might, in simplified terms, characterise the claims being debated as:

CAH versus ILH versus CCH

One way of comparing them would be to see what predictions emerged from the hypotheses as regards mother tongue influence. The original Contrastive Analysis Hypothesis (CAH), best expressed in the works of Robert Lado, explained second language learning as the development of a new set of habits. His prediction was that virtually all errors were explainable as interference from L1. Ease of learning was guaranteed where first language habits led to correct L2 performance.

The Interlanguage Hypothesis (ILH) saw learners operating with their own set of rules, some of which reflected the L1 rules. Hence some but not all L1-based deviations from the L2 norms would be expected.

The Creative Construction Hypothesis (CCH) relegated L1 influence to a very minor position. Apart from accent, L2 learners would not show very much L1 influence in their spontaneous performance. Where they did appear to show L1 influence could be explained in some way that did not involve their current L2 system.

Another way of contrasting the 'big three' would be in terms of the differences or similarities as regards, respectively, L1 and L2 learning. Here the CAH and the CCH agreed in just one respect: all language learning could be explained as the working of the same underlying mechanism. In the case of the CAH, this was also true of non-linguistic learning. The ILH, however, involves the claim that L2 learning is radically different. The most obvious proof of this is the fact that, unlike L1 learning, L2 learning does not bring with it the absolute guarantee of complete success. These various ways of looking at the big three hypotheses of the time are summarised in the table shown in Figure 5.1:

	CAH	ILH	CCH
Role of environment in learning	Major	Partial	Partial
L1/L2: same developmental processes?	Yes	No	Yes
L1 influence in development?	Major	Partial	Minimal

FIGURE 5.1   The Contrastive Analysis, Interlanguage and Creative Construction hypotheses compared.

To take the concrete example of a Spanish speaker learning English, the following learner utterance might be explained in quite different ways:

'No is true!' (= 'it is not true')

We may imagine the reaction to this L2 data from three different people, each supporting one of the three approaches listed above:

CA: 'Here, the Spanish word order pattern ("No es verdad": literally "No is true") is quite clearly behind this utterance. The negator "no" has been placed in front of the finite verb and not after it. Moreover, the learner has also transferred the Spanish habit of leaving out subject pronouns where they do not contribute to the meaning. So, we have two highly predictable Spanish habits interfering with the correct production of English ("It is not true"). Since transfer habit here results in an error, it can be classified as "negative" transfer. Virtually all of the errors we encounter should be like these.'

IL: 'I don't agree. It is true that the learner gives us evidence of two interlanguage rules that may well be the result of transfer. In this case it is the transferring L1 Spanish rules (negative placement and subject pronoun omission) into the developing IL system. Here we have evidence for one of the processes that underlie IL. It is difficult to imagine how this could have been the result of another central process, namely the overgeneralisation of an English rule. English does not have much to prompt the dropping of the subject pronoun. And, on the whole, there doesn't seem to be good reason to say that putting "no" in front of the verb is provoked by other words in

English that can appear in that position. No, it is probably transfer. Still, since not all the learner's errors will be explainable in terms of transfer, we cannot say that it is "automatic" or just blind habit. The learner seems to have made an assumption that, in this case, L1 and L2 are identical.'

CC: 'No, this is *not* transfer. So, I don't agree with either of you. Despite appearances, the placement of the negator before the finite verb is in fact evidence of the same language acquisition mechanisms that help the young English-speaking child develop L1 competence. A look at L1 acquisition data will tell you this. English children produce exactly the same construction when they are in the early stages of developing their mother tongue knowledge of negation. So, although the L2 data look Spanish, it turns out that this gives us a misleading impression. Again, as far as the missing pronoun is concerned, this phenomenon also occurs in child (L1) English. This is, therefore, another sign that we are dealing here with natural, universal orders of development which have nothing to do with L1 interference from Spanish. They may be expected from learners coming from all kinds of different language backgrounds. You may call it overgeneralisation or something else. The important thing is that it is part of the developmental programme for both L1 and L2 acquisition! You two jump to a transfer explanation far too readily.'

In this way, the same product is explained as the outcome of different processes. Each of the three theoretical positions interprets the selfsame observable behaviour in a different way. In the first case, the explanation is blind habit. In the second case, it is a learner 'hypothesis' (belief, assumption) that L1 and L2 systems overlap in some respects. In the third case, it is a manifestation of an automatic developmental program for building new language systems out of input, a programme which takes no account of the presence of the L1 system in the learner's mind.

5.1   Lines of development

By the mid-1970s, researchers were beginning to work out refinements and alternative approaches. One line was to investigate the way in which L2 acquisition and performance might systematically vary. Learners might, as was suggested in chapter 3, vary in the way they acquired L2 targets. In acquiring aspects of the L2 (like negation, *wh-* questions, etc.), they might go faster or slower along the same route, passing through the same intermediate stages. Alternatively, they might pass through different stages. This might be true even given the basic similarities between learners coming from quite different backgrounds that was posited by the CCH. Again, the ILH might show learners developing in varied ways. The whole issue of variable language performance obviously needed serious consideration.

Another line of development was when people looked into the *functions* of different forms. It was in fact quite naive to let the fact of an observed developmental sequence in L2 acquisition play a major role in theorising without first investigating the different ways in which the various forms, like the verbal *-ing* form in English, for example, were actually used in the language of the learner. After all, the 90 per cent suppliance of a morpheme of some type that could be taken as 'standing for', say, the progressive (or 'continuous') form of the verb or the definite article, was taken as signalling acquisition. It neither had to be exactly the same as the form a native speaker would utter, nor did it have to function in precisely the same way. The main thing was that an obligatory context that previously stood empty was at last filled on a regular (at least 90 per cent) basis. In other words, the learner had grasped that there was a form that had to be placed in a given position.

Finally, the role of conscious learning had to be made clear in any L2 theory that was to emerge either from the ILH or CCH position. This was a more strictly psychological issue than the question of how to handle the linguistic problems of variation and function/form relationships. In principle, both interlanguage behaviour and behaviour supposedly reflecting creative construction had to be spontaneous in character. This implied that the learner was focusing on expressing meaning and was not consciously attending to the constructions he or she was using. But, if conscious reflection played little part in the L2 performance that researchers were interested in, did it have any role in the development of L2 knowledge over an extended period of time? And what was the status of conscious analysis of language? Was it a discussion of grammar and rules and such like? These questions lay behind the developments in the CCH and ILH to be described in this chapter.

5.1.1 Variability

In trying to analyse the IL product of a given language learner, we may observe both systematicity, which has received most attention so far, and variability. In fact, as several have pointed out (notably Tarone 1988), these two terms are not mutually exclusive. Variability may be unstable and unsystematic but there may also be systematic variability. Just as in mature language systems, IL systems may have so-called free variation and variation that depends on the linguistic or situational context of use. These two basic types of variation are described below:

1. *free variation* Two functionally equivalent items or structures X and Y may be used in the same context so that we can say that, in context C, both X and Y may occur without any apparent change of meaning, i.e. that this set of two varies freely, at least among different native speakers of the same language: for example, one speaker might say 'she gave the book to me' whereas another might say 'she gave me the book'. One person might pronounce 'either' beginning with the vowel [ai] as in 'I', and another might, instead, use [i:] as in 'easy'. Free variation is an acceptable concept for most people only in a very limited sense: in other words, many would maintain that semantically equivalent forms normally have different pragmatic implications: i.e. they are not literally 100 per cent equivalent in every sense of the word (see, for example, Chafe 1970: 219 on the passive; see also Labov 1970). In any case, learners of L1 or L2 have been noticed to display a tendency to avoid free variation by assigning different meanings to given variants (see, for example, Karmiloff-Smith 1979, Andersen 1983b, Kellerman 1984, 1985). Also, where true equivalence between forms is established (as in the 'either' example), it is reasonable to argue that the two forms do not really exist side by side in the same variety or dialect of the language, and therefore should not be compared and treated as free variants within the same linguistic system.

2. *context-dependent variation* Two functionally equivalent items or structures X and Y may be used, but their occurrence is determined by the identifiable features in the context. The context may be various types of situational or more strictly linguistic context. For example, in one situation, the command 'give!' might be appropriate, in another 'give it to me (please)'. Another example is provided by the synonyms 'also' and 'too', which behave differently as far as position in the sentence is concerned: compare 'I *also* did it' with 'I did it *too*'.

It might be supposed that interlanguage variability that appears to show no system (as in 2, above) is theoretically uninteresting. In fact, it may be a sign of development since a formerly stable item or structure may be 'on the way out' or a new structure may be beginning to be established, i.e. in an early phase where it has not quite been incorporated into the learner's stable IL repertoire (see Corder 1981). The sudden appearance of variability, in other words, may signal an ongoing change in the IL system. An IL rule may suddenly become 'critical', to use's Klein's terminology (Klein 1986). The learner loses confidence in a previously firm assumption about how the L2 works. Some researchers (e.g. Dickerson 1975, Hyltenstam 1977) have detected a stable spread of new items from one context to other contexts in a predictable manner in line with the kind of changes observed in language change (see Bailey 1973). L2 variation has been studied from many different angles, some of which will be mentioned below (see Gass *et al.* 1989a, 1989b for a book of readings on the subject).

5.1.1.1   *A Labovian view*

In her pioneering work on L2 variation, Tarone developed the idea of IL variability into a model within a Labovian perspective (Labov 1970, Tarone 1979) and has claimed that a given learner is not in possession of a single IL (system) at a given time but of several: the crucial factor here is *the degree of attention accorded to form* by the learner. Hence a learner may be using one IL system when paying very careful attention to form (i.e 'correctness') and another IL system in casual speech where little or no attention is paid to form. One IL system may reflect less L1 influence than another (see Tarone 1985). This approach emphasises the fact that speakers of a language, be it a native language or an interlanguage, use different styles or varieties rather than speak a homogenised language to suit all occasions. If one follows the theoretical line adopted, this means that it is senseless ever to talk of some uniform underlying competence since both native speakers and non-natives acquire languages as flexible systems which vary according to context of use. In this particular model, the variation is endemic: it is not reduced to any common denominator for whatever reason.

5.1.1.2   *Discourse domains*

Again, in a somewhat different way, Selinker and Douglas have proposed that IL varies systematically according to the 'discourse domain' (roughly the particular subject area like personal relation-ships, job talk, etc., see Selinker and Douglas 1989). Hence, IL produced by a given learner may differ in systematic ways according to what the learner is talking about: the learner is seen not so much as a learner of a single language but rather as a learner of given varieties of a language, and these varieties may be manifested in the learner's performance as IL varieties corresponding to particular discourse domains. His or her IL may well be lexically and grammatically (and phonologically) more native-like (say) in one discourse domain than in another.

Note that, if we were to collapse Tarone's perspective with that of Selinker and Douglas, which, in principle, we can, we would get quite a complicated set of learner styles (Discourse Domain 1 in casual mode, Discourse Domain 2 in formal mode, Discourse Domain 2 in casual mode, etc.). If it could be established that each style existed – in other words, that there were sets of distinguishing characteristics that would justify such a typology of IL for an individual learner or group of learners – then we would still need a psycholinguistic explanation to establish the status of these styles in the theory. Tarone, following Labov, made her chief criteria a socio-psycholinguistic one, i.e. degree of attention to form. Attention is essentially a psychological concept. In other words, sociolinguistic behaviour is being measured using a psychological yardstick. In Chapter 6, we shall see that there are other ways of interpreting this type of variability.

5.1.1.3 *Individual variation*

Last, but definitely not least, there is the question of individual variation (see Ellis 1985 for a fuller background discussion). Individuals learning and performing in a given L2 may fall into two subtypes, following one acquisitional route or another in the case of *acquisition* and also exploiting their current resources in one way or another in the case of IL *performance*. In other words, while denying the existence of complete randomness, it will be an important task for IL theory to describe and explain systematic developmental variation within groups, if it is found to exist. And the same holds for variation in how individuals behave at a given time.

5.1.3 A functional perspective

Some mention has been made of the different functions of various forms and that, for whatever reason, researchers initially ignored this.

Indeed, the early investigations of L2 development that attracted attention in the literature did pay scant attention to the function of particular forms being acquired. A much-quoted example is the acquisition of the determiner in English. Following Brown's L1 work on the development of target forms in child language (Brown 1973), creative construction researchers typically treated the regular occurrence of 'the' and 'a(n)' in spontaneous production as formally acquired. This convenience could not last and inevitably researchers have begun to look more closely at functional development, how forms actually function in the learner's system. It is, of course, quite likely that a given target form functions in a markedly non-target manner in the learner's IL as was suggested earlier in discussing the acquisition of the present progressive -ing form (see, in particular, Lightbown 1983). Another example would be the definite article in English. The next section provides an appropriate illustration.

5.1.3.1   Huebner's Ge

To take a well-known example in the literature, Huebner, over a period of one year starting from the onset of acquisition, made an in-depth study of a Laotian adult Hmong tribesman, Ge, in Hawaii. Chapter 5 of Huebner's study (Huebner 1983) is on the apparently highly variable use of the determiner. Using a set of semantic categories such as Specific Referent and Information-Assumed-Known-to-Hearer, borrowed from Bickerton, he discovered a developmental order and thereby revealed much more systematicity in the learner's performance than appeared at first sight (see Bickerton 1975). For example, in the beginning, Ge used the determiner 'da' to mark nouns with a specific referent and which represented information that is assumed to be known to the hearer. Later, all noun phrases were marked with 'da'. Huebner discerned six stages in all and this included a stage whereby the learner backslid to an earlier stage. This provided us with a good example of an issue discussed in the second chapter, namely how going to the data with a theoretically based question yielded insights where an 'objective' look at the data indicated an illusory lack of systematicity.

In a later application of Huebner's approach, Parrish studied a 19-year-old Japanese woman, Mari, who had formal written training in Japan but only 3 weeks of real English in the USA (Parrish 1987). Data were collected every 10 days for 4 months (20–30 minute sessions). Mari was asked to tell two stories (Japan, USA) and to describe a place. Parrish looked exclusively here at Mari's use of articles and adapted Huebner's system to reveal systematicity in the IL supporting Huebner's basic points about deceptive irregularity in performance data.

There have been a fair number of studies looking at the functional developments of various IL subsystems (see, for example, Dickerson 1975, and Felix 1981 and H. Anderson 1986) and it is now generally accepted that no investigator, and no theory, can afford to ignore this crucial aspect of IL performance.

5.2 Modes of knowledge

Given that the more linguistic aspects of learner performance were treated simplistically, it is also true to say that the psychological thinking behind the earlier research was also very unsophisticated. In particular, some space needs to be devoted to the various discussions concerning the role of conscious awareness (see also 1.2.3) in IL development. As Littlewood points out, the notion that there were intuitive and conscious forms of learning had been recognised long before second language acquisition studies had started. Everyone who has some experience of L2 learning in formal and informal circumstances has a general sense of the difference between 'picking up' a language and 'studying' it in a formal, analytical manner. Palmer, for example, spoke of the 'studial' capacity for learning (Palmer 1922, see Littlewood 1984: 76) and Lambert, the great Canadian pioneer in bilingual studies, also spoke of the same basic distinction (Lambert 1966, see Selinker 1972). It was, however, Stephen Krashen who first developed this distinction within a more general model of L2 acquisition and performance.

5.2.1 Krashen's monitor

Krashen maintained that the common 'L1-like' developmental sequences that were reflected in the results of various investigations showed how common notions of interference and formal grammar learning actually played no part in L2 acquisition. In other words, where conscious knowledge of grammar rules was concerned, there was no 'interface' between that kind of knowledge about language and the intuitive competence built up via experience with the language and without conscious reflection (see Figure 5.2).

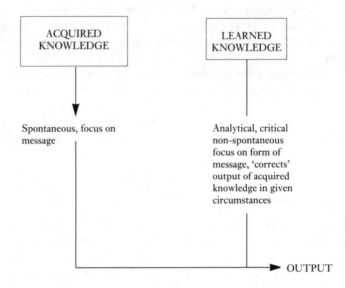

FIGURE 5.2

Conscious knowledge, which was of a highly limited character and used only by certain learners and in certain favourable circumstances (basically: sufficient time, deliberate focus on form as well as meaning, and, of course, the learner's possession of the relevant rule), was originally termed 'learned' knowledge (see Krashen 1982, 1985). The idea was that it served as a kind of first-aid kit, patching up the output of intuitively acquired knowledge. When learners have the time and the ability to apply learned knowledge, they can, if they focus on the form of their message, produce more native-like performance than is supported by what they intuitively 'know', i.e. the stage of development they are really at.

5.2.2   Defying the natural order

Krashen has always preferred to maintain a no-interface position whereby learned knowledge cannot make the learner ready for a particular linguistic target form before all the forms that are supposed to precede that particular form have already been acquired (Krashen 1985). According to him, *you cannot re-order the natural sequence*. Investigations supporting this no re-ordering point of view are still being reported but not necessarily from Krashen's perspective (see Ellis 1989, for example).

5.2.3 Implicit and explicit

A somewhat similar distinction to the conscious/subconscious knowledge concept was made by Bialystok when she distinguished between *explicit* knowledge of the language and *implicit* knowledge (Bialystok 1978, but see Bialystok 1988 for a much revised version of her model). However, in her early conceptualisations of IL development, these were actually different ways of storing information which could actually interact: there was an interface between the two types of knowledge and hence the learning of formal grammar rules could in principle be converted into implicit knowledge via practice (see Bialystok 1978, and see McLaughlin 1978, Sharwood Smith 1980, Rutherford and Sharwood Smith 1988 for various different perspectives).

5.2.4 Knowledge storage versus knowledge access

There is always the possibility that knowledge of a language is a single entity but one can develop it and have access to it in two different ways. Hence, for example, if I can produce questions like 'What am I doing?', this means at the very least that I have some intuitive knowledge of English interrogatives. If I can talk about it and perhaps even give a rule, this means that I have explicit knowledge of this area of the language. But it is the *same* knowledge as the intuitive knowledge: I have simply uncovered it, i.e. made it 'visible' to conscious analysis. I can also acquire new knowledge either intuitively or by using my conscious analysis. This third, commonsense, lay understanding of the knowledge as a *single* store may also be shared by many researchers. Most of the literature on the topic has, however, tended to support some idea of two separate knowledge stores, the argument being about whether they can influence one another and, if so, how.

According to which proposals that one favoured, one could see IL knowledge as consisting of:

(1) two entirely different non-interacting kinds of knowledge;
(2) two entirely different kinds of knowledge but still capable of influencing one another;
(3) the same knowledge but one which could be developed and accessed in two different ways (intuitively and consciously).

The development of explicit knowledge (metaknowledge) of a language has still not been extensively researched, either in and for itself or, indeed, in relation to the development of spontaneous, intuitive (L2) ability. However, if a theory allows a direct connection between intuitively acquired knowledge and explicit analytic knowledge such that one type of knowledge can be transformed into the other, then that theory should allow for the possibility that the natural order can, in principle, be overridden. This would mean that there was nothing sacrosanct about the natural order but that it was the result of the learner having no other input except exposure to the language. This approach could be reformulated as 'leave the poor learners to fend for themselves, and they will be forced to fall back on the natural order' and 'clever teaching techniques can provide learners with much more efficient solutions to their learning problems than is offered by natural, unaided processes of acquisition'. In principle, then, the third person singular *'s* that comes *late* in the proposed natural order for acquiring English morphemes could, if required, be made to come *early* via practice (and in a way that could be made to last). People supporting such claims would have to show that there are areas of the language that appear to be linked with a natural order of acquisition but which can be manipulated in all kinds of ways by teachers and learners. This would also open up the possibility of there being two alternative kinds of natural order which might coexist:

(a) An *unadjustable* natural order: one truly preprogrammed order, not to be tampered with.
(b) An *adjustable* natural order: one which is a default order that takes place in the absence of external intervention.

The simplest example of an order that can be manipulated would be in the area of lexical knowledge. A learner in a given situation may naturally tend to ignore certain aspects of the lexical input as being unimportant for communication. The communicatively important items may be acquired before those that are less relevant. On the other hand, some less relevant words may be made more relevant through special emphasis placed on them by the teacher/researcher. The normal sequence of development in this case would be *adjustable*. The order would, in a sense, remain constant in that less significant items would be learned later than significant items – significant to the learner, that is. In another sense, the order is adjustable because the teacher can artificially make certain items more important to the learner and hence change the order of acquisition. In other situations – one thinks here more immediately of areas of grammar rather than of the learning of words – no amount of emphasis by the teacher/researcher would achieve stable results and therefore we would have to conclude that the natural order was of the first, unadjustable, kind. In short, where, if anywhere, may we find naturally arising processes open to intervention from outside? This is clearly a rich area for research with clear implications for practical language teaching not to speak of theories of cognitive psychology (see for example, Sharwood Smith 1986, Lightbown 1985, Lightbown and Spada 1990). These issues will rise again when we examine more closely the strengths and weaknesses of the theorising in the 1970s and as we look at what followed in the 1980s.

5.3 Unanswered questions

It is instructive to ponder on what the early models of L2 acquisition left unsaid. For instance, with particular reference to Selinker's model, the following questions may be raised:

1. To what extent are transfer and overgeneralisation really different processes? Are there just two kinds of generalisation: generalising too much from L1 rules versus generalising from L2 but going beyond what is indicated by the L2 input (Taylor 1975)?
2. To what extent is transfer of training as a process just a type of overgeneralisation, the only difference being the *source* of the overgeneralisation (teacher emphasis versus learner's independent interpretation of an L2 rule)?
3. Do the three processes mentioned above interact or not? Surely one error can indeed be the outcome of more than one process?

And, with respect to the creative construction model:

1. What is the *explanation* for the actual sequences observed in L2 development? (Cf. Hatch 1979, and 2 below.)
2. Is there a *single* explanation for a whole developmental sequence or are there many quite *different* explanations for various parts of the sequences?
3. Are there common sequences for *all* aspects of IL development or is it restricted to those areas already investigated? (See 4 below.)
4. If some areas of IL show a different order of development, what are they and what is the reason for them?
5. Is the L1 a trivial factor in all aspects of IL development as it is claimed to be for these areas already investigated? (See Schachter 1976 for an important contribution to this question.)

6. Do all the central claims of the model apply to all aspects of language (for example, with respect to conscious learning)?

These are the kinds of interesting questions raised as a result of the most publicised research done in the 1970s. They are questions that are now being addressed in current theories of language acquisition, to be discussed in later sections of this book.

6 Theoretical developments

6.0 Introduction

The previous chapter dealt with early refinements in theoretical thinking. It is now time to move on and consider how the field has developed up to the present day. This will involve a more differentiated approach to notions that were hitherto treated rather vaguely and confusingly. It was necessary, however, to consider those early models if only as a theoretical foundation for the next stage of development.

6.1 IL and creative construction theory reappraised

In this chapter, the models of the late 1960s and 1970s, which are relevant for the study of interlanguage and which were discussed above, will be subjected to a preliminary reappraisal in the light of some theoretical developments that have been taking place since the late 1970s. Consideration is then given to two alternative views: one concerning the notion of competence and the other a different way of looking at the acquisition of language skills. A fuller review of the current scene in second language acquisition studies will be undertaken in the chapters that follow.

6.1.1 The early IL hypothesis reviewed

In discussing what drives language acquisition, it is necessary to separate the physical brain from the various alternative ways in which the (same) brain may function. The functional structure is commonly referred to in modern psychology using terms such as 'mind', 'mental' and 'cognitive structure' (knowledge structure).

The IL hypothesis, as framed by Selinker (1972), entails that most L2 learners have recourse to a 'latent psychological structure' underlying their language development which is distinct from the psychological basis of L1 acquisition. This effectively means that the mechanisms that drive the development of the new language system are not the same as those that drove mother tongue acquisition whether or not the physical structure of the brain is the same. At the same time, regarding the physical brain, Selinker did also ally himself with the comments of Lenneberg suggesting that those aspects associated with language acquisition have also undergone changes that affect learning success.

In Selinker's view, the psychological basis for L2 behaviour may be characterised as comprising a number of central interlanguage processes, namely, language transfer, transfer of training, over-generalisation, strategies of learning and strategies of communication. The first three processes were discussed in the first chapter. The last two, the two types of strategies, had to do with:

(1) conscious attempts by learners to commit parts of the L2 to memory or to increase their fluency (learning strategies);
(2) various ways of facilitating communication, given perceived gaps in L2 resources (communication strategies).

As was shown earlier, problems arose with Selinker's 1972 proposals (as is inevitable with preliminary models designed to stimulate discussion) because of the indeterminate nature of the scope and interaction of his IL processes. For example, one has to ask the following questions:

1. To what extent are transfer and generalisation really processes controlling *performance* rather than processes building *knowledge?*
2. to what extent is language transfer, as a generalisation of L1 rules, actually the *same* central interlanguage process as his over-generalisation, which generalises L2 patterns beyond what is sanctioned by the L2 input (see Taylor 1975)?
3. Are central IL processes unique and discrete or can they be contributory factors, i.e. conspire to yield an IL pattern? Can an IL pattern actually have more than one underlying explanation?

6.1.1.1   *Driving performance or building knowledge?*

The status of IL processes in performance was unclear, or became unclear when Adjemian (1976) placed the IL model within a Chomskyan perspective. Adjemian raised the question of whether IL was primarily *knowledge* underlying behaviour or the systematic aspects of *performance* behaviour themselves. Was, for example, the IL process that Selinker called 'language transfer' essentially something that steered performance in L2 'on-line'? Or was it (also) a process that worked to changed underlying IL knowledge and create mental rules so that IL competence (knowledge) could be said to be influenced by L1?

If the IL processes are 'knowledge-changing' processes, then IL competence would, as it were, contain copies of L1 rules (mental representations) which were now employed with L2 lexical and phonological material, as part of a separate rule system. Put another way, the learner's intuitions about the L2 (with regard to a given linguistic phenomenon) would be the same as the learner's intuitions about L1. French-speaking learners of English would immediately 'know' that the non-native sentence 'John stroked often the cat' was good English just as they would 'know' that the strict equivalent in their own L1 was also good French. And this would be so despite the fact that their English knowledge is actually different from native-speaker English knowledge. The adverbial 'often' is in an unconventional position and sounds wrong. A French native-speaker would therefore say of the learners of French that 'they believed this sentence to be acceptable but were wrong in their belief'. A more technical way of speaking would be that the French learners in this example possessed 'IL knowledge' and that this IL knowledge included a rule copied over from their French system where adverbials can occur in just this position. If IL knowledge is a difficult concept to stomach then one can think in terms of native and non-native 'mental grammars'. It is not at all clear, however, that Selinker endorsed the distinction between knowledge (mental grammar) and on-line processing mechanisms by which knowledge is used at a given moment in time.

If Selinker's IL processes are not knowledge-based but have to do with on-line processing (production and reception during actual language performance), then learners would not assume L1/L2 equivalence in advance. They would not copy over L1 knowledge as in the previous example. They would, against their better judgement, find themselves processing L2 material willy-nilly via performance mechanisms originally set up to cope with the L1. This would result in, for example, L1-based accent and L1-based word order. Transfer errors observed by the researcher or teacher would then be *performance* errors not reflecting underlying knowledge. In other words, transfer would be viewed in a similar manner in which it is viewed by supporters of the creative construction position. French learners would know that adverbials cannot interrupt verb and direct object in simple sentences of the type illustrated above and would not still go ahead and 'do' it, i.e. make the mistake simply because their habitual performance in L1 dominates their production and reception of L2. Any learner will recognise the frustrating situation of persistently saying things that they know perfectly well to be wrong.

A third possibility, the one that most immediately arises out of the 1972 paper, is that there is, in Selinker's view, simply no valid competence/performance distinction to be made – a view voiced by various linguists over the years (see Halliday 1978, Hymes 1972, etc.) and hence no ambiguity. Interlanguage is simply 'systematic behaviour'. Knowing a language and being able to perform in it are one and the same thing.

This discussion should illustrate the necessity of having first to choose one or other theoretical position on what language, language behaviour and language knowledge are all about before going on to analyse models of learning or, indeed, to analyse learner data.

6.1.1.2   *Two types of overgeneralisation?*

It is also unclear as to whether, in Selinker (1972), instances of language transfer and overgeneralisation are simply two different types of overgeneralisation, distinguished only by *what* is over-generalised (L1 or L2 rules). This was pointed out by a number of people, including Taylor (1975). Why not talk of one 'central process' of overgeneralisation operating on either:

(a) L1 rules
(b) L2 rules

or, in the case of transfer of training, on

(c) some perceived regularity artificially created by the teacher or textbook to promote learning (e.g. making an uncommon but difficult structure artificially frequent in the classroom input: see Selinker 1972 for examples and Lightbown 1985 for related research).

Ignoring, for the moment, more fundamental differences between L1 and L2 acquisition, this would mean that the L2 learner simply had more resources to draw on when generalising. These would be resources that are not available to the L1 learner, i.e. instructional input and knowledge of at least one previously acquired language. To reiterate the idea of the learner (language-learning device) as a generator of hypotheses, all of these IL processes might well be examples of a single process of overgeneralisation where the learner posits an overgeneral rule and then has to come to realise that the hypothesis has to be modified and the rule limited to certain situations and not others.

6.1.1.3 *'One phenomenon, one cause' versus conspiracy*

As Dulay and Burt pointed out, learner errors can be multiply interpreted. They are in their very nature typically ambiguous (see discussion in 2.1.5). This raises the question of whether a given phenomenon in learner performance could be the outcome of different factors 'conspiring' to target the learner's attention in one direction rather than another (see Hakuta 1976, for example). The idea of 'one phenomenon, one cause' may be a totally unreasonable assumption (Sharwood Smith 1983).

6.1.2   Creative construction reviewed

As was demonstrated earlier, creative construction theory did not involve the notion of interlanguage in the sense of an overall learner language system although it did allow for IL in some sense, that is, in the form of specific developmental (transitional) forms. These forms represent deviant but predictable stages which occur prior to the attainment of a particular subtarget within the broad framework of L2 as a whole. The development of subtargets such as negation and question forms provide classic examples of such 'mini-routes', occurring apparently independently of one another following their own specific principles.

6.1.2.1 *Weaknesses in the standard creative construction position*

To focus, in retrospect, on the gaps in the creative construction position (as put forward in Dulay *et al.* 1982, and elsewhere), the various claims made by creative construction theorists in the 1970s did not, at least in any serious fashion:

(1) differentiate between subsystems within the grammar (in the absence of disclaimers, we must assume that the inbuilt syllabus for morpheme acquisition – and hence the absence of L1 influence – was claimed to hold for *all* of the grammar);

(2) differentiate between the development of knowledge (competence) and the development of processing control over

knowledge, especially with regard to the interpretation of developmental sequences;

(3) allow for systematic individual variation in the development of competence;

(4) involve a proper application of the principles of the linguistic framework to which it claimed allegiance, i.e. generative grammar.

It might be argued that creative construction did all of these things, at least to some extent. However, the message propounded in the literature concentrated first and foremost on similarities observed in L1 and L2 development, and the nature of the underlying processes were left largely unexplained. The same black box drove development in L1 and L2, and understanding how the black box worked was not a first priority. Attempts to explain the L1 or L2 orders always ended up itemising a number of quite different factors like the salience of the input, relevance to communicative needs, etc., which could explain one or other of the developmental patterns but none of which could explain *all* of them (see Brown 1973, Slobin 1973, Hatch 1978; for a discussion of hypotheses about general acquisitional principles underlying L1 morphological acquisition, see Ingram 1989: 499ff).

In an attempt to update creative construction theory, Schwartz pointed out what might be seen as the unused potential in this approach. She attempts to make good some of these deficits (see Schwartz 1986) by couching the model (as presented in Dulay *et al.* 1982) in terms of Fodor's ideas on the modularity of mind (cf. Gregg 1988 for criticisms of this interpretation of Fodor). In fact, Schwartz's suggestions constitute more of an adjustment or enrichment of the original creative construction position as set out in Dulay *et al.* (1982) than a description of what it actually claimed to be in the 1970s.

The fact of the matter is that, despite its undeniable value as a thought-provoker to researchers and language teachers, the creative construction model of the 1970s fell far short of anything approaching a theoretically interesting explanation of the phenomenon of L2 acquisition. It held out some promise but, as it stood, was seriously in need of adjustment and elaboration.

6.1.2.2   *The role of the mother tongue undervalued*

As already mentioned, the priority of claiming similarity between the two types of language acquisition seems to have led to an insistence on the reduced status of language transfer. Transfer needed to be explained away to keep the claim of L1/L2 equivalence pure and unsullied as though transfer in L2 implied non-creative, habit-formation and a corresponding commitment to an outmoded learning theory, i.e. behaviourism.

In fact, downgrading the status of transfer was an unnecessary precaution against behaviourism. The possibility of applying principles specific to the L1 system in the creation of L2 knowledge is, by definition, simply not available to an acquirer of an L1. There is no previous 'L1' available. This means that transfer occurring in L2 acquisition may easily be the application of processes available *in principle* to L1 acquirers but not used crosslinguistically. This would be because, *in practice*, there was simply no prior linguistic knowledge of this type available to the L1 learner to transfer. Moreover, by talking of the transfer of knowledge (competence), we are violating a major canon of behaviourism by referring to a concept that is not open to direct observation and measurement, i.e. 'knowledge'.

Clearly, a single process using different input and working on different assumptions may lead to different results. L1 patterns observed in interlanguage (all through the 1970s as well as later – see, for example, Wode 1978, Sajavaara 1981) suggest that the learner may be assuming that L1 principles also apply to L2 and hence creating the IL system with the help of L1 principles. This does not happen in L1 acquisition because there is nothing to transfer. The L1 acquirer is forced to rely on input from outside and the outcome is inevitably different (see Odlin 1989 for an extensive review of work on crosslinguistic influence in second language acquisition).

6.1.2.3 The role of conscious processes

Ignoring potential L1 effects in L2 competence on such slender grounds is a major weakness of creative construction theory especially due to the limited nature of their empirical evidence (superficial areas of morphosyntax). It did, however, as a result of Krashen's Monitor Model, make some headway in defining the role of conscious explicit knowledge in acquisition. The resulting hard line, i.e. that conscious knowledge plays no role at all, provided and still provides a useful challenge to the standard layman's (including linguist's) assumption that learners just have to be 'told the rule' and everything will be all right.

Despite the little evidence that was first gathered, it is now a standard assumption in second language research that subconscious processes are very important and that many of them may well be impervious to outside intervention (either by the learners themselves attempting to apply rules consciously or by teachers attempting to explain, demonstrate and drill rules). This, of course, is not the same as saying that all second language acquisition is beyond such manipulation. The blanket claim that conscious processes have been shown to play no role at all is clearly misconceived (see Sharwood Smith 1980, Rutherford and Sharwood Smith 1985, Rutherford 1987a, Gregg 1984, 1988, Ellis 1989).

6.1.2.4   The role of comprehensible input

As White (1987) has emphasised, the notion that L2 acquisition is driven purely by comprehensible input has serious weaknesses in that

(a) a *breakdown* in comprehension can trigger acquisition; and
(b) it may often be the case that the input itself provides no clear evidence of how the grammar should be changed.

White gives an example of acquiring the passive in English. If, according to the current IL, the first NP is taken to be the subject of the sentence, then 'the book (NP1) was read by John (NP2)' is going to create a breakdown in comprehension: the book cannot possibly be reading John (except in a crazy fairy-tale world). The sentence does not make sense in the real world. The learner does not comprehend it and is thus pressured (or the learning device is pressured) to reassess the current IL which may be held responsible for the breakdown in comprehension. The evidence suggests that learners need more than just comprehensible input to allow them to approximate further to native speaker norms (see White 1987, 1990). They also need incomprehensible input. More properly, we should say that the learners' drive to comprehend input is crucial for their further development.

6.2   Some other alternatives

6.2.1   Heterogeneous competence

In reaction to the notion of an idealised, homogeneous competence which has been taken by some people to be a core concept in the

Chomskyan literature, an alternative view of native-speaker ability has arisen, namely one which views competence as *heterogeneous* in character. This means that linguistic rules vary systematically according to the particular use to which they are put. Language users do not, in this view, have a single competence which varies only when it is applied to real-life situations; rather, they have a competence which contains usage information such that rules are stated in terms of the various manifestations they have according to the situation and context and the speaker's communicative requirements (see Hymes 1972 for an earlier version of this idea; see Halliday 1978 for another integrative approach to language). It is not always easy to compare linguistic models since people have quite different notions in their minds when they talk of 'the grammar' and 'the language'. However, broadly speaking, one can distinguish models which present one system within language as unaffected by other systems or levels and following different principles and, on the other hand, models which see different systems as interacting, as following the same basic design and therefore not really separate or autonomous.

6.2.1.1 Chomsky misunderstood

People not immediately involved in Chomskyan generative grammar generally draw their knowledge from earlier models, e.g. models based on *Aspects of the theory of syntax* (Chomsky 1965) when it was possible to talk of 'transformational' grammar. Current views have involved a drastic reduction in transformations and a whole new (modular) approach to how different parts of the grammar interact (see Newmeyer 1983 for a readable account). However, there are some enduring areas of misunderstanding, one of which is the role of pragmatic or sociolinguistic knowledge in language use.

Allowing for situational variation has, in fact, never been a problem in Chomskyan linguistics although it is true that what amounts to 'usage' aspects have been outside the main thrust of theoretical investigations. This was particularly clear in Chomsky (1965) where he basically delimited the scope of 'competence' to exclude such concerns. He did not claim that all we have is a homogeneous competence underlying language. He never excluded the possibility of rule-governed variation according to situation, nor did he exclude the idea of the native speaker possessing different dialects or varieties of a language. And even where homogeneity was adopted for methodological purposes, he never included all of language in its scope.

There are good reasons for supposing that accounting for linguistic behaviour in the broadest sense (i.e. not just aspects of syntax) needs us to separate out different types of competence or 'knowledge systems' (see discussion in Chomsky 1980, 1981). Treating some large-scale linguistic subsystems as being very different in kind, i.e. different kinds of competence, allows us to clear up these issues in that variation according to use can be treated as a separate system obeying different laws. At some level, of course, the language user has access to these different systems. In themselves, they are independent but they all contribute to a larger picture. The language user must integrate everything in trying to match knowledge with speaker intention and the general situational context.

One simple illustration of using distinct linguistic systems to account for a phenomenon that has been noticed both in mature languages and in the language of acquirers is the omission of pronouns. Hence, if the dropping of a subject pronoun in a particular (inter)language (as in '. . .is coming now' or: 'They saw. . .') cannot be accounted for by recourse to some basic principle of the *grammatical* competence system, it may well be accounted for perfectly well as a principle of the *pragmatic* system: 'leave out redundant information', 'drop pronouns denoting topics known to the hearer'. In this way, apparently random variation in (inter)language performance at a syntactic level can be explained coherently at a pragmatic level. The grammar allows the variation, i.e. says what is possible and what is not possible, and the pragmatics decides when, where and how *possible* structures should occur. In other words, it is the interaction between two distinct linguistic systems that explains variation.

An alternative to explaining variation as the interaction of different systems is the one chosen by linguists such as William Labov (see Labov 1970). Here, the factors causing variation are integrated into one system of 'variable rules'. A variable rule can collapse all the relevant information about possible structures, appropriacy and probability of co-occurrence into one statement. In other words, it can tell you the forms and structures that are possible, in the situations in which they apply, the alternative forms that are used accordingly and even the degree of probability that a particular alternative will occur. These are rules describing the complete facts as well as a number of sociolinguistic and psycholinguistic regularities.

What this all amounts to is that any respectable account of the phenomenon of language, in one way or other, informs us about our knowledge of the *possible*, the *appropriate* and the *probable*. Chomsky's account is one of these. Choosing between different accounts depends on a number of factors, some of which may be quite technical while others deal with what a given model is trying to explain.

6.2.1.2   *Variation according to degree of control*

There is another kind of variability which has to do with purely psycholinguistic factors rather than situational usage *per se*. It is what would here be called 'control variability' (see Bialystok and Sharwood Smith 1985), that is, variability caused by factors having to do with the on-line processing of competence.

Apparently random behaviour may be caused when the language user experiences some kind of stress or overload due to fatigue or distraction. When the principles of on-line processing are more fully understood, it should also be possible to see some system in this erratic behaviour. Presumably, there are predictable strategies that a processing system will resort to if its available on-line capacity is reduced. This, at least, is what is indicated by slips-of-the-tongue research (see Fromkin 1973a, 1973b).

By way of illustration, let us consider two possible reasons for the way in which an IL user might vary his or her use of particular constructions to convey a given message. Assume, for instance, that there are two alternatives available to express a request in IL English: 'I want' and 'I would like'. The IL grammar and lexicon allow both these possibilities: the question is *when* and *where* they are actually used in performance.

In the first case, as a result of hypothesising rules of usage from observed native-speaker behaviour, the IL user uses 'I want' in formal and informal speech, and 'I would like' in formal writing. Systematic variation in IL is therefore determined by sociolinguisti- cally based rules which make reference to the context of use. The variation is only detectable at a purely grammatical level. The pragmatics of the learner's IL determine that there is no choice after all.

In the second case, the IL user uses 'I want' only when processing capacity is, for one reason or another, overloaded. Hence, 'I want' functions as the default form, usable in all contexts. 'I would like' is used both in formal and informal speech, and in writing as well. In speech, when there is no processing overload, it varies only with the contracted 'I'd like'. The learner, unlike a native speaker, treats 'I want' as always inappropriate and is aware of this even when forced to use it in overload situations. In this case, he or she performs in defiance of current IL sociolinguistic knowledge (pragmatic competence). We may speculate that the learner has overgeneralised the perceived inappropriateness of 'I want' in some contexts, to all contexts of use. Notice that writing variable rules (see discussion in previous section) to account for learner performance will not help us to understand the different psychological factors underlying variability.

6.2.1.3   *Variation and developmental effects*

The main point illustrated above is that systematic variability will have to be explained in terms of at least two kinds of linguistic system. To this we may add *cognitive* variability, that is, variation due to the indeterminacy of particular areas in knowledge (see Bialystok and Sharwood Smith 1985, Sorace 1985). The IL learners may be in the process of developing a new grammatical, pragmatic (or other type of) rule. This itself may trigger backsliding behaviour (Selinker 1972) whereby a learner, when pressed, uses the more established or previously fully established IL form as the default option. This is different from the situation in which learners are pressured to fall back on an L1 structure which they *know* to be deviant. In cognitive variability, their intuitions are still fuzzy and their performance reflects this. Their confidence in the old rule has been undermined and they have not yet made a satisfactory readjustment. In Klein's terms, the relevant rule has become critical (Klein 1986).

The reader will immediately appreciate the effect of certain types of experimental task on the elicitation of learner performance designed to shed light on variability (see Chapter 2). Faced with the task of explaining variation and hesitation and given the horrendous ambiguity of live linguistic performance, no one can set up a test to help unravel the underlying processes without having clear hypotheses about what the explanations *might* be. The test designer must use these hypotheses to justify the test design as a way of assessing the learners' current intuitions or their ability to reveal their beliefs about the language system under varying conditions of stress and in various social situations.

6.2.1.4   *Psycholinguistic versus sociolinguistic variability*

The explanation of variability in terms of different mental knowledge systems, 'modules', possessed by the learners and operating according to different laws may seem more feasible than an approach which seeks to present language users as possessing non-modularised, i.e. heterogeneous competence. Labov's heterogeneous approach is reflected most obviously in the work of Tarone (Labov 1970, Tarone 1983, 1985, 1988) and this relies on *attention* to form as the crucial determinant of variation and hence the type of IL style used.

Just as Labov's native speaker of Black English in the United States will give evidence of, say, systematic phonological variation with regard to the formality of the situation, so, too, an IL speaker will produce a different kind of IL when in a casual relaxed mode than he or she will when in a strained, formal situation. In both cases one might ask, in present terms, if the kind of variability we are seeing in the formal situation is occasioned not by sociolinguistic style but rather by processing overload. The speaker requires more conscious attention when performing in a style that he or she has not fully mastered. In this case, we would have to say that calling the formal IL a 'style' and linking it to a context of use is committing a category error, since it is not *sociolinguistic* in origin, but *psycholinguistic* (see discussion in Bialystok and Sharwood Smith 1985). The phenomenon has, of course, sociolinguistic relevance but social factors are not the immediate concerns underlying variation.

If control variability is being confused with variation according to rules of appropriateness, this prompts the question of whether the native speaker of one dialect is actually performing as a non-native speaker of another dialect. This other dialect may be seen as more appropriate to formal situations but he or she may not necessarily be in complete command of it. In the same way, IL speakers may lose control over their competence in formal situations. This leads us to suggest that the term 'native command' be used not merely to refer to knowledge of correct and appropriate L1 or L2 forms in all relevant types of situation, but exclusively to those who can perform in those situations fluently and spontaneously. In this way, reflecting on IL usage in various circumstances leads us to pose interesting questions about the notion of 'native speakerhood'.

6.2.1.4   *Variation in acquisition: a summary*

To sum up, variation can have various sources in both native speaker and IL speaker alike. It can have to do with the variable use of (inter)linguistic competence in specific contexts, given specific types of situation and speaker intentions. This deployment of linguistic competence in rule-governed ways follows sociolinguistic or pragmatic principles and hence may be accounted for as part of sociolinguistic/pragmatic competence. IL research can look into ways in which this kind of competence unfolds in the learner. It can also look at the extent to which a given IL user controls the sociolinguistic/pragmatic competence at a given time. This mirrors research into the control of more purely linguistic competence.

Variation in control of knowledge of whatever sort must not, in this scheme of things, be confused with the knowledge itself. IL users of English may then variably produce the deviant utterance 'Has no car' alongside the non-deviant 'She has no car':

(a) because their IL grammar allows optional dropping of subject pronouns (a linguistic competence fact);
(b) according to a rule which says that subject pronouns are dropped when the context makes them redundant; the hearer already knows the identity of the subject (a sociolinguistic competence fact).

Alternatively, variation in the occurrence of the pronoun may take place because the learners, despite the fact that their current linguistic competence disallows the dropping of subject pronouns, have not yet gained full control of this new rule in their grammar. In this third case, variation may vary systematically with the amount of processing load they are faced with in a given situation.

6.2.2   Cognitive psychology applied

During the late 1970s, two alternative frameworks were proposed along general cognitive psychological lines (see also Faerch and Kasper 1986, Kohn 1986, Sajavaara 1986). The first was that proposed by Bialystok which was based on two dimensions, namely the 'analysis' of knowledge dimension and automaticity. The second one was proposed by McLaughlin (see McLaughlin 1987) and dispenses with a separate notion of knowledge, applying information processing theory to L2 learner behaviour (see also McLaughlin *et al.* 1983).

6.2.2.1   *Degree of analysis versus automaticity*

Stated very roughly (and following Bialystok 1990), various language tasks can be placed on a grid defining exactly how analysed the relevant knowledge is that is required for their successful completion, and also the degree of control determining how the knowledge needs to be handled. A particular small area of, say, syntactic knowledge can be more or less integrated with a larger syntactic system. An area that is minimally integrated with the rest of the syntactic system is less open to different uses, one example being a structure in early L1 or IL English like 'itsa', which is stored in more or less 'prefabricated' form {itsa}, but not further analysed into subject pronoun plus copula. As was made clear in a study reviewing current notions of interlanguage (Bialystok and Sharwood Smith 1985), IL can be studied as the development of analysis and automaticity (knowledge and control) irrespective of whether the 'knowledge' referred to is in conformity with the native speaker norms and allowing for the restructuring of knowledge away from those norms rather than towards them. Note that analysis is applied to knowledge, and control involves the exploitation of knowledge in actual performance and the degree to which the learner is able to switch attention to and fro to the relevant bits and pieces of knowledge available. Tasks (like responding quickly to unexpected questions) requiring a high degree of control involve the language user in a lot of complicated mental juggling. If control is inadequate, then the smooth manipulation of linguistic resources will be interrupted.

6.2.2.2   Controlled versus automatic processes

The second framework was first advanced in a paper by McLaughlin (1978; see also McLaughlin 1990) criticising Krashen's Monitor Model. Cognitive psychologists' first preference seems to be to try to present linguistic knowledge in non-modular fashion as being essentially the same as other kinds of knowledge, analysable according to the same laws and processes and acquired in a similar manner. This means that (all types of) grammatical knowledge, as well as skill in using that grammatical knowledge, may be accounted for in a general model that encompasses all other aspects of human cognition. In other words, there is no rationale, in this view, for presenting grammatical knowledge as somehow different from other, more general types of knowledge.

McLaughlin makes use of information-processing theory as advanced by Schneider and Shiffrin (1977; see also Rumelhart and Ortony 1977, for example). Knowledge is stored in memory as a series of interconnecting nodes. The information is handled by the system via *automatic processing* and *controlled processing*. In response to external stimuli, knowledge may be processed automatically. Various nodes are activated automatically, spontaneously and in a manner difficult to suppress (cf. Fodor's notion of an input system: Fodor

1983). Controlled processing, however, involves the activation of memory nodes in a more deliberate manner. Although controlled processing is relatively slow and laborious, it does not have to involve conscious awareness. It therefore cannot be equated neatly with Krashen's Monitor which by definition, involves conscious introspection during performance.

Controlled processes allow greater control of the information by the user; they can easily be applied and adapted to new situations. On the debit side, they are costly in terms of the processing capacity they use. A learner driver may be so taken up with the business of driving using controlled processes, that there is no capacity left for making higher level decisions, like which route to take, what to say to the boss later, etc. From this it may be (correctly) inferred that learning starts with controlled processes which are then converted into the more efficient and specialised automatic processes. This allows room for higher level decision procedures such as those just mentioned. McLaughlin's original example (in McLaughlin 1978) was German word order. The English-speaker learner first places the verb at the end of the subordinate clause using controlled processes, but hopefully passes on later to a stage whereby this is done automatically, i.e. via automatic processes in the Schneider and Shiffrin sense.

This intuitively satisfying explanation of controlled processing preceding automatic processing in language acquisition appears to clash with the idea that, at the very least, the acquisition of important areas of grammatical knowledge proceeds exclusively in a manner well beyond the control of the learner or the teacher and hence in what looks more like an automatic-processing mode. In particular, it is difficult to reconcile the idea of learners getting sudden insights into the L2 system with the notion of slow-and-difficult preceding fast-and-skilful. In other words, controlled processes may follow on from an earlier stage where there has been an assembly of some new piece of linguistic knowledge.

As Jackendoff has pointed out recently, information-processing approaches suggest a rather undifferentiated view of information (Jackendoff 1987). According to him, they focus much more on the flow of information in real time than on the probably highly complex make-up of the information being processed. Language acquisition research on the other hand has focused on the internal structure of information (for example, prefabricated chunks versus well-analysed areas of grammar).

It would seem, then, that the information-processing model would be more helpful in understanding the development of *control* rather than the development of grammar-as-competence. In fact, it does not seem to have much to say about the development of knowledge *per se*, perhaps because the competence/performance distinction is simply not recognised (for an interesting discussion on a related approach, i.e. connectionism, see Fodor and Pylyshyn 1988). If this is so, it is difficult to integrate research into (human) information-processing theory with the existing body of research into language viewed as a type of knowledge. In any case, research associating the work of cognitive psychologists with the work of linguists is in its infancy. McLaughlin has recently pointed out that the information-processing perspective is not yet sufficiently integrated with linguistic theory to provide a suitable theory of second language acquisition (McLaughlin 1990).

If the mind is seen only as a massive network of connections without any complex linguistic structure, as is the case in the connectionist approach, then a whole new theory of language acquisition is needed. For the time being, the onus is on the connectionists to prove that we can dispense with the more familiar idea of linguistic knowledge as a set of interacting rules and principles which are separate from and interact with the mechanisms designed to produce and comprehend language in real time. It may be, as just suggested, that allowing information-processing concepts to refer to the control dimension rather than the development of linguistic knowledge *per se* is a possible avenue for integrating the two research traditions. In this way, 'controlled processing' of German verb placement would not lead anywhere *without* the learner having prior grammatical knowledge of the rule. This rule would have been attained according to principles quite different from those governing the on-line processing, in some cases instantaneously, perhaps as a consequence of something in the input triggering a sudden insight. In brief, competence in area X (say, verb placement) would never follow control of area X.

On the other hand, the development of control over knowledge might indeed begin with controlled processes. And, by the same token, the apparently rapid development of control over parts of a new linguistic knowledge system may be explained as the redeployment of automatic processing routines used to process information from another linguistic system, e.g. L1. In other words, the information-processing approach may be useful in our understanding of crosslinguistic influence at the level of control of for example, why, German learners have fewer problems from the start with regard to verb-final position in Dutch subordinate clauses (disregarding finer word-order distinctions between the two languages). Where like is related with like at the competence level, the possibility emerges of deploying the same automatic-processing routines at the control level.

6.2.3 Pienemann's Teachability Hypothesis

There is one recent trend in second language research which does develop an approach which focuses on processing problems but relates these specifically to linguistic structure. This approach has been developed by Manfred Pienemann following up research done on the German of migrant workers in the ZISA project (see Meisel *et al.* 1981). Here, an apparently stable order was discovered in the acquisition of German word order whereby learners irrespective of language background, seemed to begin with a 'canonical' sub-ject–verb–object order, placing adverbials outside this complex, and then move on to later stages where this canonical order could be manipulated.

The explanation favoured by Pienemann is that 'processing complexity' determines this order (see Clahsen 1984). It would appear that, given this canonical order as the starting point, when manipulation of the order takes place, it is first easiest to place elements externally in initial or final position, harder to move elements from the outside in (or vice versa) and harder still to juxtapose internal elements, i.e. inside the sentence. These process-ing laws, it is claimed, dictate the fixed order of acquisition schematically represented below, X being the element that is added or manipulated and '_' being a space abandoned by X – the reader may care to think of X as, for example, a time adverbial like 'often' and the rest of the utterance as 'John may miss his train':

1. X xxxxxxxxx or xxxxxxxxx X (adding X on outside)

2. _ xxx X xxx (bringing X from outside to inside)

   X xxx _ xxx (bringing X from inside to outside)

3. xxx X xx _ xx (moving X inside the sentence)

Initially the relevant elements had to do with word order but more recently morphological elements have been seen as also reflecting these processing laws. Hence, the addition of a suffix or prefix which involves a global operation across sentence structure as in subject–verb agreement as in 'JOHN (SINGULAR) generally hopeS' are more difficult, in processing terms, than local operations like adding a suffix or prefix to the beginning or end of words as in the expression of time/aspect in English 'arriv-ED' or German 'GE-kommen'. (Pienemann 1987a)

It is instructive to follow these ideas through to what they imply for actually teaching word order (for instance). In one study (see Pienemann 1984), he asks the question whether natural second language acquisition (as it occurs in an immigrant situation) can be affected by formal instruction. Note that this is not the same as asking, as Felix and others have done (see, for example, Felix and Hahn 1985) whether classroom instruction displays the characteristics encountered in natural situations. Pienemann quotes Long's survey of various input frequency studies and the general finding that instruction is beneficial, but points out that the focus is on 'learning success', the desired outcome of acquisition, and not on how instruction may specifically change known processes of acquisition.

Pienemann's claim, his 'Teachability Hypothesis' is that, although there are aspects of the target system that can, in principle, be picked up at any time (variable or variational features), there are certain structures in a language (developmental features) which can only be acquired when the learner is ready, i.e. has gone through the appropriate stages *en route* to the target structure in question and has therefore acquired the processing prerequisites. Learners cannot, as it were, be expected to run before they can walk. Teaching a given construction may well be effective, according to this theoretical position, but only when the learner has progressed through the prerequisite stage(s). Experimentation has indicated that learners who have still not independently reached a certain stage are impervious to instruction that attempts to drag them into that stage, whereas learners who have shown signs of having arrived do profit from teaching (see also Johnston 1987). If the learner has signalled arrival at a stage by independently producing a relevant construction, the teacher can then try to help the learner to apply his or her new processing skill to all the relevant areas of the language, for example, moving sentence-internal elements, as in 'Where DID/YOU see him' and 'You DID NOT see him' (see useful discussion in Ellis 1990). The effect of teaching is then to speed up acquisition at specific points in the learner's acquisitional career, a type of timed intervention that was mentioned above in connection with consciousness raising. Although a particular processing stage may have been reached, it is not immediately applied to all relevant areas. Compare this with Krashen's view that teaching has a minimal effect on acquisition. For Krashen, 'readiness' for a given structure simply means having at last become ready to process some input which might well have been available to the learner for some time: it does not mean that it becomes teachable. Pienemann's ideas on teachability offer the teacher more hope actively to assist the learning process.

Readiness to learn may not necessarily be solely linked with developmental features. In an experiment focusing on copula-inclusion, a variational feature, teaching was shown by Pienemann to be successful in promoting a decline in non-native omission of that structure by immigrants. The point here is that when learners have shown they can produce the copula sometimes, they are ready for instruction. Even here, there is some doubt. One subject, Monica, interviewed 9 months after the copula experiment, showed a rise in omission to 34 per cent (backsliding). It seems that instruction is not only unable to disrupt the natural acquisitional sequence of development but it might also be ineffective with variational features such as copula-omission.

It might seem that instructional benefits would accrue only to immigrant learners in a naturalistic learning situation. However, Pienemann (1987a) found that formal instruction seemed to make no inroads into a natural order which emerged in his Australian learners of German as a foreign language. This confirms what Felix, Lightbown and others have found, namely that foreign language classroom does not preclude natural acquisitional processes taking place even though they may not always have the same result as in untutored situations. It also suggests that Pienemann's ideas on teachability may prove valid for foreign learners as well (see Long 1985, White 1991b and Hulstijn 1987 for critical discussion of Pienemann's teachability research; see Pienemann 1992 for refinements of his position and recent applications of lexical functional grammar to his model). Pienemann's ideas will be taken up again in the final chapter.

6.3 Summary

Earlier chapters provided a streamlined, rather simple view of the current accounts of second language learning. This chapter dealt with the manner in which researchers into second language learning began, even in the 1970s, to explore other ways of accounting for learner behaviour which elaborates on, or deviates from the standard accounts. The seeds of further development were sown in the 1970s: the interest in variable behaviour, in more sophisticated aspects of linguistic competence, in the role of consciousness and crosslinguistic influence – everything, in fact, that should lead to the conclusion that things were not as simple as they first seemed. The doors were thus opened to a Pandora's box of research in theoretical linguistics, psychology and sociology although, understandably, the benefits of such interdisciplinary perspectives have been slow to accrue.

PART III:
The Coming of Age

7 Theoretical applications of linguistics

7.0 Introduction

In this part of the book, we move on to look at more of the ideas that are presently dominating the field. In this chapter, various applications of linguistic theory to second language research will be the issue. The following chapter will delve more specifically into one linguistic and psycholinguistic framework, namely the Chomskyan perspective in which the concepts of 'Universal Grammar' and 'learnability' will come to the fore.

7.1 Theory and 'application'

Second language research was born within the confines of what is generally called 'applied' linguistics. Applied linguistics, in this sense, is aimed at using linguistically based explanations and descriptions of language to solve practical problems of relevance to society. The example that first springs to many people's minds concerns the development of language-teaching methods and techniques, although applied linguistics covers many other areas such as language planning, speech therapy and automatic translation, to name but a few.

'Application', however, does not have to mean *practical* application. It might also have been the hope that linguistic theory and linguistic descriptions could directly help us to unravel the mysteries of success and failure in L2 learning *irrespective* of any practical application. In any case, this hope is quite evident in research today. The question is, can linguistics help us to understand what is going on in second language learning? And, what about the role of other relevant fields, like psychology and sociology? Solving *language teaching* problems should more properly be called 'applying second language research'. This identifies second language research as, in part, a theoretical field in its own right. Perhaps linguistics can be 'applied' to second language learning problems and these in turn may form the basis for practical applications. Only in this very indirect way, then, could applied linguistics conceivably be thought of as linking up linguistics with the practical world of teaching (see Corder 1973).

The failure, in the 1960s, of contemporary American structural linguistics reliably to predict learner errors led to a general desire to develop special L2-based tools for this special job of analysing non-native linguistic behaviour. Also, sticking to simple structures, as exemplified in the morpheme studies, was convenient: it meant not having to go too deeply into the technicalities of linguistics. And linguistics could not, it seemed, be applied to predict learner performance in any straightforward manner. However, since the onset of the 1980s, more and more researchers have been turning back to theoretical and descriptive linguistics for ways of asking precise questions about L2 development. Also, linguistics itself has developed a great deal since the 1960s and this has stimulated further interest in seeking useful cross-fertilisation between the two fields.

The more one looks at complex structure – especially in its more advanced stages of development – the less one can do without a well-worked-out linguistic framework. This means applying theoretical concepts and descriptive techniques from linguistics to the performance of L2 speakers. Just because there are linguistic patterns in learner language that do not seem to belong to native-speaker systems does not mean we have to devise an entirely new linguistic framework to handle description and explanation. After all, linguistic theories are supposed to handle *any* language that is used by human beings and, as has perhaps become clear, learner language patterns certainly fall within the scope of the term 'human language'. So, linguistic principles and descriptive mechanisms can be grafted on to an L2 theory which has a whole set of principles of its own. And, in that learner language is still human, i.e. 'natural' language, the results may even lead to insights that are of relevance to linguistics proper.

One linguistic notion in particular has attracted attention in L2 research and that is the notion of 'markedness'. For example, some forms belonging to a particular category, seem to be more basic than others: 'cow' seems to be the basic form whereas the plural 'cows' seems to be derived from the basic form. This unmarked/marked distinction holds for forms within a given language and also for forms in a whole range of languages. For example, every language that has prepositions and (the equivalent of) *wh*-clauses has sentences where the *wh*-word and the preposition are next to each other, as in:

'*About what* are you talking?'
'*On what* are you sitting?'

However, only some of those languages allow separation of the two words, as in:

'*What* are you talking *about*?'
'*What* are you sitting *on*?'

This has led to the speculation that such splitting (leaving the preposition 'stranded' at the end) is somehow less usual, an extra possibility, and hence a 'marked' phenomenon in languages in general. The same could be said of rounded and unrounded front vowels. There seems to be no language that has just only *rounded* front vowels. This makes them special, i.e. marked. Every language that has rounded front vowels has unrounded ones as well. Some languages only have unrounded ones. This seems to make unrounded front vowels unmarked.

Again, in the lexicon, 'dog' or 'cow' might be considered more basic forms than, respectively, the feminine 'bitch' or the masculine 'bull'. Since the first member of each of those pairs is the generic one, it can stand for the species (as in 'cows are stupid but dogs are clever') and not just one particular sex.

The real question here is whether this distinction between marked and unmarked forms is reflected in any way in learner behaviour at a given moment or in learner development over time? The following sections will deal with this question. They should provide the reader with interesting examples of how linguistics has stimulated thinking in different ways since the abandonment of the habit-formation views of the 1950s and 1960s.

7.2   Markedness in linguistics and acquisition

The general notion of markedness in phonology, morphology and syntax, i.e. that certain principles, forms or structures may be seen as 'basic' forms, in some sense, i.e. *unmarked*, has been available in linguistics for some time. The label 'marked' is used in many ways, as is suggested by the examples given above: for instance, it is used to mean forms that have more structure, or that require an extension of a rule or possess more informational content than forms directly associated with them, or which occur less frequently in the world's languages and by virtue of this are less typical; further examples of the distinction include active versus passive versions of a sentence, full devoicing of final stops before a silence as in German *Bad* [bat] versus English *bad* [bæd] , etc.

In acquisitional terms, markedness has been seized upon as a possible element in the learner's strategies in coping with system building. Markedness invokes the notion of complex versus simple, and structural simplicity itself inevitably invokes, for better or for worse, the psychological notion of learning simplicity. Hence, for example, some have wondered whether learners prefer to begin with more basic, unmarked items/structures as a way of simplifying their task.

Note that one might also assume the opposite line, namely that 'marked' meaning 'less usual' might mean more striking, more noticeable and therefore more readily learned. The first hypotheses, however, took the first approach that 'simple' or 'frequent', or whatever 'unmarked' was, was more attractive to the learner/learning device.

Since learners are not usually linguists, they cannot know in any *conscious* fashion what is marked or unmarked. This means that some idea of subconscious foreknowledge is inevitably involved in this idea of markedness playing a role in acquisition. Also, assuming without further ado that what is *structurally* simple is also *simple* to acquire is to confuse linguistic, structural notions with psycholinguistic notions. In other words, there has to be a theory that explains why it is that linguistically unmarked structures are somehow attractive in purely learning terms. It could always be the case that what linguists or laymen using their common sense find difficult might, for the human brain, be plain sailing. In the same way, we often find that we can understand something easily when it is explained to us but somehow, five minutes later, we find it difficult again. Our brain has, after all, not appeared to accept what we thought we had successfully taken in. Where the human mind is concerned (and its engine, the brain), we can, it seems, take nothing for granted. There is, in any case, evidence that marked structures may be in fact acquired before related unmarked structures. Children acquire stranded prepositions before they acquire non-stranded ones (see examples in previous section). This may, of course, be because the marked versions are so much more frequent in the input. At the very least, frequency would seem, then, to override questions of markedness.

7.2.1 Markedness in linguistics

We could say, as far as linguistics is concerned, that there are almost as many definitions of markedness as there are linguists using this term (see Comrie 1981). They refer to phenomena ranging from single morphemes expressing, say, tense, number and so on, to basic grammatical characteristics such as surface word-order types and deep phrase structure configurations. They refer to pragmatic phenomena, lexical phenomena, phonological phenomena, morphological phenomena and syntactic phenomena. They invoke such notions as frequency, complexity and quantity. Hence, any discussion of markedness has to begin with defining how markedness is to be understood. This, in turn, invokes the notion of language universals, those characteristics noted by linguists studying a large variety of languages that appear to be typical properties of linguistic systems. In certain cases, it seems useful to talk about forms that are more or less 'basic': variants that stand out as being 'less basic' are commonly termed 'marked' variants. 'Unmarked' means 'basic' or 'more basic'. As suggested above, this may mean that unmarked forms/constructions are, for instance, simpler, more frequent or simply shorter whereas the marked variants are correspondingly more complex, more infrequent or longer.

In the late 1970s and early 1980s, several researchers were trying to apply the study of language universals in an L2 context (see, for example, Eckman 1977, Gass 1979, 1983, Luhan *et al.* 1981, etc.). The first explicit discussions of a possible relationship between markedness and various 'developmental scenarios' (see general overview in Van Buren and Sharwood Smith 1985) made absolutely no reference to Chomsky (see also Hyltenstam 1977, Kellerman 1979). Rather, they followed an approach to universals pioneered by Greenberg (1974; see also Comrie 1981). Here, universals are characteristics that have been inferred from a study of a large number of different languages allowing the linguist to devise a language typology based on surface configurations of sentence constituents. Hence, a subject–object–verb (SOV) language is a language in which the basic (most frequently occurring) form of an active declarative main clause sentence would be S + O + V, i.e. with verb in clause-final position as in 'the little dog the postman bit'. In fact, English is to be classed as an SVO language since this, not SOV, is the normal order: 'the little dog bit the postman'.

Certain phrasal configurations, for example, the order of constituents within a noun phrase, may be associated with this main basic clause order such that the position of the head versus the modifier in a phrase (e.g. noun versus modifying adjective in a noun phrase) will typically come in first position or second position (head–modifier or modifier–head, e.g. 'dog little' or 'little dog', as it were). Hence languages could be sorted into types and the types could, on the basis of a count on those languages in the corpus, be sorted into more frequently or less frequently occurring types and subtypes.

The method of language typology described above – i.e. typology based primarily on a survey of structures in a large group of languages – yields certain characteristics that all languages in the corpus (and by implication *all* human languages) have, and certain characteristics that *most* languages have. The less common characteristics might be called 'marked'. For example, Keenan and Comrie proposed that languages could be placed in a hierarchy depending on the number and type of possibilities they offered for the formation of relative clauses (cf. Keenan and Comrie 1977; see also McLaughlin 1987: 85). This would place languages that allowed subjects to be relativised in a less marked position in the hierarchy than languages that allowed indirect objects to be relativised. English, as it happens, allows both:

'The man who (SUBJECT) fed my little dog.'
'The man whom (INDIRECT OBJECT) I wrote to.'

We can assume, then, that any language which allows the second type of relative (above) will automatically allow the first. If we encounter a language that allows the first, it may not necessarily allow the second. Perhaps it is more difficult to acquire a language that allows fewer positions to be relativised than one's own language allows. Or could it be the other way round (see Gass 1979, 1983)?

Hawkins has proposed that an additional principle known as 'cross-categorial harmony' may be invoked to shed insight on the way that main clause order is in harmony with certain phrasal orders. If verbs and nouns are seen as 'heads' then those elements that modify them may come before or after the head, giving us the two options head+modifier versus modifier+head. For example, if a given language has SOV main clause order, that is, with the verb (V) following its object (O), this would imply that it always has, or at least *tends* to have, adjectives and possessive markers respectively following a head noun (hypothetically: JOHN GIN LIKES (OV), DRY GIN (adj+noun) and OF JOHN (possessive marker+noun)) (see Hawkins 1983). Thus, modifier+head order in one part of the grammar implies modifier+head in another part. All in all, following Hawkins, grammars tend towards this kind of harmony although there will always be exceptions. In other words, in addition to frequency, there may be various kinds of *implicational* relationship between the types of linguistic (sub)systems (see Hawkins 1983, 1987). These are referred to as *implicational* universals of language in contrast to *absolute* universals, which would be what *every* language has been found to possess. The relative clause hierarchy and the rounded/unrounded front vowel example mentioned earlier would be instances of implicational universals.

7.2.2   Markedness and acquisition

As mentioned earlier, linguistic markedness has nothing in principle to do with language acquisition. It can simply be part of an analysis of commonalities observed in the world languages. Yet, as already suggested, one could suppose that the less frequently occurring or more basic patterns might be less frequent precisely because they are harder to acquire. And, if one accepts the cross-category harmony principle, for instance, it might be that learners tend to build up a new language system to conform to it. Language acquisition researchers are naturally on the lookout for linguistic principles that were originally devised to account for patterns in existing languages to do extra duty by explaining patterns of language development.

The basic idea behind linking markedness with language learning is to try to find an explanation regarding the typical early assumptions or hypotheses made by given learners which can be tied up meaningfully with those features of the L2 that are relevant for a given theory of markedness. This is to see if markedness affects the order of acquisition. Do learners, in an attempt to simplify the learning task, 'demark' (Zobl 1984) their early IL grammar ('demark' despite evidence of marked features in the L2 input or *in advance of* any relevant L2 evidence) or do they initially assume/hypothesise that L2 will have the same degree of markedness or unmarkedness in the system as the L1 does? Since we know learners devise their own versions of L2 grammar despite the evidence offered by the input, does the notion 'unmarked' actually reflect a natural psychological bias towards more basic rule systems?

As always, researchers are searching for explanations about how learners initially make sense of the input and why they depart from the evidence and produce forms that are not sanctioned by the input. Of course, if markedness theory – any particular markedness theory, that is – does help explain early IL development, it should do this for a wide range of data. It is no use employing a concept like this to explain one or two forms in early IL. As we have seen previously, there may be many competing, logical explanations for isolated phenomena; what is important is to find a theoretical explanation that has a wider coverage.

The concept of a 'demarked' IL obviously requires an explanation. One idea voiced in the literature is that unmarked aspects of human language reflect not merely a kind of fall-back system but in fact some underlying skeletal grammar (a literal 'universal' grammar at the core of every language) on the basis of which particular languages are developed and 'complexified' (cf. Traugott 1977, Naro 1978, Corder 1981: 107ff), a skeletal system which, moreover, is reflected much more transparently in *pidgin* languages, that is – languages with relatively fixed word order and impoverished morphology that have been developed by adults for a very restricted type of communication.

It has been claimed by some that *early* ILs have a non-coincidental resemblance to pidgins (cf. Schumann 1978, in particular, and Andersen 1981a, Huebner 1983; see discussion in the contributions to Andersen 1983b, and in McLaughlin 1987: ch. 5), that is, they evolve along similar lines as pidgins and creoles, exhibiting fixed word order, missing copulas, lack of inflection and so on. A demarked IL in this kind of perspective would be a skeletal IL stripped of all marked characteristics and built up with marked characteristics as they are evidenced in the input (see also Stauble 1978, Macedo 1986).

In Schumann's 'Pidginization' model, the elaboration of the basic grammar is dependent on socio-psychological factors, roughly a perception of closeness with the community of L2 speakers. The more pidginised the IL, the more one observes alienation from this community: a Mexican Spanish woman who comes to the United States to earn some money and then return home to Mexico, and having no basic sympathy for North American culture, will develop pidgin-like forms in her IL and not develop further (fossilise early). A migrant worker in Europe who in principle is willing to integrate as much as he can into the host community may still remain outside an unsympathetic host culture and, as a result, end up willy-nilly more integrated with a fellow group of migrants speaking his L1 and only a little L2: here, again, Schumann's Pidginisation Hypothesis would predict the development and maintenance of pidginized IL.

In Andersen's terms, the movement from the skeletal system is not so much due to feelings of greater psychological and social closeness to the target culture, but is more due to the fact that the problem of restricted L2 input is reduced and an inevitable internal process of 'denativisation' starts to operate by which the learner ceases to assimilate available L2 input to some internal model of language (the basic system). The IL begins eventually to accommodate to the properties of the input that diverge from this internal 'native' norm.

So, in Schumann's case the trigger to further development, i.e. a complexification of the learner's IL, is the learner's perception of closer socio-psychological distance to the target culture (less alienation, if you prefer). The trigger in the case of Andersen is rich L2 input (see Figure. 7.1).

It should be clear that the models developed here seem to focus their explanation more on the early, primitive forms of IL than on the way the elaboration of IL unfolds at later stages.

The models of both Schumann and Andersen, whatever prompts the developmental trend they are describing, rely on the notion of some basic, simpler linguistic system. This can be seen as a set of unmarked properties characterising linguistic systems as a whole.

Markedness does not have to cover a whole language or level of language (like syntax). It can refer to much more specific phenomena. Eckman's Markedness Differential Hypotheses (see Eckman 1977 and the discussion in Long and Larsen-Freeman 1991: 102-3) provides a good example of a markedness theory yielding very particular predictions about L2 learning that is different from a straight contrastive analysis prediction of the old type. For example, the complete devoicing of voiced obstruents in word-final position, requiring for example, German 'Hand' to be pronounced [hant] before a silence or another voiceless sound, is claimed to be unmarked. Maintaining voicing in this position as in English, and especially French, is therefore marked. Eckman points out that

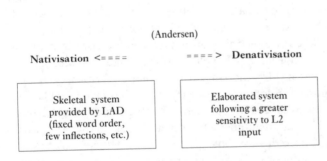

FIGURE 7.1 Developmental trends in IL with respect to skeletal language systems: two explanations for movement away from and towards the norm.

learners with an unmarked L1 structure have a tough time acquiring equivalent marked structures in L2. Hence German and Dutch learners will persistently pronounce English 'hand' as [hant] whereas English learners going from marked to unmarked, will have relatively less trouble learning to produced [hant] appropriately in German.

In this way, Eckman claimed that markedness allows us to make better predictions, based on contrasting L1 and L2, than a simple matter of finding out what is the same and what was different in the L2 and attributing learning difficulty to what is different. If what is different is also what is difficult, then English and French learners should have the same degree of difficulty in learning devoicing as the Dutch and the Germans have in learning to maintain voicing. Presumably, too, a language that allows both unrounded [i] and rounded [y] is going to pose problems for learners whose L1 only allows the first. And indeed, English learners do have difficulty pronouncing French 'u' or the German umlaut. On the other hand, as Eckman points out, they have no problems with the initial sound in French 'je' even though it is not permitted in English phonology. So, new sounds are not necessarily difficult: this is only true when going from an unmarked L1 situation to a marked L2 situation (see Hammarberg 1988 for an opposing view claiming that phonological markedness *per se* always means difficulty whatever the L1/L2 relationship).

As mentioned earlier, the main point is that the notion of marked languages, or rather marked structures in languages, as proposed by different linguists may (optionally) be translated into claims about ease and difficulty of learning. Are unmarked linguistic systems, such as final devoicing or SVO syntax, say, or languages with a syllable structure that involves no consonant clusters, more easily acquired? Some approaches, following Greenberg, take observed regularities in natural languages and try to find L2 developmental patterns that correlate without attempting any deeper explanation of why markedness should have this psychological relevance. Others look at ways of linking markedness with explanations of how learners deal with the input.

7.2.3   Markedness and parameter setting

In the approach adopted by generative grammarians in the Chomskyan tradition, markedness is seen as something quite different from the kind of markedness discussed within a Greenbergian perspective (although Hawkins has proposed a connection: Hawkins 1983, 1987). Firstly, there is no corpus of world languages from which frequent and less frequent types are induced. Secondly, the theory of grammar employed involved a new distinction between deep and surface structure: hence an SOV language in this second perspective is normally understood to be a language with a verb-final configuration in *deep* structure, irrespective of the verb's eventual position in surface structure, and not SOV in main clause *surface* structure: in Greenberg, the typology was worked out on the basis of main clauses in what would now be called surface structure (ignoring theoretical niceties).

According to this newer approach, a theoretically interesting classification of languages must, then, follow from a consideration of more abstract analyses and not simply on the way constituents are ordered 'on the surface'. Hence, one cannot simply use a study of surface characteristics of a particular corpus of world languages (see Coopmans 1984). For various technical reasons, this makes Dutch and German, for example, into SOV languages despite the fact that, in a Greenbergian analysis, they would figure as SVO languages.

Thirdly, there is no skeletal system from which all subconscious grammar-building begins. Universal Grammar (UG) is not a common core set of rules at the heart of every language. It is supposed to be a set of construction principles that are applied to the building of any grammar by any L1 learner. Very often, UG actually decides what should *not* be in the grammar.

According to some working within the current Chomskyan model of grammar (Chomsky 1980), the characteristic of being 'unmarked' (or 'less marked', see Kean 1989) is possessed by certain given aspects of grammar which admit of 'parametric variation'. Parameters are ways in which certain grammatical principles vary. In other words, they are ways in which the grammatical make-up of natural languages seem to differ. Some languages allow a wide variety of word orders without any change in the basic meaning of the sentence, for example. Other languages use word order to signal what the subject and object of a verb are. Grammatical parameters are usually thought of in much more specific terms, however. On a more detailed level, some languages place, say, relative clauses after the noun ('the man who arrived yesterday') and others opt for the reverse of this (as it were: 'the who arrived yesterday man'). In this way, although grammars of natural languages show a great deal of diversity, there are areas of grammar where the diversity can be treated as variations on a fairly small number of themes, i.e. along a small number of parameters.

The limited set of parameters admitting of variation is no accident, according to the Chomskyan view. A normal, immature child has to be able to learn any natural language without grammatical instruction. Anything that limits the task of guessing how a mother tongue grammar fits together must be good news. Parents may help with vocabulary building but they can hardly help when it comes to the complex structural make up of the L1. The child, it is argued, must be predisposed to look for various feature in the input data, the language it is exposed to. These predispositions lie behind what Chomsky has called Universal Grammar (see Cook 1985, 1988, White 1990).

Grammatical parameters, then, allow for one or more variant. To make things easier, it is claimed that, in certain cases at least, particular options are assumed by the child. That is to say, the preferred (unmarked) option would be assumed by the child unless counter-evidence turned up in the input. This means that the unmarked option of a given parameter allowed for in Universal Grammar will be adopted automatically unless there is actually evidence in the input indicating the presence in the language of some marked setting of the particular grammatical parameter in question. The moment the evidence comes along and is noticed, and this may happen sooner or later, the child can adapt its grammar accordingly.

What is the value of having an in-built preference to choose one option rather than another? In Chomsky's approach, the rationale is always the problem of making grammars 'learnable', that is, for the immature child. Generating hypotheses from the input on general logical grounds would take forever. Unbounded creativity in LAD would give rise to myriads of false starts, so the learner or rather LAD's task is simplified by *reducing the amount of hypothesising that has to take place*, firstly by the existence of a limited set of parameters for *any* language and secondly by means of the provision of preferred 'fall-back' ways of setting parameters. The foreknowledge that limits the ways in which human grammars can work is precisely what UG is.

The key criterion for deciding which option is the default (unmarked one) is whether the child could learn the given mother tongue without being corrected. So it is an essentially theoretical principle that determines markedness, not a statistical count of properties observed in the current set of world languages. This principle, learnability, is closely related to the 'no-negative-evidence' issue – in other words, children are rarely corrected where their syntax is concerned; correction occurs generally where communication is hampered (see Brown and Hanlon 1970) and consequently has often more to do with the misleading use of vocabulary and pronunciation. Even if parents respond by producing the correct versions of a child's incorrect utterance, it is by no means clear whether the child interprets this as a correction or, indeed, understands exactly where the correction is.

Parents, and adults in general, seem to assume that the child's syntax will take care of itself. Hence, mother tongue acquirers construct a non-adult rule and nothing in the speech addressed to them shows them that their utterances are syntactically odd. In other words, when they have created their own version of a rule, they ought never to be able to learn the adult version. Provided there is no serious breakdown in communication, all seems to be well. They will simply not be able to change without guidance. If the guidance does not come from outside, it must come from within, so goes the argument.

The lack of regular correction makes it important that the unmarked option is always the *stricter* option of the two (or three, say). This is because the child, in its creative construction of rules, may construct a rule that is too general. If the child observes, in the input provided by adults, a more relaxed use of the grammar than it would normally sanction, then it can relax its own system accordingly. If, for instance, as a foreign visitor, I think that you can only drive a car on weekdays, the experience of seeing people driving on Sundays is all I need to relax my initial and unduly strict interpretation of the traffic rules.

Imagine, on the other hand, that I think you can drive *any* day of the week. I begin with a relaxed rule. But, in fact, there is a no-weekend-driving rule. I may think up a thousand reasons why people are not to be seen on the road at the weekend. Maybe in this country they just prefer to rest quietly at home. To learn the real reason why there are no cars around, someone or something has to *tell* me that there is a no-weekend-driving rule in the country. Only then will I know exactly why the roads are empty of traffic. In other words, I really do need correction of some kind (negative evidence) if I start with the relaxed version of the rule. I shall not see anything in the normal course of events that signals to me unambiguously that I have 'got it all wrong'. And, in the case of traffic rules, sooner or later, I also get corrected (ideally, not in a manner that will cost me money).

That is to say, the input – the experience I get while driving around – may not set me on the right path. A sign that I understand, or a policeman, will correct me, however. The child acquiring the syntax of its mother tongue cannot, it seems, avail itself of warning signs or a linguistic police to set it on the right path when it has adopted the wrong rule.

Not all UG parameters have a default option: the position of a head of a phrase (in deep structure) relative to its complements seems not be present: learners must wait for evidence in the input telling them (their LAD) whether the head comes first or last. Japanese input would say the grammar is a head-final one whereas English data would say the language is a head-initial one (see Flynn 1986 and the discussion below). There is no learnability problem concerning which of the options the learner should take. The input can always provide the information. In either case, the input will show the learner which way to go. For example, noticing 'bit the postman' (the verb head coming first) signals to the English child which way English goes. The converse is true of Japanese and the Japanese child.

Here, the evidence in the input, then, tells the L1 learner how a particular option in UG is to be set, and, where markedness applies, whether the default option supplied by UG should be rejected. This evidence which (where markedness applies) has the effect of *disconfirming the unmarked option* is usually called 'positive evidence' – 'positive' signifying simply 'present in the input' and 'showing by virtue of its appearance what is permissible'. It will serve to confirm or disconfirm hypotheses and assumptions in the learner's developmental grammar. At least, this is the case when the occurrence of one option immediately signals to the learner that the other option must be wrong.

To sum up, what the input provides in the case of the default (unmarked) options of the grammar is the presence of some aspect of grammar possible but not necessary in natural languages (part of the natural repertoire, as it were) and which is open to variation.

Note that this aim of explaining how languages are learnable given the difficult situation the child finds itself in provides a goal and a limitation for the linguist, too. The linguist trying to uncover the principles that underlie human languages must not devise complicated albeit beautiful syntactic systems *if the result is a system that is unlearnable by a small child*. Without this learnability constraint, linguists are free to devise a myriad of grammatical explanations, all of which may account *equally well* for the observable facts of the language(s) in question. Many linguists, it has to be said, are not interested in imposing what they would see as this 'psychological straitjacket' on their descriptions and explanations of language.

It is useful to compare the notion of UG markedness with the notion of a skeletal language system mentioned earlier. However simple the early IL grammar is, it is not, if created within the framework of UG, a fall-back to some pre-existing basic pidgin-style grammar. It is simply the outcome of LAD making the best of a bad job where L2 input is particularly deficient and, hence, where relevant evidence for developing an appropriately marked grammar for L2 is scarce (see Bickerton 1975, 1981). We might get this situation with migrant workers in a country where they spend all their time with other non-native speakers or with native-speaker colleagues who simplify or 'pidginise' their own utterances in order to get basic information across efficiently. In this case, efficient or socially restricted communication paradoxically ensures their failure to gain access to information required to develop a more native-like command of the language. The general context of learning is clearly an important issue in such cases and research projects into migrant worker language – such as those already referred to, and the European Science Foundation project – should play an important role in shedding light on this issue.

It should be remembered that, as far as we know, parameters of UG are relevant to only a part of the language. Languages vary in other ways which the learner can learn without any help from UG (like, perhaps, many of the options illustrated in the well-known list of English morphemes discussed earlier). The L1 learning task as a whole is not supposed to be handled exclusively by principles and parameters of UG. And it still remains a distinct possibility that UG parameters may be irrelevant when learning a new language after the mother tongue has been acquired. The whole question of learnability will therefore be re-examined in the next chapter.

7.3   Other areas of language

For a time, IL grammar has had the lion's share of attention. There are clear signs that other aspects of learner language are now rapid growth areas. For practical purposes, these areas are not accorded the attention due to them in this book. Nevertheless, the same basic issues arise. What is the role of the first language? Are there orders of development? Do factors outside grammar actually play a role in assisting or hindering grammatical development?

7.3.1   Lexis

As indicated at the outset of this chapter, the major thrust of second language research has been in the area of morphology and syntax. Work on the lexicon was slow to get under way. Positive evidence tells the learner what is allowed. It says nothing directly about what is not allowed. Where the learner is assuming something different, positive evidence (when noticed) forces a revision of the learner grammar. It is still possible that the learner may have many wrong assumptions that are not ruled out by positive evidence simply because he or she can keep these assumptions on board as options that have coincidentally not yet shown up in the input. In first language acquisition, the way children acquire words and the conceptual apparatus behind words has had a longer tradition. In second language research, matters began to improve with the pioneering work of such scholars as Levenston, Blum, Kellerman and Meara (Levenston 1971, Levenston and Blum 1978, Kellerman 1977, 1984, 1987, Meara 1984, Ringbom 1986). More recently much has been said about lexical usage within the framework of communicative strategy research (see, for example, fuller treatments of this issue in Tarone 1988, Bialystok 1990, Carter and McCarthy 1988, and Nattinger and DeCarrioco 1992). Lexical acquisition in part follows its own course, determined by many factors – phonological, semantic and pragmatic. In part, it is intimately linked with the growth of grammar because the behaviour of words in sentences and their actual shape inform the learner about the grammar of the target language. If, for example, learners are used to a language with a relatively free word order, they will be used to inspecting the morphology of individual words to give them clues about whether a given noun is a subject or an object. This is vital for interpreting utterances. The learner, in acquiring words in an L2 where word order is fixed, will have to learn to search elsewhere for clues about subjecthood or objecthood, i.e. the position of the word in the sentence. By way of contrast, in the reverse situation, learners coming from a fixed word-order background will have to learn to pay special attention to the morphology of words in languages where order is relatively free. This means that lexical acquisition involves more than establishing the meaning of individual lexical items. Not only does it include discovering rules of usage, their frequency of occurrence and their phonology, it also includes working out what parts of words are grammatically significant and how exactly they function in the target grammar.

7.3.2   Phonology

Studies in the international literature analysing learners' speech have also been slow to take off but since the 1980s this has been a rapid growth area with an international L2 symposium devoted exclusively to L2 learner speech first taking place in Amsterdam in 1990. Such studies have ranged from more variationist perspectives, for example the work of the Dickersons, to UG-based work, as evidenced, for example, in the work of Broselow (1988). The Dickersons studied the spread of a rule from single to multiple contexts as the learner approximated in a systematic manner towards the L2 norm. This indicated that IL stages of development were better seen in terms of continua rather than jumps from one discrete stage to another. Japanese learners, for example, did not suddenly appear to acquire /th/ in one fell swoop but acquired it first in one context and then another. Such studies provide a good indication of how many of those things that are of interest to the developmental researcher can be left out by simply charting the learner's full acquisition (acquisition and control) of given target norms. Broselow's article shows how theoretical constructs in phonology can shed light on learner's production and perception of sound patterns and goes on to suggest that L2 errors can help the linguist decide between competing analyses of L1s (that is, more for purely linguistic purposes and less in connection with learning developmental patterns). The L2 evidence provides a source of data that may not be available in the L1 itself. She concludes that it is therefore directly relevant to the discovery of principles of Universal Grammar (p. 306). Useful sources on IL phonology include contributions to edited volumes by, respectively, James and Leather (1986) and Ioup and Weinberger (1987).

7.3.3   Pragmatics and discourse analysis

It is not surprising that pragmatics has experienced a long delay in L2 studies. Although clearly of both practical and theoretical interest, it is a tricky area where a long established theoretical tradition is lacking. While applied linguists might immediately appreciate the importance of pragmatics in designing teaching courses and actually try to adapt current insights from pragmatics to that end, the problem here is how (L2) pragmatic and sociolinguistic information are actually acquired. It is true that much of the work on communicative strategies has dwelt on what are essentially pragmatic issues, matching the linguistic system to situational context and speaker intentions. Also, Schachter and Rutherford (1979) produced a classic work relying on Li and Thomson's typology whereby languages are divided into topic-prominent and subject-prominent languages. They showed that Chinese learners of English were producing structures that, in fact, reflected L1-inspired topic prominence; that is, they used structures which brought the topic to initial position at the expense of the rules of English syntax. This is the more 'syntax' side of pragmatics (see also Givon 1979, 1984, Dittmar 1992 and the work of Huebner, discussed elsewhere in this book: see Huebner 1983, 1985). More strictly sociolinguistic research has been carried out on, for example, the way L2 users express politeness and on the causes of pragmatic failure (Olshtain 1983, Thomas 1983, Kasper 1985, Blum Kulka and Olshtain 1986, etc.). Given the expansion in recent times of literature on this area, there is promise that more explicit links will be developed between sociolinguistic research and second language acquisition (see Gass *et al.* 1989a, 1989b) so that we can understand more about

(1) how learner speech intentions determine the observed variation in their behaviour;
(2) how factors external to the learner shape their learning and performance in L2.

No theory of language development can dispense with research that sheds insight on the context of language learning even though they may differ in how sensitive or insensitive the learner is to changes in the environment; in other words, the learner, one way or another, relies on input. Input comes in different forms, some of which may be more conducive to learning than others. As mentioned earlier, Selinker and Douglas have claimed, indeed, that interlanguage is only analysable in context and that learners develop different ILs according to their 'domain of discourse' (Selinker and Douglas 1989). Klein (1986) deals with the notion of the early stages of acquisition as being presyntactic, i.e. with the structure of utterances governed more by pragmatic than by syntactic principles. Word order when the learner is in this 'pragmatic mode' might, for example, be determined by a rule which requires 'old information before new information' (see Givon 1984, Klein 1986). Clearly this is a vast and rich field for research and the signs are that, following on from early work, much will be developed in this area in the next decade (see Trévise 1986, contributions to Gass *et al.* 1989a, 1989b, Crookes 1990, Kasper and Dahl 1991).

7.3.4   IL and modularity

The modularity hypothesis touched on elsewhere in this book provides us with a way of integrating the various strands of IL research as they are now developing, including the areas mentioned in the previous sections. If, indeed, the psychological make-up of our language capacity is such that we acquire and process different aspects of language in different ways, then we can expect that different accounts of how the great questions of the field (L1/L2 differences, crosslinguistic influence, markedness, conscious manipulation of development, etc.) should be answered with respect to these different linguist domains or 'modules' may not be psychologically incompatible. We shall be able to live with an overall account whereby, for example, phonology is only marginally influenced by L1, L2 articulatory phonetics is radically influenced, pragmatics fairly extensively and some areas of syntax not at all. This is a hypothetical situation but it allows research to proceed without research findings in one area of learner language automatically upsetting theoretical claims made in other areas.

7.4   Summary

Any language acquisition theory needs a theoretical model of language, or indeed, several models of language where no suitable single grand theory of language can be found. Learning theorists need linguistic theory to be able to define the linguistic aspects of the learning problem. At one time there was a general feeling that sophisticated linguistic questions were being avoided and that researchers were relying on fairly simple low-level aspects of language which required little in the way of specialist knowledge. It might just be possible to put up a defence of this position where the initial stages of language acquisition are concerned, but certainly not when the *totality* of language learning is being considered and this includes pragmatics, lexis and all the areas of language beyond the standard areas of focus, morphology and syntax. All this puts the researcher in the unenviable task of trying to be a double or multiple specialist; a learning specialist and a linguistics specialist. The discussion of markedness should have shown the dangers as well as the potential of adapting linguistic theoretical definitions to the business of second language development. Not only have researchers to cope with different psychological models of development, they also have to sort out the different ways of defining concepts such as linguistic markedness. At the same time it is perfectly valid to ask whether a linguistic distinction is there for psychological reasons, and make it a way of setting up a project in second language acquisition. The next chapter will continue this discussion with special reference to one particular model of linguistics and language acquisition.

8 The role of UG in second language learning

8.0 Introduction

This chapter looks specifically at the role of Universal Grammar (UG) in second language development. Even if UG is only supposed to play a role in the development of certain areas of the language, it deserves special treatment by virtue of the debate that it has provoked and continues to provoke in the 1990s. The discussion will inevitably involve more attention to technicalities and the reader may care to consult elsewhere for additional information (see Flynn 1986, Liceras 1986, Cook 1988, 1993, White 1990, Eubank 1991 for fuller treatments of the issue). What will develop during the course of this chapter is a recasting of the basic L2 issues raised in the 1970s in new forms, drawing on advances in linguistics, and specifically Chomskyan linguistics.

8.1 Psycholinguistics

Linguists normally focus on the structure of natural languages. Psychological dimensions are usually covered by others. 'Psycholinguistics' is often used in a misleadingly narrow sense involving the measurement of performance, as is done, for example, in reaction time experiments. In fact, a more logical definition would be the field which associates linguistic theories with theories trying to explain acquisition and performance as psychological phenomena. Where reaction time experiments are carried out, we may then talk of the psycholinguistics of language processing – that is, studying how language users access and integrate structures in order to produce and understand utterances. Looking at how linguistic structures arise and change over time as part of the learner's mental repertoire, should be called 'developmental psycholinguistics'.

It is relevant now to consider how linguistic and developmental psycholinguistic research might interact. The aim of linguistic theory in Chomskyan generative grammar is to investigate the nature of the hypothesised principles of UG and how they are instantiated in particular languages. Recall that UG is not 'a' grammar but a set of limits. Without these constraints, the child would be able to generate all kinds of ideas about the target grammar, including many that would crucially need correction, i.e. the sort of corrective feedback we know children do not need and usually do not get. This also means that the linguist must only propose accounts of language and of particular languages that are compatible with the notion that children must learn from the 'normal' input, i.e. utterances in the target language as produced by parents and caretakers.

Each language, apart from having its own vocabulary ('cat', 'chat', 'kot', 'Katz', etc.), represents a unique instantiation of UG: in other words, UG allows for various structural options in the make-up of natural grammars. This in turn allows for many different combinations from this quite limited set of options hence the great variety shown by natural languages despite the constraints imposed by UG. Also, some options simply do not apply to certain grammars. Each grammar is a selection of a larger set of possibilities. An analogy would be the kind of landscapes we have on earth. Choosing one type of landscape makes certain further choices relevant and others irrelevant. For example, the choice of one type of raincoat rather than another is irrelevant in an arid desert. In the same way, there may be some linguistic constraint which is valid for a given L2 but is quite irrelevant to the structure of the learner's L1. The L2 may have syntactic rules moving elements around to create different constructions, relatives, questions, passives, etc. However, the L1 may have the type of grammar that does not require such rules. This means that those UG principles constraining movement would be irrelevant for L1 but would be valid for L2. The learner would never have to apply them until encountering L2 data (as in the raincoat option with a learner who had grown up in an arid desert and only then moved to England). For example, principles constraining movement in English would render unacceptable an equivalent *wh*-question to: 'You support the claim that she likes who?' That is, if the *wh*-word moves to the front, we get the ungrammatical sentence: 'Who do you support the claim that she likes?' Such restrictions (the technicalities are unimportant here) are quite irrelevant in a language like Korean where word order is not governed by syntactic principles. Moving elements play no role in determining what the 'subject' or 'direct object' is and the basic syntax remains unaffected. The child learning an L1 like Korean never has to 'consult' UG to find out about movement restrictions on moving *wh*-elements. When the Korean learner encounters English data, these UG principles suddenly become relevant for the first time.

What theoretical linguists *can* provide is a theory to explain the abstract principles such as those associated with the concept of UG. What they *do not* provide is a theory to explain how grammars actually grow over time in people's heads. That applies to both L1 and L2 grammars. The aim of the type of linguistics under discussion is to outline logical possibilities, i.e. what is possible and what is impossible. Someone else has to account for the patterns of language growth that show up, the rate and route(s) of development. For example, one aim in psycholinguistics may be to investigate the way in which these principles of UG operate over time as the individual's grammar gradually develops. In the case of L2 acquisition, this means how the working of these principles might be affected by other native and non-native competence systems possessed by the learner which represent different instantiations of UG.

The basic question then is: where do successful second language acquirers, who clearly create novel utterances, get the necessary information for them to bridge the information gap and acquire those principles? By 'successful' is meant the attainment of grammars, fragmentary or otherwise, which depend at least partially on evidence that is not available in the input. There are a number of possible answers to this question of second language learnability and these are sketched out below. It will be necessary to explain how the question arose in L2 studies in the first place, and to expand a little more on the notion of learnability itself.

8.2   The role of UG in IL development

Adjemian was the first to make a really specific proposal to adopt a Chomskyan approach to IL development (Adjemian 1976). His suggestion was that IL (grammatical) systems were 'natural' in the special, theoretical sense used by Chomsky (see Chomsky 1965): that is, they involve grammars that allow the user to generate an infinite range of novel sentences and they have the basic design characteristics of grammars created by children acquiring their L1. These design characteristics can in part be explained by the fact that cognitively immature children have to be able to learn their native language with no explicit instruction and confusing evidence.

According to Adjemian (1976), IL grammars differ from L1 grammars only in their 'permeability' to invasion from the L1 system.

This means that the developing L2 grammar is not sealed off from inside such that it is sensitive only to L2 input coming in from outside. Rather it is subject to infiltration from an 'alien' system, i.e. the learner's L1 (see also Liceras 1986). In a sense this re-expresses some of the basic tenets of creative construction theory but suggests more directly that ILs be analysed using the concepts and tools of generative linguistics which are, by definition, designed to investigate natural languages.

Any linguistic framework could, in principle, be of help to IL studies, that is, for the purposes of linguistic description and analysis. What makes the particular brand of generative linguistics as pioneered by Chomsky relevant and interesting for acquisition researchers is that it treats language (and particularly 'grammar') as a human, *psychological* phenomenon and not just as an object 'outside' (like the physical world). 'Grammar' is more than just a 'system of rules' (such as the rules of chess); it is a specification of a language user's knowledge. Specifically, it treats language structure as the product of human mental developmental processes, as something which comes into being as a result of a individual's linguistic experience. Hence, although the theory makes no specific claims about real-time development, the way in which the grammar evolves over time, it seems (potentially at least) to provide a particularly fruitful basis for linguistic description and analysis because it crucially involves attempts to gear its description to the problem of learnability. Its way of defining markedness is a prime example of this.

One should mention, finally, that linguistic models like Gazdar's Generalised Phrase Structure Grammar (Gazdar *et al.* 1985) and Lexical-Functional Grammar (see treatment in Pinker 1984), although not quite so specifically focused on the logical problems of child language acquisition, have also been seen as having psychological relevance. As Newmeyer (1987) has pointed out, the differences between these models are not as great as some suppose, so there is some hope that acquisition research will have the support of an increasingly larger group of linguists. To date, however, very little work seems to have been done in L2 acquisition using these other models.

The idea, mentioned above, of treating transitional systems in L1 and L2 acquisition as natural grammars together with the 'end-state' grammars (the ultimate product of L1 development) offers intriguing avenues for research. It permits the use of a set of precision tools devised in order to analyse and describe linguistic phenomena (see White 1982, 1990). However, the most important function that this particular brand of linguistics could have would be the explanatory one. In other words, it should be able to provide more than descriptive techniques: as mentioned above, it could provide explanations of the psychological processes that underlie some important aspects of the linguistic product that is described and analysed.

If certain important aspects of *grammatical* acquisition can be explained using a Chomskyan framework, then, as implied earlier, other aspects about which (this) generative theory has less or nothing to say may therefore, by a process of elimination, also be easier to handle. A large number of problems, especially semantic and pragmatic ones, will in fact need to be handled using other approaches.

More recently, after a gap of four or five years, the issue of how theoretical linguistics can be tied into acquisition research has been addressed again using Government and Binding theory (Chomsky 1981; see Cook 1988 for a useful introduction). This has allowed a number of specific, theoretical questions to be asked about language development, such as:

1. To what degree do learner grammars stay within the constraints of natural language grammars as defined by the theory?
2. To what degree does linguistic 'markedness', as defined by the theory, play a role in developmental sequences?
3. To what degree do the grammatical 'parameters' (selected from the total repertoire available for natural languages and set in specific ways) of the learner's L1, again, as defined by the theory, influence the shape of the emerging L2 grammar?

Finally, three things should be stressed here. Although 'grammar' in the Chomskyan sense is by no means identical with 'language', it does cover a wider range of linguistic phenomena than some other definitions which include only syntax, or syntax and morphology. Grammar, here, covers phonology and some aspects of semantics (so-called 'logical form', see Van Riemsdijk and Williams 1986: 183ff), as well as certain systematic aspects of the lexicon.

8.2.1 More on learnability theory

Using linguistic theory to look at the complexity of IL grammars, especially as they have evolved in the intermediate and advanced stages of acquisition, forces us to consider the validity, for L2 studies, of Chomsky's 'poverty of the stimulus' argument (cf. discussion in Hornstein and Lightfoot 1982b; see also Pinker 1979, 1984). This argument was originally put forward with respect to L1 acquisition but it can also be applied to second language acquisition albeit with certain interesting qualifications. It works backwards, as it were, looking at natural grammars as reflected in the linguistic behaviour evinced by mature native speakers and it asks the question: what evidence would be needed to create such a complex system?

It is crucial to keep in mind the fact, already discussed earlier, that the language learner is not someone who simply parrots words and patterns that have been heard. Learning involves invention: old words or invented words are combined in new ways to form novel utterances, 'novel', that is, in the sense that these utterances have not been personally encountered before by that learner. The consequence of this is that we have to ask questions about the nature of learners' inventiveness. Does it obey laws? Is it constrained? How does the learner's individual experience provide relevant evidence about the norms of the language?

The bottom line in this argumentation is that we cannot unfortunately hold on to the convenient assumption that the learner works out the target system by relying completely on a general process of hypothesising, that is, by creating rules purely by considering the evidence in the input and drawing logical inferences about how the system works. This would be convenient, because it would show that grammar learning is like many other kinds of learning and does not require any special learning theory to account for it.

The argument for L2 acquisition would go roughly as follows: however rich the communicative context of utterances addressed to the language learner, and however helpful the native speakers are that may be in his or her environment, there are subtle and complex principles and features of human languages that cannot be provided by the usual kind of input or even by the usual type of correction and explanation given to language learners, that is, even in a formal classroom where there is a lot of metalinguistic explanation. Hence, the input is *structurally* impoverished: whatever it *does* provide in semantic or pragmatic terms, it *does not* furnish the learner with enough relevant evidence to work out the many subtle principles and constraints that characterise the native-speaker grammar.

One way of expressing the logical problem of L1 acquisition, and perhaps L2 acquisition, is to say that the target grammar is 'underdetermined' by the environmental input: on the basis of the input alone, as it actually appears to come to the learner *qua* rule-hypothesiser, many different rules could be created, many of them quite outlandish and not actually encountered either in mature languages or indeed in the language produced by children. That is, the learner has a limited amount of relevant information coming from the environment and it is certainly insufficient to project the kind of grammar that the learner does in fact develop. It is as if one were asked to design a complicated suspension bridge with a pile of bricks, girders, and assorted parts – all of which would appear to be sufficient – but

(a) without any instruction on the appropriate principles of mechanics to ensure the completion and survivability of the bridge;
(b) without any explicit correction by experts of errors that are crucial to the design of the bridge;
(c) without ever seeing unsuccessful designs fail: many trial designs (with errors) seem to be accepted by others;
(d) with few clues: a model to follow that is not sufficiently informative, i.e. consisting of simplified bridges and fleeting and fragmentary examples of more complex bridges and certainly no labels describing the functions of the component parts.

In these circumstances, the inexperienced bridge builder ought to try out a vast number of bridge designs, many of which would be completely impossible. What we actually see, to maintain the parallel between bridge construction and first language acquisition, is a highly limited number of trial constructions: all of these bridges are feasible constructions. They are 'possible bridges' although they do not actually conform to the target model being attempted.

The problem of how languages can be learned may not be immediately apparent to someone not sufficiently versed in the complexities of grammars of natural languages. It does, however, seem difficult to resist the notion that young children would be quite unable to learn the complex grammar of a given target grammar, the complexities of which are only partially understood even by linguists, by using a general hypothesis-formation process. This process would be informed only by the fragments of language that actually come their way. In fact, given the lack of continual, intensive correction of errors and any other relevant information about what is not possible – and here we are considering the situation in which learners have not yet made errors necessary for a general hypothesiser to induce a grammar from input – it seems implausible that human grammatical acquisition of any kind, i.e. including second language learning, is at all feasible in normal circumstances (but see Schachter 1988, Bley-Vroman 1986, 1988). This is so even if we assume a tireless learning device that is permanently operational, i.e. is sensitive to absolutely all relevant data that come its way, and never fails to pay attention to everything – an idea that, in itself, is scarcely plausible. The learning device seems to select certain input data for processing and not others. Sometimes, it simply seems to be dormant, or insensitive to the information presented to the learner by the outside world, however much that learner consciously wishes to extend his or her L2 ability.

Ultimately, the position one takes on this issue depends on what one considers to be valid evidence for various given categories of language learner. In other words, a theory of language learnability has, among other things, to state

(1) where the evidence is to be found, logically speaking;
(2) the extent to which the evidence is in the input;
(3) the learning mechanisms that must be posited in order to account for the degree of success observed in the learner type under investigation.

The conclusion that is usually drawn, given the particular perspective under discussion, is that acquisition takes place via an interaction between (a) the evidence provided by the input and (b) a set of grammatical principles available to all normal language learners which forms part of our genetic endowment. These principles, together, are referred to as Universal Grammar (UG).

As mentioned in the previous chapter, UG, despite its name, is not a universal mini-grammar underlying all languages but rather *a set of limitations on the form of mental grammars*: it is a kind of necessary 'straitjacket' placed on how a grammar may develop in order to prevent the wild and endless generation of all logically possible hypotheses about every bit of data the learner has to deal with (see White 1990 for an extended discussion).

This means that in the creation of a grammar for any given language, the learner does not need to entertain all such hypotheses about how input may be interpreted. In a similar way, to use another illustration taken from traffic rules, a traveller to a new country would, in advance, know a set of constraints holding for all traffic systems (e.g. 'red means stop' and 'traffic goes on one particular side of the road') in order to be able to go from one city to another. The general knowledge the traveller already has, prior to arrival, is neither a knowledge of the traffic rules of that country nor a map showing the route from City A to City B. It does, however, provide him or her with a reasonable chance of finding out these particular facts about the country without getting killed in the first five minutes.

The traffic-rule learning process will take place via an interaction with the knowledge he or she has about traffic systems in general and the experience of the particular system in the country concerned, i.e observing what actually happens. One observation of two-way traffic will be enough to enable you to decide how to drive and how to cross the road safely. Imagine, however, that you were a vulnerable Martian with no preconceived ideas on traffic behaviour, on the necessity of driving on only one side of the road, etc., and with no way of handling explicit advice proffered by earthlings about what *not* to do. You would most likely end up with most of your fellow space-travellers as something green and flat and very dead. The chances of your surviving your trip to Earth would be about the same as the chances of a child learning its L1 without some inbuilt idea of where to look and what not to do.

Observation of millions of successful travellers should tell us that they drive into a new country with at least some general knowledge about traffic. And they survive. Here, of course, the similarity ends. Traffic knowledge is normally gained via formal instruction or the conscious internalisation of rules from a book of regulations: most people can tell you what they know. Normal native speakers have no conscious awareness of UG, the 'traffic rules' that govern grammar construction. They cannot tell you about it. It is assumed that it is not learned but given: it is part of our biological endowment.

We know that first and second language learners do make hypotheses (subconscious or conscious as the case may be). We may frequently observe them producing utterances which exhibit systematic features not obviously available in the input and certainly not in accordance with native-speaker norms. As was discussed earlier, they are 'creative': they go beyond the input. Given some insight that they may think they possess – an insight into the grammatical structure behind that input – they could, in principle, make many different guesses about how the 'rule' might be applied in other contexts.

To sum up, the notion of UG, i.e. the general constraints that underlie the basic design characteristics of any grammar, entails certain logically possible hypotheses being excluded in advance, making the learning task feasible. This goes for any human language (see Pinker 1979, 1984 on the notion of equipotentiality).

To take a commonly used example, learners do not need to try out the 'absurd' hypothesis that questions are formed by simply reversing the word order of a declarative sentence, a 'structure independent operation'. This would involve moving an element in the situation without regard for its new position. For instance, a learner might find it justifiable to create a rule which would regularly *move* the verb to the front of the sentence irrespective of that sentence's internal structure – yielding both the correct utterance 'IS the man tall?', as in 1b (below), and the incorrect utterance 'IS the man who tall is in the room?' (cf. Emonds 1976, Chomsky 1975, White 1982), as in 2b:

DECLARATIVE   1a. The man IS tall

INTERROGATIVE 1b. Is the man ⌐ tall?

Grammatical English utterances of the type illustrated in 1a and 1b mean that the illegal rule 'to form questions, change the order such that the verb is moved to the front of the sentence' is certainly warranted by the input: the processing operation required to make the rule work would be something like 'read the words (of sentences like 1a) from left to right; stop when you come to a member of the lexical set containing is, was, can, may, (etc.) and move that word to initial position.' Admittedly some primitive structural information is needed even to do this, but it does not require knowledge of such hierarchical notions as 'noun phrase' or 'verb phrase'.

At first sight, this simple movement seems to work. However, a problem arises when the learner begins to create new utterances according to this rule. He or she would then produce sentences like 2b, moving the verb out of a subordinate clause ('. . .who is tall. . .'):

DECLARATIVE: 2a. The man who IS tall knows Wendy

INTERROGATIVE 2b. *'Is the man who ⌐ tall knows Wendy?'
                   rather than:

                2c. 'Is the man who knows Wendy ⌐ tall?'

We see from 2b that the general hypothesiser has created a structure-ignoring rule, which does not work with all questions. It really needs a structure-dependent rule, in other words a rule which recognises the noun phrase in 2b ('the man who knows Wendy') as a single unit, just like 'the man' in 2a, for the sake of movement. It is not easy to imagine a grammar hypothesiser that works out structure using only the input and is unaided by corrective feedback, in-built taboos and preferences.

Given the misleading nature of pairs of utterances like 1a and 1b, why do neither first nor second language learners regularly produce or accept the logically possible 2b type of sentence? Clearly it is not because they have read learned books on verb movement or attended lectures on linguistic theory. It is also not because they are completely uncreative and never produce what they have not actually heard. Apparently, then, they cannot have a general hypothesiser for building grammar rules. It has to be a hypothesiser that is prevented from forming rules which ignore the structure of the utterance.

One might suppose that ease of communication plays a role in grammar rule-building. This does not seem to be the case. Take for example utterances which discuss the claim or belief that a certain Tineke once knew the pop-star Madonna. Compare the (complicated but correct) English question in 3a (equivalent statement-like questions are included in parentheses below) to the incorrect question in 3b. In each case, it has to do with the object of 'know', i.e. Madonna (Tineke knew Madonna):

3a. ('Henk believed that Kevin said that Tineke knew WHO?')
    QUESTION: *Who did Henk believe (that) Kevin said (that) Tineke knew?*

with the (somewhat) simpler, shorter but incorrect sentence in 3b:

3b. ('Henk believed the claim that Tineke knew WHO?')
    QUESTION: **Who did Henk believe the claim (that) Tineke knew?*

In this way some *semantically* acceptable constructions are ruled out by fairly subtle *grammatical* principles: and every child appears to handle the learning of systems with such principles and *seldom* makes errors that violate them (see Chomsky 1975: 90).

It seems, then, that

(a) language learners are able in advance to impose structure on the stream of speech;
(b) constraints on possible grammatical rule-systems guide the learner's acquisition system away from avenues that would lead to operations such as the one exemplified in 2b (and 3b) where the internal organisation of the sentence is disregarded.

Hence learners are able to impose structure without any physical signals coming from outside (like bleeps announcing the beginning and end of a noun phrase) and they are able on the basis of their analysis to construct certain types of rules and not others.

8.3 The logical possibilities

8.3.1 The fossilised UG view

One possibility may be that common principles typical of all languages, i.e. 'universal grammatical' principles (principles of UG) have been activated during L1 acquisition to make the learner's *first* natural grammar, and that some or all of these principles are *transferred* over to the L2 in the form they have taken in the L1 grammar. In this way, L1 grammar serves as an 'initial template' for the L2 system, as it were. Harking back to the bridge-building metaphor (in 8.2), the learner may begin with the 'successful' design used for creating L1, or, to use the traffic metaphor, the learner may adopt the L1 traffic rules and busy himself or herself with just learning the new 'vocabulary' – the foreign traffic signs. Learners then have to adapt or 'restructure' those aspects of the L1-based IL grammar which turn out to be specific to the L1 in the light of incoming L2 evidence available to, and perceived by, them (see discussion of Corder in 2.1.1). This means that principles of UG which, for example, rule out structure-independent operations as demonstrated earlier, operate in IL 'by proxy'. At the same time, UG itself is no longer active. It has fossilised in the form of L1 grammar (or its core at any rate). Therefore, UG cannot help the learner in creating *new* areas of the IL not based on L1.

Without the L1 template, the L2 learner would have to build all of the IL using some other principles, perhaps just those principles of hypothesis-formation and testing that are not allowed free rein in first language acquisition. In this first scenario, then, by incorporating L1 structure into the IL, learners can produce utterances that conform to UG and give us the false impression that they still have access to it.

Therefore, in the 'fossilised initial template' view, IL development – since it is influenced by UG – is 'parasitic' on the L1 grammar. The consequence of this must be that L2 conforms to UG until some adjustment to the L1-based system in the learner's developing IL grammar (as a result of L2 input calling the L1-based system into question) actually leads to a violation of UG. That is, the learner changes the IL to fit some newly perceived input following some general hypothesis not bound by UG and, by so doing, introduces a rule which could never appear in any L1. The IL, taken as a whole, would then cease to possess a natural grammar in the Chomskyan sense of the word: it would have elements that violate UG, elements that would, by definition, never appear in French, Korean, Swahili, Vietnamese, English or any other natural language. Such violations would be tolerated by the L2 learner precisely because UG would no longer be active in the L2 acquisition process. Utterances of the 2b type (see above) ought then to appear regularly in IL production.

People supporting the maturational view of UG in first language acquisition, in other words, the idea that UG is not available *in toto* from the start but becomes available at relevant stages in development (allowing for some wild L1 developmental grammars on the way: see, for example, Felix 1984) would certainly have to say that UG was accessible in a different way in L2 acquisition than in L1 acquisition, but they would not necessarily be committed to a fossilised initial template view.

8.3.2   The recreative view

A second logical possibility is that L2 systems are acquired *in the same way* as L1 systems and that the constraints on possible shapes the L2 grammar may take (i.e. principles of 'universal grammar') are imposed *directly* (and not via transfer). We might term this the *recreative* (or 'starting afresh') view. The idea behind recreation is that each time a given learner learns a language, the language is recreated in the learner's head. In other words, just as the child uses the linguistic input to recreate its native language (in its head), the learner 'recreates' the L2 grammar as if he or she were a native learner of the language (for a discussion of recreation versus reconstruction, see Corder 1981: 87ff) *because* UG is still active (i.e. accessible). This is also called the 'Back to UG' position. This means back to an unbiased UG unaffected by any preferences acquired during the course of applying it to the learner's L1. The L2 learner's native language is therefore *ignored* and plays no part in the developing grammar of L2.

This recreation view is essentially the idea of UG and learnability as applied to the creative construction position (see Schwartz 1986). Using Adjemian's terminology, IL competence would not be permeable to invasion from L1 (see Mazurkewich 1984). Note, however, that small children growing up bilingually, that is, from the very beginning, also need to create two separate systems. If they kept the two systems apart from the start then non-mixing would look like a special characteristic of L1 acquisition as opposed to L2 learning by older learners. Nevertheless, bilingual children do mix systems, especially at the outset. In other words, 'pure', unpermeated development is not necessarily a sign that different principles are at work. After all, the monolingual L1 learner simply has nothing to mix, hence there is no mixture. What you have to look at is not mixing but whether L2 development is limited by the principles of UG or not. This is taken up below in the discussion of the third possibility (resetting).

The first and second possibilities just discussed are sketched out in Figure 8.1. Here, UG helps to cut down on the hypotheses needed to build the new grammar and direct the learner along a limited number of paths. In this way the core L1 grammar is built (with, of course, other processes at work in areas not relevant to UG). In the fossilised UG scenario (see the left side of Figure 8.1), the L1 grammar then forms the basis for the emerging L2 grammar (IL) and this is the only reason why we find the kind of structures in IL that could have been created within the confines of UG. There is no evidence that the learner makes hypotheses about the L2 that are *not* based on L1 and that are limited by UG. In the alternative view (see the right side of Figure 8.1), the merging L2 grammar is created within the confines of UG and we see no evidence for the learner carrying over

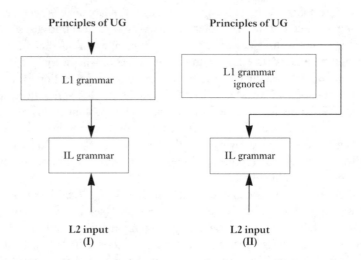

FIGURE 8.1 Two views on the possible role of UG in L2 acquisition: (I) parasitic development (UG not active in IL grammatical development) – present in fossilised form; (II) recreative development (UG active in L1 and grammatical development).

principles that are specific to L1, which is ignored. The L2 is recreated in the mind of the learner in essentially the same way as it is recreated in the mother tongue learner. In all cases, of course, the L2 input plays an important role since it provides crucial information, on which the learning device must operate.

Even assuming that L2 learners have direct access to UG, it still remains an open question as to whether, as Adjemian originally implied, developmental (IL) grammars must also conform in their totality to the constraints imposed by universal grammars at every stage of development. The position that IL grammars (or child grammars, for that matter) *literally conform* to UG at every single step on the way means in effect holding the view that every new adjustment to the grammar triggers a complete scan of the grammar and any necessary reorganisations, so that the grammar remains natural.

8.3.3   Wild grammars

The 100 per cent conformism approach would mean that, by the use of appropriately sensitive tests, one could elicit data from a learner at any time and still find that, whatever the spontaneous performance suggests, the underlying IL grammar always conforms to the constraints imposed by UG. However, it is worth considering the possibility that there may be room for some deviation along the way with conformity to universal grammar as the *guiding* principle, but one which can be temporarily overridden, ignored or abandoned during periods where internal restructuring of the grammar is complicated in some way (cf. Sharwood Smith 1985b).

One school of thought contends that L2 acquisition is not constrained by UG, the proof of this being the development of subordinate clause (embedded sentence) grammar in L2 German. Clahsen and Muysken (1986) claim that children learning L1 German have already grasped that German is a verb-final language by the time they start producing complex sentences, i.e. with correct adult-like embedded sentences reflecting the basic underlying (verb-final) position as in 'that he come *will*'). This turns out to differ from L2 situations. German L2 learners coming from various language backgrounds, as shown by the data from the ZISA project, typically produced subclauses that mimic the syntax of the matrix (main) clause, irrespective of this situation in their respective mother tongues. The result could either be viewed as a strangely English-style (UG-conforming) grammar with the verb in various possible places in both main and subordinate clauses (e.g. second or third position: 'he always *sees* me', 'he *sees* me often', 'he always *says*. . .') or as a mixed, wild grammar with matrix clauses conforming to native German norms, i.e. a finite verb form moved into obligatory second place from its original final position (He *comes* today, he *has* today come) and a clause following the same pattern, hence ignoring the principles which, in the subclause, disallow movement out of the basic, final position. This failure to master verb-final syntax in the earlier stages of acquisition is, for Clahsen and Muysken, compelling evidence that L2 learners are using other learning principles (cf. Duplessis *et al.* 1987).

Despite the appearance of no-access-to-UG, however, one could argue that L2 learners with their more urgent and sophisticated, adult communicative demands are ready and willing to produce complex sentences at early stages in their development. For this reason they will outperform their current UG-based competence. The gain will be an extension of their current communicative ability in L2. In this case, one might argue that they do have some kind of makeshift subordinate clause syntax but one that is not yet UG controlled. One might, of course, also argue, that the on-line assembly of the subordinate clause along the lines of main clause word order is a production strategy of some kind, forced on the learner as the result of overambitious communicative demands placed on their current learner grammars. In the latter case, you might say that the learner *grammar* itself is not actually wild at all, it is only the performance of the learner under certain conditions that produces nonconformity. It is precisely questions of this kind that can only be resolved by a good theory and empirical testing.

The motive for allowing for the possibility of 'wild grammars' (see Goodluck 1986, Sharwood Smith 1988, White 1990 for this possibility in L1 acquisition) would be to try to capture as many interesting developmental phenomena as possible without abandoning the potentially fruitful notion of an active UG in interlanguage growth on the basis of occasionally recorded deviations from UG. This would be especially desirable if it were observed that L1 development contained wild periods, i.e. periods in which children went astray and were entertaining analyses of the input that appeared to ignore UG constraints. They would either produce evidence that they had a rule system that is not a feature of any mature natural language, or, they might entertain structures that were consistent with two alternative and mutually incompatible settings of one UG parameter, driving sometimes on the right and sometimes on the left, to use the 'traffic rules' analogy. One example of a theoretically impossible feature would be the creation of structure-independent rules whereby a word appeared in a given position (say, first or second) irrespective of the syntactic constructions in which it appeared. One example would be 'why' always appearing in first position, whatever follows, in: 'Why do you go?', 'Why can you go?', '*Why you can go?', '*Why you go?', 'Why that you go, surprises him?'. It might be, for example, that certain observed stages in the acquisition of question constructions are in fact 'wild, structure-independent' stages. The only proviso in this kind of argumentation is to relate claims of 'wildness' to those areas of syntax that are claimed to be UG controlled, i.e. not to areas that are of no relevance to UG.

8.3.4   Methodological issues

Intermittent deviance, as defined above, refers to deviance in the learner's systematised intuitions about the L2, i.e. his or her IL competence. If UG is still active, then, logically speaking, there have to be moments where recalcitrant areas of the grammar have to be brought into line. A close study of learner development would have to look for evidence of sudden shifts in IL intuitions not apparently occasioned by any outside impulse (teacher intervention, conscious problem-solving, etc.) that would suggest such crisis points. By definition, such an investigation would have to use tests that were specifically designed to examine relatively stable learner intuitions rather than fast, spontaneous speech.

There is a disadvantage in the notion of an intermittent reorganisation view, however plausible it might seem as a working explanation of how UG could work. It has to do with the interpretation of IL data. Violations of UG in IL as reflected in learner data elicited by the researcher with a view to uncovering facts about IL competence are less helpful: they can be interpreted either as support for the view that UG is no longer active in L2 acquisition or, alternatively, for the view that it *is* active but does not work instantaneously across the whole system. If you can argue both ways, then resolving the problem of whether there is or is not access to UG in second language acquisition or not is rendered impossible.

The problem of intermittent deviance can be resolved by looking at developmental patterns longitudinally, i.e. over a period of time, and answering the following questions:

1. To what extent do UG violations remain in the IL while the IL as a whole still seems to be developing?
2. To what extent do UG violations have a limited life span in the developing system when compared with other phenomena, especially those also in conflict with the input?

In other words, just as occasional utterances which look like the product of an unconstrained hypothesis builder (without access to UG constraints) might be attributed to performance failure – i.e. learners producing what they actually would not accept as grammatical – so too might learners be led into entertaining some movement rule, violating UG, that is, because the focus of the acquisition device is elsewhere. The violation is a consequence of some other changes taking place. Looking at those learners later might show that the 'wild' rule of movement, or whatever it is, is eventually expunged as the grammar is tidied up. The tidying up would be because the UG censor, as it were, had finally noticed the discrepancy or that there was a maturational schedule for a given structure: UG only looks at a given area of the grammar once other things have been taken care of (Borer and Wexler 1986). This complication does not make life easier for the researcher, of course. One may still prefer the 'never-wild' option, i.e. the view that the learner grammar is, at any given moment, 'optimal' (to use White's term) for that learner given the input that has been perceived to date. 'Optimal' would mean here that learners fit all L2 facts currently known to them into a UG-compatible format (Sharwood Smith 1988).

8.3.5   The resetting view

It may be seen from the two basic views as sketched above – the parasitic view and the recreation view – that L1 influence only plays a role in the first view. But it is not the case that L1 influence automatically implies an inactive UG. For some people who believe in continuing access to UG, L1 represents the starting point, the 'initial state' of the second language learners. Kean (1986) makes the point that the L2 learner brings a *different UG* to the task of developing an L2; different, that is, only in the very specific sense of being no longer unset: it has been set in L1 terms. This means that the parameters of UG set for the first language are applied where possible to the parameters of L2. The learner will then have to reset some of those parameters. This, in turn, means a kind of reorganisation of the template provided by an 'L1-like' interlanguage system. If the contrastive hypothesis is applied here, it means we might expect development to proceed in those areas where this reconstruction has to take place and certainly no problems where the L1 and L2 systems match (see, in particular, discussion in Flynn 1986). The learner essentially has to compare L1 and L2 in all kinds of ways and by noticing discrepancies, he or she thereby identifies the learning task.

The possibility exists that the initial template for the new language system may in fact not be the mother tongue but another language known to the learner and which the learner perceives to be genetically close, like Spanish and Italian or Dutch and German. For the moment, however, we shall assume that the initial template is 'L1'.

If L2 and L1 do not match in certain respects, there may be, according to some researchers, a real L2 learnability problem. There is the possibility that internal UG-inspired reorganisation is seriously held up or even blocked because of L1 influence – a reinterpretation of an idea put forward by a few researchers in the 1970s whereby the natural 'universal' path of development, if it coincided with a structure that happened coincidentally to be in L1, was held up at that stage as the learner had stumbled upon an unexpected and attractive overlap between L1 and L2 and had consequently decided to rest there. In this way, Spanish learners might discover that their natural pre-verbal stage of negation fits in nicely with Spanish negation and they would remain in that stage longer than learners for whom L1 and L2 did not coincide at this point (see Schumann 1978, Wode 1978, Zobl 1978).

White and others have argued for L1 influence in a manner that suggests that UG is still active in L2 acquisition but its operation is constrained by certain instantiations of UG in L1 carried over to L2 (cf. White 1985, Liceras 1986; see Hilles 1986 for a study of how learners can pick up positive evidence to reset parameters). The problem rests crucially on the fact that there may be no counter-evidence in the L2 input to certain types of L1-based assumptions. This means that L1 learners have default assumptions which make them see certain areas of the target grammar in very restricted terms. L1 evidence from the input sometimes allows them to relax those strict assumptions. However, If L2 learners are misled by their L1 into assuming a relaxed version of the grammar from the start, they will never encounter evidence in the L2 input that their relaxed version of the L2 is not, in principle, possible. In this case, a comparison of L1 and L2 could uncover certain areas where learners would need very special help to recover from their error (see Rutherford and Sharwood Smith 1985, Lightbown and Spada 1990; see also discussion of the overgeneration problem below).

The parameter-resetting view involves three developmental phases:

Phase 1:   Initial application of any L1 instantiation of those UG parameters that are perceived to be relevant.

Phase 2:   Recreative application of UG in areas where L1 provides *no* basis for hypotheses about L2 structure.

Phase 3:   Reorganisation, revising the effects of Phase 1: where the evidence demands it, resetting UG parameters.

'Relevant' simply means 'as indicated by the perceived input'. Since UG contains a set of principles to cover a large range of alternative grammars, some of the principles of UG will not be relevant for a particular L1. L2 evidence will make it clear if they *are* relevant for L2: in this case, the learner will process them according to the recreative view (above). For example, Koreans learning English are faced with a system that requires syntactic movement rules, e.g. *wh*-movement in questions. This is new. As mentioned earlier, Korean does not require movement rules in its syntax and hence makes no appeal to UG limits on movement (cf. Schachter 1990). Korean L2 learners of English, if they have access to UG, have to address the movement aspects of UG for the first time. The shape their IL takes should tell us if they are able to limit their hypotheses about, say, *wh*-movement and not simply dream up a rule which is logically possible given the evidence they have but which nevertheless violates some known UG constraint.

Phase 3, the reorganisational phase, may be conceived of as an instantaneous one, or, as sketched out above, i.e. as gradual and 'intermittent'. It crucially depends on evidence showing where the L1-based parameters are wrong. The degree to which the third phase can really proceed must depend on the learner's sensitivity to the relevant corrective feedback (see White 1991). If corrective feedback is found to be of no use, then the third phase will never be completed. In this case, the model would provide a precise description and explanation of (a particular area of) fossilisation in L2 acquisition. This third view is illustrated in Figure 8.2.

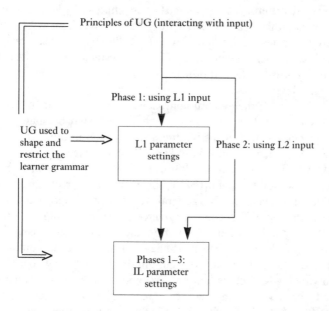

FIGURE 8.2 (III) The resetting view (UG active in L1 and IL grammar) –
          stages 1 and 2.

In this third view, IL grammatical development, where it departed
from L1, would still be constrained by UG and this would then
contrast with the first, parasitic view, where UG plays no active role
in reorganisation, i.e. in Phase 3.

8.4 Theoretical issues

It should be noted at this juncture that questions of the kind
discussed above only emerge when one has a very specific theoretical
model in view. Without a theory, one can only ask very general,
common-sense questions. This chapter is supposed to be a
demonstration of both the complexities and sophistication of
addressing theoretical issues properly. This, of course, applies with
any theory relevant to the study of second languages. The advantage
of using UG and associated concepts in the study of IL is that one
can apply a quite sophisticated linguistic model to IL problems. In
doing so, one can find interesting theoretical questions to ask in
connection with the more general and crucial question of whether L2

acquisition proceeds in the same or similar way to L1 acquisition. Any observed differences between IL and child (L1) language can then be seen within a larger explanatory perspective. The three main views on the roles of L1 and UG as outlined above can be re-expressed as (working) hypotheses for IL investigations, i.e. respectively, the *Fossilised UG* Hypothesis, the *Recreation* Hypothesis, and the *Resetting* Hypothesis.

The main idea of the general approach outlined above that tries to associate L1 and L2 acquisition is strongly contested by some, who say UG principles are not active the second time around (cf. Bley-Vroman 1986, Clahsen and Muysken 1986; see also discussion in Felix 1984, 1985, Schachter 1988). If, however, the approach is adopted, it cannot be imported lock, stock and barrel, given the observable differences in the general acquisitional context and the way in which first and second languages actually develop. In other words, there still has to be a separate theory of 'second language learnability' (cf. Sharwood Smith 1985a–d) in which key notions such as 'evidence' – as well as more specific notions which may change as the theory changes, such as 'parameters' and 'markedness' – must be redefined for second language research taking into account the possible role of the learner's L1 (and other known languages).

With regard to the applicability of UG research, there are other strands of second language research that can mesh with this particular approach. The study of pidginisation, mentioned earlier, can be seen from a UG perspective (see Macedo 1986). Work on the pragmatic aspects of acquisition may employ insights from pragmatic research that are quite compatible with a UG perspective, notably 'relevance theory' as developed by Sperber and Wilson (1986), a rich vein yet to be tapped. Even work done on language processing can be done within a perspective (Berwick and Weinberg 1984, Frazier 1986). It is, then, being overcautious to say that Chomskyan research only bears on a small and very abstract area of syntax.

Finally, with regard to the risks attached to applying linguistic theory to IL research, a distinction should be made between the overarching *meta-theory* and the various specific theories or 'sub-theories', imported or adapted from linguistics, which may change rapidly as the field develops. What has been described so far is meta-theory in that it spells out the basic unchanging assumptions of the model (major learnability problems, the existence of UG, the competence/performance distinction, etc.) that are more proof against shifts and upsets in the more detailed working out of the separate parts of the framework. It is this meta-theory that remains protected from the rapid developments in linguistic theorising that are discussed from month to month in the international literature. At the same time, when doing research which employs some more specific area of grammar, and hence becoming more exposed to changes in linguistic theory, one is still better off than one would be if one gave up the benefits of such a close link with linguistics. In any case, as Pollock has said, such cross-disciplinary research should be a collective enterprise. No single discipline should have a privileged status of 'handing down' ideas to be investigated while not being open to useful information in the other direction (Pollock 1990).

To sum up what has been said so far, the question is: How do the complex principles of natural language systems (in the Chomskyan sense) develop in the IL grammars of second language learners, given the apparently infinite range of hypotheses that can be entertained by them (or rather their learning mechanisms)? Is the second language learner *disadvantaged*, seen from an L1 point of view, and are there other learning mechanisms available to, say, adolescents and adults to compensate any apparent disadvantage that the L2 acquirer may have? If these questions are to be answered with more than speculation, a carefully worked-out theoretical framework is needed to test them. In any case, these are questions concerning areas of L2 where UG is not a relevant issue and here different learning mechanisms probably need to be posited to account for IL development.

8.4.1   The overgeneration problem

One thing that learnability theory has to explain, given the creative talents of all language learners, is how a learner recovers from a self-created form which is non-native. As we have seen, learners may hypothesise a rule or form which is not directly sanctioned by the input. If the learner (*qua* language acquisition device) is sensitive to negative evidence, say in the form of correction, then the self-created forms that do not conform to the L2 norms will be eliminated. This is illustrated below:

SCENARIO 1 (Negative Evidence accepted by learning device)

A. Learner creates non-native form.

B. Learner encounters evidence that the form is incorrect.

C. Learner *abandons* form.

If, however, the learner is not sensitive to negative evidence, another situation may still provide the trigger for development, namely when a native ('correct') form appears in the input and the learner notices it. This gives us new possibilities:

SCENARIO 2a (Negative Evidence ignored by learning device)

A. Learner creates non-native form.
B. Learner encounters and recognises equivalent form in input.
C. Learner adopts new form as an *alternative* form.

SCENARIO 2b (Negative Evidence ignored by learning device)

A. Learner creates non-native form.
B. Learner encounters and recognises equivalent form in input.
C. Learner *replaces* non-native form with native form.

Note that it is entirely consistent to follow the 'a' version of the second scenario, since language typically has synonymous expressions (like 'manner', 'way' and 'fashion' in the frame 'in the right . . .'). Note also that following this course of action would ensure that all non-native forms remained in the learner's repertoire. Scenario 2b would result in successful development in the sense that non-native forms would continually be replaced by native forms as they were encountered-and-recognised in the input.

To provide this last course of action (in 2b) with some explanatory force, a principle of one-form–one-function has been put forward in both first and second language acquisition. Pinker has called it the Uniqueness Principle and researchers in second language acquisition noting the same phenomena in their studies have come up with related concepts (see Kellerman 1984, 1987, Andersen 1983 and related discussion in Karmiloff-Smith 1986, Baker 1979, Bowerman 1983 and Rutherford 1989). The general idea is that the language learner in early stages of development is very conservative and has little tolerance for what normally obtains in fully developed systems, namely a single expression covering many functions and a single function expressed by many forms.

Karmiloff-Smith (1979) provides an interesting example of the Uniqueness Principle where learners 'refuse' to have a perceived form in the input fulfil more than one function. In the L1 acquisition of French children in their use of 'même' (meaning both 'the same sort of' and 'exactly the same/identical') they apparently create two separate expressions for a single meaning of it, as illustrated below (for 'X' read some noun, say 'colour'):

child version	*adult version*
le/la même de X (same sort)	le/la même X
le/la même X (identical)	le/la même X

There still remains the problem of what happens when learners begin tolerating synonymy in their new system, when they abandon the Uniqueness Principle. After all, uniqueness does not exist in fully developed languages and this principle would prevent the learner ever attaining an 'end-state' in his or her language acquisition. If the French child starts to admit synonymous expressions into the developing system, then what happens to 'même de'? Encountering a synonymous expression like 'the same sort of' will not expunge 'même de' any more. At the same time, the same child will become more open to the use of 'même' with two functions in the input and will be able to incorporate the two meanings of 'même' into its own developing system. The disappearance of 'même de' can only come about if we accept that the learner either:

(a) is sensitive to direct negative evidence saying that 'même de' is wrong;
(b) is sensitive to the *continuing absence of* 'même de' in the L2 input: this is known as 'indirect negative evidence'.

The interesting thing about the overgeneration problem and L2 acquisition is that even very mature and sophisticated L2 learners, with all their knowledge of synonymy and multifunctionality in languages still appear to adopt a sort of uniqueness principle. Kellerman (1985) has indicated how Dutch learners of English appear to 'resist' the adoption of two meanings of the past tense ('past time' and 'hypothetical') and use 'would' to convey 'hypothetical meaning in conditional *if-clauses* even though their L1 has just such a distinction and allows past time on the main verb ('if they were there' as opposed to the broadly unacceptable 'if they would be there'). Apparently, this principle has nothing to do with cognitive immaturity, since the learners in question are fully grown and highly educated, but has more to do apparently, with making the learning task easier.

8.4.2 Subsets and supersets

The idea of the learner as a conservative system-builder takes on a special significance when it comes to the thornier aspects of syntax, i.e. those areas where it is relevant to posit the notion of UG constraints. Here the notion of subset has been invoked to explain how learners, given the possibility of creating looser systems, with exceptions and alternatives, opt first for tighter, more restrictive systems. These preferred and more restrictive systems are subsets of a larger set of possible ways of building a particular area of the learner grammar. The ramifications of subset theory are quite involved (see especially White 1990 for useful discussion of subset theory in second language acquisition; see also Rutherford 1989). Recall that, without negative evidence, a learner cannot know that something in the developing grammar is *not* in the target grammar, that is, when nothing in the L2 input actually *contradicts* it.

The subset idea is relevant where there are two linguistic systems that have a particular relationship with one another. The so-called subset condition obtains when one system is a more restricted version of the other. Let us take a lexical example (not the usual area for subset theory but a convenience here for the purposes of illustration). We might consider that lexical items that have only one meaning form a class within lexical items in general that have more than one meaning. This subset–superset relationship is illustrated in Figure 8.3.

The subset principle is a learning principle which may, we hypothesise, be applied by the learner/learning device wherever we have a subset–superset situation. It could also be called a 'conservative' learning strategy. Conservatism, here, really means beginning with the subset, that is assuming all lexical items belong to Class 1, and moving outwards when experience shows this to be permitted. If learners assume that 'bank' only has one meaning, the one they have encountered in the input (bank of a river, say), they will not invent new meanings; that is, they will never put themselves into the situation where the meaning they have assigned to a word cannot be directly contradicted by experience. So, if learners do start to imagine that certain lexical expressions have more than one meaning *when they actually only have one meaning*, they will need to be corrected in order to recover from the error. Their error is not, to use Baker's

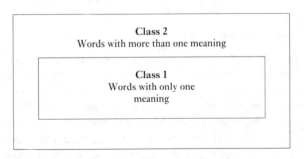

FIGURE 8.3 A lexical subset–superset relationship.

terminology, 'benign' but rather 'embarrassing' (for our learning theory, see Baker 1979). Encountering evidence for a new meaning for 'bank' (financial institution, say) will not have the effect of ruling out some previous incorrect meaning, e.g. bank meaning 'side of a building'. The two meanings can, in principle, live happily alongside one another.

If one considers lexical acquisition, it is quite easy to imagine that experience may often (but not always) provide negative evidence of some sort. So, recovery does not seem too much of a problem since lexical learning is so crucial to communication that learners, by soliciting and asking, obtain plenty of indications about whether they have used the right word. A learner may well have more problems if he or she forms the incorrect syntactic construction 'I proposed him a toast' to live alongside the correct construction 'I proposed a toast to him' (on analogy with the perfectly correct pair of alternatives: 'I told him the story/I told the story to him') (see Bowerman 1983). That learner will need negative evidence and it would be important to see if recovery from error happened at a time when such syntactic correction was indeed available.

8.4.3 Learning scenarios and modularity

In L2 acquisition, learners may transfer two meanings for one item from L1 to L2 (but see Kellerman 1984, 1985, 1987). This gives L2 learners an additional nudge in the direction of beginning with the superset (Class 2) and having problems (perhaps) in recovering. As suggested above, the problem becomes more serious in syntax. If the learner's language acquisition device does not react to syntactic correction from outside (from teachers, native speakers, etc.), how should it come to know that, say, 'I proposed him a toast' is wrong rather than a correct alternative to 'I proposed a toast to him'? What should already be clear is that learner creativity can bring with it a serious learnability problem; it may be different for different areas of the language and we need to have rigorous definitions of what those problems are. It is quite possible, for example, that the same learner who, in lexical terms, follows a conservative path is also highly liberal in his or her creation of syntactic forms. A 'lexical miser' can be a syntactic 'wastrel', and vice-versa.

If we take the modular view of the learner seriously, we can conceive of learning strategies being applied by the learner in quite different ways, depending on which module in the system we are talking about. The approach adopted by the learner/learning device –

i.e. the 'learning scenario' for that learner – is not uniform. In the same way, different learners may have their personal subconscious preferences for adopting different scenarios or combinations of strategies. Some, of course, may be more successful than others. We shall return to this topic in the next chapter.

Whatever the learner's general or individual preferences are with respect to different areas of the L2, we may find it appropriate and even necessary to apply different constructs from different linguistic theories, depending on which part of the L2 is being investigated. UG, for example, even if it turns out to be relevant in L2 learning, leaves an enormous area of the language unaffected by its principles. A general theory of L2 learning has to have a principled way of accounting for all areas, and there is no question of only one particular theory helping us to uncover all L2 problems on its own. For example, Sokolik and Smith (1992) use a computer simulation to show how a connectionist model – which works essentially in a behaviouristic manner and in a manner quite opposed to the manner in which UG is supposed to work – can learn French gender. Since the functioning of this particular model is designed in such a manner that it resembles the operation of the human brain, the more or less explicit claim here is that learners may also learn French gender in this way simply by being exposed to samples of gender assignment and building up the appropriate associations without ever forming hypotheses and rules. Whether this is the case or not, the point is an important one. There is a vast area of language which needs to be learned by means other than UG-constrained syntax acquisition. And, as has already been suggested, if some or all L2 learners have no access to those constraints, or have limited access, then even more must be handled by other mechanisms. A learner without access to UG must be able to work out the syntax of the L2 in some other way. This will have to involve being sensitive to correction where an IL rule has been created that is too general or simply wrong. In other words, the learner will have to process the L2 data using more general processing mechanisms and also, perhaps, relying on L1 knowledge to help out. This is essentially what the Fossilised UG Hypothesis is about.

8.5   Summary

Already, there have been quite a few studies investigating second language development from a learnability perspective drawing on generative linguistics for inspiration. The aim of this chapter was not to detail these studies but to outline the conceptual framework and introduce the various theoretical positions that can be taken. In a way, the theoretical battle lines of the 1970s can be seen here in a new guise. Accessibility to UG leads us straight back to the L1=L2 controversy. People who adopted the creative construction view are likely to be sympathetic to arguments that point to the accessibility of UG in the older second language learner. People who took the original interlanguage position, as detailed in Selinker 1972, are likely to prefer the 'no-access-to-UG' position since it reflects the idea that the second language learner, at least the post-childhood learner, has to rely on general learning mechanisms that are not specialised for language development. And, just as it was possible to have positions in between these two extremes, it is now possible to talk about 'partial access to UG' or about some learners preserving access to UG while others have simply lost it. In the 1970s, however, it was normal to refer vaguely to the 'language acquisition device' (or 'the organiser' or 'creative construction') without specifying very much about its contents. Linguistic theory, particularly the one discussed above, has remedied that situation. While UG, in the Chomskyan sense, is itself not an acquisition device but more a resource or filter for the activities of LAD, it had focused attention on a crucial aspect of acquisition theory, namely 'evidence'. How does a learner/learning device extract evidence from a mass of information flowing in its direction. What does it need to know in order to recognise how, say, the passive works? Can it really react to corrective feedback? Does L1 knowledge provide the initial grammar and obscure some crucial evidence about L2 linguistic structure? Does the learning device adopt conservative strategies by first seeking the structurally simplest solution? And so on. The fact that grammatical L1 and L2 acquisition, or at least important aspects thereof, appear not to need, and be resistant to, correction via negative evidence precludes the straightforward application of general psychological theory to language learning. The learnability literature associated with the concept of UG provides a serious challenge. Any theory of language development for any area of the broadest concept of language has to show clearly and convincingly whether correction of some kind or other has any effect at all.

9 Implications and applications

9.0 Introduction

In the previous chapters, after the introductory survey of crucial terms and notions, and a look at the kinds of technique used to study interlanguage, the early models of the 1970s were analysed. The aim throughout was to illustrate the kinds of problem that second language researchers have to wrestle with. In Chapter 6, the unsolved issues were reviewed and this was followed by an extended discussion of some more recent models and the issues they have uncovered. This final chapter, in a more or less speculative vein, will now consider where we have arrived today. It will attempt to shed light on what current research findings imply for future research and on the practical conclusions that may be drawn. The discussion will be framed within the perspective that reflects dominant themes of this book, namely *knowledge, control, learnability* and *modularity*.

Second language research may be seen as an area which informs other areas of theoretical and experimental research that deal with language structure and language use. It has also been seen as having a special relationship with more practically oriented areas of activity, such as foreign language teaching. What, then, does learner language research have to say to language teachers? What other more practical applications might there be? Can it, for instance, help parents of bilingual children to decide when and how to use different languages at home? In actual fact, the present state in which the field of L2 studies finds itself still makes it difficult to turn research findings into advice for teachers, language planners, and parents in bilingual situations. Yet these various 'nuts-and-bolts' areas of activity must ultimately be ones in which people ought to gain enormous benefit from IL findings. The following sections focus more on the potential of learner language studies within these more practical spheres of life. Some implications on a more purely theoretical front will be mentioned briefly in 9.1 and 9.3. The important proviso is, however, that most of it should be read as avenues for future investigation. It would simply be dishonest to make a neat set of confident claims about what second language research can 'offer' the practitioner apart from confirming the fact that second language acquisition is complex and not fully controllable by either teacher or (conscious) learner.

9.1   Theoretical and practical relationships

Given the fact that language and language learning impinge upon so many aspects of life, learner language analysis may be of relevance to a great number of types of applied and non-applied researcher. Its interdisciplinary character suggests that research ought to be conducted in a way that reflects this fact. For example, one might argue that IL analysis most naturally belongs to the more general field of *language acquisition* despite the fact that, in most institutions nowadays, child language and interlanguage acquisition still seem to be treated as totally separate areas.

There are other umbrellas under which second language research might profitably take its place. As mentioned earlier, not all of language, in the broadest sense of the word, can be divorced from other kinds of knowledge. IL analysis could be undertaken within a more general *cognitive psychological* investigation, where general knowledge and skill-building processes (not specific to language) were also seen to be involved. In this case, general cognitive theories of learning might be applied to the study of IL development. One example might be the study of the semantics of word usage; for instance, how to work out new concepts expressible in L2 but not in L1, such as verbal aspect in Russian (see Carpay 1974). Another example might be the conventions for turn-taking in conversations that are specific to the target language culture. It is difficult to see how language-specific mechanisms could be responsible for this kind of learning. Findings could be related to the analysis and refinement of teaching strategies with regard to relevant areas of knowledge and control. And, finally, the analysis of learner language can be done from a *sociological* point of view in the light of the social categories and functions it expresses. IL analysis would thus contribute to our general understanding of the sociology of language.

With any of the above-mentioned interdisciplinary connections, the relationship may well be two-way. Just as insights gained into the social behaviour of second language learners of various kinds can inform general sociological theory, so demonstrations of psychological processes at work in IL development and IL use can inform general theories within cognitive psychology. Finally, two-way relationships are not confined to links within non-applied areas: they also may exist across the fundamental/applied research divide, i.e. between non-applied and applied areas. Quite clearly, designing and testing the effects of, say, educational policy in bilingual communities or a given language-teaching technique can yield data that are of theoretical interest. One can conclude from this that a healthy relationship should exist between theoreticians and applied researchers if any progress is to be made in either the more fundamental type of research or in those applied areas where theoretical thinking focuses on more immediate, socially relevant concerns.

9.2   Guidance in acquiring competence and control

Here, the implications of some of the more recent ideas, together with some studies not yet mentioned, will be spelled out in the form of a series of research questions. This means asking, in different ways, what a consideration of the different kinds of IL competence and control, as defined in the previous chapters, suggests for future investigation.

9.2.1   Guiding development at the level of knowledge: logical options

Let us begin at a general level. Just as answers to a given set of research question may be different as far as the different types of knowledge (competence) are concerned, so, too, will attempts to *guide* acquisition from 'outside' have to take into account the various aspects of modularity discussed in this book. As far as the *knowledge* level of L2 proficiency is concerned, research should make clear the degree to which knowledge is open to a more straightforward kind of manipulation, that is, via overt correction, negative evidence. Vocabulary is a case in point. Assembling a repertoire of items in the mental lexicon ought to be open to considerable outside intervention. Manipulability can, of course, be a learner-initiated activity pure and simple, or it can be a learner activity that is guided from outside (via teacher and syllabus, cf. Carter and McCarthy 1988).

What is the most fruitful way of tackling pedagogic problems with respect to the development of the learner's knowledge? The default assumption, for teachers and many methodologists, seems to have been that all knowledge-getting can be facilitated if only the right type of intervention is found. It now seems safer, in advance of proof to the contrary, to assume the null hypothesis option: knowledge-getting is, in principle, beyond our control, i.e. *teachers and textbooks can only provide input and meaningful contexts*. This, of course, is an assumption open to counter-evidence, but it seems to be the safest starting-point for the researcher. The null-option was essentially the claim of Krashen and associates (see Dulay *et al.* 1982). In this view, learners in formal classroom situations tend, as it were, to learn despite the syllabus and not because of it. Telling the learners which bits of L2 to learn and the order in which they should be learned is tantamount to asking people to put new electronic components into their television sets when they have neither access to the inside of the sets nor the knowledge to do the job even if they *could* access the sets. A small step away from the null hypothesis would be Pienemann's approach, discussed earlier, whereby learners first (independently) cross the threshold into a given pre-programmed stage of development and then and only then are open to teacher intervention so that they may more rapidly pass on to the next stage. This claim is made possible by viewing stages as more complex entities, namely by seeing them as involving the stabilisation of knowledge and the development of the requisite performance skills (control). The question of what form intervention should take is, of course, a separate issue. It might involve making the learner more aware of the formal properties of the target system, including the provision of information about the type of constructions that are not permitted in the L2.

To take the kind of knowledge that both logical considerations and empirical findings have shown to be seemingly least accessible to outside intervention, we can, in a strong attempt to erode the null hypothesis, pose the following provocative questions concerning the allegedly inaccessible, impenetrable LAD. The questions assume that children do not need negative evidence or conscious introspection to work out the grammar of L1.

1. Is the successful L1 acquisition of grammatical competence an indication that the development of such intuitive knowledge *ipso facto* can never take place with negative evidence and introspection in any circumstances?

Alternatively:

2. Is it the case that children simply acquire this intuitive kind of competence this way because:
   (a) they cannot rely on their caretakers to provide sufficient corrective feedback (negative evidence), that is, appropriate as regards quantity and quality, and
   (b) they are too cognitively immature to be able to profit from whatever metalinguistic help they might get, that is, however much and of whatever kind?

If the answer to Question 2 is 'yes', then the learnability issue could be seen as involving a *guarantee* of successful L1 acquisition, given impoverished evidence and cognitive immaturity but without implying that, if the L1 child were unusually gifted, it could not manage even better using the extra aids normally available only to adults. Cognitive maturity might, arguably, open up the mysteries of L2 structure to conscious inspection: the door to LAD could be thrown open, and our expert knowledge about the given language being acquired might provide the learner with appropriate information at appropriate moments. This, at least, is a logical possibility. Hence we have two basic strong hypotheses:

I.   The Null Option: acquisition takes place in a manner not open to external manipulation.
II. The Open Door option: subconscious acquisition can be supplemented or replaced by the well-informed provision of relevant evidence for conscious inspection and learning.

The modular approach also allows a further refinement of these hypotheses, namely:

Ia. The Null Option holds for all types of L2 knowledge.
IIa. The Null Option is only true of certain types of knowledge; other types fall under the Open Door hypothesis.

If Ia were true, then language planners and teaching methodologists would opt for language educational programmes based entirely on the principles proposed by Krashen and Terrell (1983), i.e. simply ensuring 'natural' exposure in communicative situations with teachers providing input for LAD to operate on. If, on the other hand, IIa were true, then teaching procedures of the more interventionist kind could be applied with respect to particular kinds of knowledge. Identification of relevant areas would then depend on your theory. Everything that fell outside the domain of UG, for instance, could be open to direct intervention. Or, following Pienemann and associates, all areas of knowledge that could be seen in terms of variable features could be targeted using direct intervention, whereas the developmental knowledge seen in terms of developmental features should be left to develop naturally.

Finally, the hypotheses may be extended in terms of competence versus control, to cover 'skill' as well as 'knowledge'. This is already strongly implicit in Pienemann's claims. Stated at the most general level, this could run as follows:

Ib. The Null Option: the acquisition of control (performance skill) takes place in a manner not open to external manipulation.

IIb. The Open Door option: the acquisition of control (performance skill) acquisition is open to external manipulation.

The teachability hypothesis, as it currently stands, needs to be separately stated in terms of hypotheses IIa and IIb. In areas which are claimed to be guided by fixed orders of acquisition, the learner crosses the threshold into stage X by independently producing evidence of new knowledge. What then happens? Does the passage through that stage to the next involve the application of that new knowledge to all appropriate areas of the grammar and lexicon and not just a few grammatical contexts and one or two lexical items (see Bailey 1973, Dickerson 1975, Hyltenstam 1977)? Or is progress a matter of control, i.e. boosting the frequency in which the new knowledge is actually put to use, i.e. old habits falling away and giving way to habits that reflect more regularly what the learner really already knows? Or does the 'passage through' stage involve both aspects, i.e. (a) establishing the grammatical and lexical domain relevant to the new insight and (b) making the presence of new insight show regularly in performance (Hulstijn 1987)? Pienemann (1985: 37) mentions both the frequency of rule application and the spread of rule application to different contexts without treating these as theoretically distinct aspects of acquisition. The implications for teaching research will be further elaborated upon in the next two sections.

It is important to note that, so far, we have been assuming what was earlier termed the 'singular' learner strategy approach. The Null Option implies also 'for all kinds of learner'. If further IL research substantiated the impression, already gained in some investigations, that the 'multiple strategy' view was the valid one, then teaching policy would have to be much more subtle, and that is even setting aside any differences there might be in learning style based on cultural norms and personality traits. Teachers would have to be able to detect learners who take radically different approaches to L2 acquisition, say, relying on intuitive processes alone or supplementing the intuitive with the conscious strategies, using L1 (or some previously learned L2) as a basis wherever possible or not, working via UG where relevant or using only general cognitive strategies, and so on. Perhaps, then, different teaching strategies would have to be adopted accordingly. It then becomes an empirical question as to whether learners can, where convenient, actually be *made* to adopt a particular developmental strategy or whether teachers would just have to accept diversity in learner preferences. In the second case, the interventionist teaching programme would somehow have to be flexibly adapted to allow for learners following different developmental strategies.

9.2.1.1   *Consciousness-raising, metalinguistic knowledge and metalinguistic awareness*

Intervention may not necessarily mean raising the learner's awareness of language structure. As mentioned earlier, the type of knowledge involved may be crucial as to whether such metalinguistic intervention is called for. Well-focused studies should quickly show if certain kinds of IL knowledge fall into the 'general, encyclopaedic' category. They will then, by hypothesis, be open to manipulation via well-tried teaching strategies which are also for teaching non-linguistic subject material. What will then be more of a challenge is to see how far subtle techniques can be devised to facilitate the more 'underground' kind of competence indirectly, assuming that its relatively impenetrable nature is substantiated.

When you rely on the 'meta-mode', you explain to learners how a part of the grammar works. If learners understand this and commit it to memory, those learners are then capable of explaining that aspect themselves on another occasion. The controversy referred to frequently in the literature in this book is whether metalinguistic information actually helps build that subconscious, inaccessible system that some linguists call 'competence' and, indeed, whether there is any other way of helping the natural processes of acquisition. The most obvious way to try to affect subconscious processes beneficially is by making relevant evidence in the input *salient*. This is assuming that we can determine what the learners are ready for at a given moment in time (see Dulay *et al.* 1982, Long 1985, Pienemann 1985). It does not involve directly manipulating the subconscious process – this is by definition impossible – but it expands or restricts the information on which the process may operate.

In Sharwood Smith (1980), it was argued that what might be termed grammatical 'consciousness-raising' did not have to involve teaching rules and grammatical paradigms but could range from subtly highlighting relevant aspects of the input without any overt explanation to elaborate explanations of L2 structure. You could, for example, use extra stress or exaggerated intonation. Or you could colour-code the target structures. In other words, this is what often happens in teacher speech and teacher behaviour in general as well as in textbooks. In present terms, one can work to heighten metalinguistic awareness of relevant input without appealing to systematised metalinguistic knowledge. This kind of minimal consciousness-raising one might term 'input salience enhancement' (Sharwood Smith 1991, 1993). Of course, in using teacher talk or foreigner talk, by talking more distinctly and with exaggerated intonation, we already make some input more salient. However, if the effect of this is the same as the effect of parent talk (motherese) on children, then we may only be highlighting aspects of our message which are crucial for communication, usually crucial lexical items. At the same time, we may be putting in the shade just those subtle morpho-syntactic signals that the learner may need to be aware of to advance his or her development (as opposed to simply understanding the gist of what is being said). Imagine the negative effect of exaggerated stress and intonation in English that serve to obscure the presence and type of article to, say, Polish learners whose L1 did not lead them to expect such 'odd' things at the beginnings of noun phrases.

Sensitivity to negative evidence remains a problem. The learner needs to know (in an effective sense of 'know') that certain possibilities currently accepted by his or her IL are not only absent from the input but are actually 'incorrect'. Rutherford and Sharwood Smith (1985) have suggested that metalinguistic activities in the classroom, such as error-detection exercises, may be directed towards providing negative evidence. Further research will tell us to what extent the teacher needs to formalise any metalinguistic activities that are attempted, which metalanguage is most effective and how much class-time is necessary (see Sharwood Smith 1980, Ellis 1987, 234ff).

Let us consider, for a moment, another logically possible way of affecting learners' intuitive levels of knowledge and, in particular, reducing a certain type of insensitivity to available evidence. This might be to try to change their current perceptions of crosslinguistic relationships between relevant languages. If Kellerman is right in ascribing some kind of role to psychotypological intuitions (e.g. 'Chinese is like Japanese', 'Dutch is like German', 'Chinese is not at all like Dutch', etc.), then, where the learner is assuming an incorrect L1/L2 relationship, a demonstration of how the L1 and L2 are actually related may unsettle any fixation on the learner's part that 'all L1 structure' or, alternatively, 'no L1 structure at all' may be used to build IL. This could be done on a modular basis showing areas where languages overlap and where they are quite distinct. In this way, teaching along contrastive linguistic lines could be linked up with second language theory.

This more global consciousness-raising may also be more relevant to areas like lexis where conscious manipulation is, by hypothesis, more likely to work. In any case, it would be interesting to see whether the strategy of making learners more aware of, say, the difference between Dutch and German syntax to German learners of Dutch (see also Jordens 1977, 1986), or the 'surprising' similarities between Dutch and Polish idiom to Dutch learners of Polish, would effectively cause them to make beneficial shifts in the way they attended to the input. All this is food for future research.

There are potential problems surrounding 'psychotypological intervention', i.e. manipulating a learner's crosslinguistic perceptions about the target language and its relationship to other languages known to the learner. For example, research seems to indicate that learners actually experience shifts in perception by themselves. This may well lead to an overreaction. Whereas before they might have refused to accept any, say, L2 idiom that had a close equivalent in L1, they can do a U-turn and begin transferring *all* L1 idioms into L2 (see the discussion in Kellerman 1984). This suggests that deliberately altering learner crosslinguistic perceptions may have side-effects in that it simply triggers the overreaction. Nonetheless this may not be as bad as it looks. It may simply help to *speed up* a natural U-shaped development even if it does not eliminate that profligate overgeneralisation that may be an inevitable intermediate stage in development. In other words, according to this particular speculation, a teaching technique would not lead directly to success but would stimulate processes that would normally take place at a later date.

One may also ask (in view of the creative construction position on the 'Monitor') whether consciousness-raising at the knowledge end of the scale – i.e. of the more formal, explicit type – may actually impede the development of implicit knowledge. If learner perceptions could be changed via consciousness-raising, then the inability to grasp the finer points of, say, the English present progressive or article usage, might arguably create doubt where there was no doubt before. And even if this did not actually affect the growth of underground grammatical competence *per se*, it might seriously affect the way subjects report their intuitions in tests of grammaticality (see the discussion in the previous chapter). In addition, it might well affect their performance in non-spontaneous situations.

Enhancing the input, and making it more salient either subconsciously (like someone talking to a foreigner in the street) or more deliberately (like a teacher or textbook writer) always begs questions. Whether the enhancement is subtle or very explicit, the learner's brain must still register it. What we know of learners includes the fact that they are very good at ignoring what appears to the outside observer to be very obvious. This is natural and there may be good reasons for it. This is also why we need to do a great deal of research on the matter to see what works best, and especially why it works best.

9.2.1.2   *More on teachability*

As suggested earlier, the most that could really be said about the application of IL research, until fairly recently, was in terms of sensitising teachers to the natural developmental patterns of language acquisition and telling them, as if they did not know already, that learner motivation seemed to be crucial.

As we have seen, the non-interventionist approach (see Krashen and Terrell 1983), following the Null Hypothesis, has been criticised *inter alia* by Pienemann who has advanced his own teachability hypothesis (see also 6.2.3). However, the possibility that formal teaching is of little lasting use is still alive in the literature. For example, a recent study by White showed that, initially, the provision of corrective feedback to French learners concerning the restrictive nature of adverbial placement in English *vis-à-vis* French (no interruption of verb and direct object in English) did lead to an apparent improvement in their English. However, a post-test conducted months after the test showed that this effect of instruction had not lasted and that the French learners were once again accepting adverbs in between verb and direct object (see White 1991a).

It is still early, as far as this kind of experimentation is concerned. In the light of the control-based (Ib and IIb) hypotheses in 9.2.1, there is another dimension within which teachability could be examined, namely the control dimension. Could teaching techniques be much more successful in giving learners control over what they have already intuited via subconscious processes? Since the competence/control distinction is not focused upon in Pienemann's model, we might consider this angle (see also White 1991b): teachability in the Pienemann sense could be reinterpreted as having more to do with the teaching of control than the teaching of that competence. Competence may turn out to be difficult or even impossible to affect via direct teaching intervention, at least with respect to the syntactic structures investigated.

9.2.2   The control dimension and teaching techniques.

It has already been pointed out by Bialystok and others that different tasks that IL users are asked to perform will require different levels of knowledge and control (see, for example, Bialystok 1988). It may be instructive, in the light of the knowledge/control dichotomy, to reanalyse the attitudes adopted by language-teaching methodologists to the use of various techniques such as structural (pattern) drills, popularly associated with the audiolingual and hence behaviourist school.

It would seem that drilling, the administering of tasks that require fast, relatively unreflecting responses from the learner, is in fact providing them with an exercise in control. Within the audiolingual perspective, drilling is supposed to induce language habits. Language habits are regarded by audiolingualists as essentially all that language learning is about. In a framework that, unlike the audiolingual (behaviourist) school, assumes both a knowledge and a control dimension, it would appear that drilling could nonetheless still be seen as a useful teaching technique despite the change in underlying philosophy. Habits, as performance phenomena, have to with control, in other words. The prerequisite for the effective use of drills then becomes the possession of the relevant knowledge. If the learner *already has the relevant insight into the L2*, e.g. that you cannot omit copulas in English, then some form of drilling will enable him or her to gain higher levels of control. If there is nothing available at the knowledge level, then drilling would serve no obvious purpose. You cannot control non-existent knowledge. The fact that the non-omission of copulas appears sporadically in learner production may indeed be a sign that the insight has been gained. However, a learner may experience a change in IL knowledge at Time 1 that does not surface in production at all, and a later change in knowledge at Time 2 that surfaces in production fairly quickly by virtue of it being inherently easy to process for a given learner (e.g. L1-like). This would mean that there is a different sequence of development for, respectively, the knowledge of those two items and the control of those two items.

The hypothetical possibility sketched above is illustrated in an adaptation of the 'armchair model' of development as presented in Sharwood Smith and Kellerman (1989) in Figure 9.1, where we see

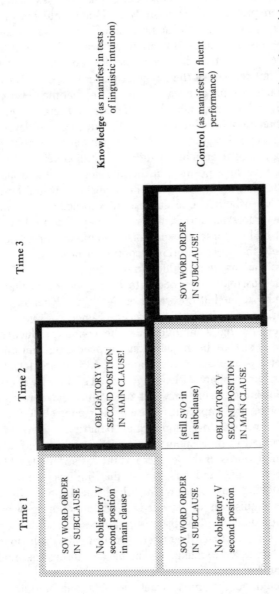

FIGURE 9.1 The 'armchair model': different developmental sequences of knowledge and control (a hypothetical example).

that the arrival in competence of 'Verb-final position in subordinate clauses' is not reflected in production until Time 3 whereas a *later* arrival, 'Obligatory Verb–second order in main clauses', actually turns up *earlier* in production. In a study of Dutch students of English, Bakker (1983) found that the acquisition of gerund was present in the final year although an examination of production tests requiring higher levels of control than acceptability judgement tests showed that it was not yet part of their regular performance. This example is elaborated here simply as a way of suggesting that the development of knowledge and control may be different and may require quite different intervention techniques (at different stages of development). The reader might imagine another (independent) structure/principle undergoing a similar armchair pattern of development but appearing *earlier* than verb-final position in the knowledge cell and *later* in the control cell. In this way the 'order of acquisition' would be different depending on whether one looked at knowledge or control. In information-processing terms, the acquisition of control would be a question of building fast and specialised 'automatic processes' where formerly only the more laborious 'controlled processes' could allow the learners to show their hidden knowledge.

A further possibility that needs to be mentioned is that, just as drilling can be applied at the wrong or right time depending whether an appropriate L2 insight has been gained or not, so, too, consciousness-raising techniques may be counterproductive where the insight has already been gained at a subconscious, intuitive level. This danger has already been mentioned with regard to interfering with learners' perceptions of language distance: their psychotypology. The consciousness-raising may not only affect the development of new knowledge, the impact may be on their control of L2 as well. One could provoke 'overmonitoring' behaviour: learners would become inhibited in their spontaneous performance (see Dulay *et al.* 1982). In other words, if the learner has the insight the teacher wants him or her to have, and has gained this intuitively, then explicit grammar teaching may (possibly) impede the acquisition of control as well as the acquisition of knowledge. Overmonitoring would also affect the credibility of subjects' responses in an acceptability judgement test in that they were thrown into self-doubt and confusion when asked to make judgements (see discussion in Chapter 2). The moral of the above tales, if research showed them to be justified, would be that many teaching techniques require a prior assessment of the precise state of (a) IL knowledge and (b) IL control. This implies a refinement of the standard ways that a teacher has of assessing where learners are at a given stage of their learning careers.

9.3   General cognitive theory

Several approaches to theory-building and experimentation have been mentioned which do not make reference to the idea of language (or grammar) as a specialised cognitive ability. At least, ideas on acquisition and skill proposed by those coming to the field from the perspective of cognitive psychology – e.g. Bialystok, McLaughlin and Pienemann – do not really involve references to special processes not existing outside language. If it were not for the learnability issue discussed earlier, the most economical way of tackling language knowledge and skill would be by deploying theories which lump language together with other cognitive areas (e.g. Anderson 1983; see overview in O'Malley *et al.* 1989). In all of these theories (leaving aside connectionist theory), a distinction is made between knowledge (mental representations) and the on-line procedural mechanisms for which the overall term 'control' has been used here. Over and above those areas of grammatical, phonological, lexical and pragmatic knowledge which could be usefully explained without recourse to specialised linguistic processes, many aspects of control need the input from the control-oriented theory in cognitive psychology. This is clear, again as discussed in this and earlier chapters, from the proposals of McLaughlin and Bialystok and from recent work in the area of first and second language production (see Dechert and Raupach 1989, Levelt 1989, Crookes 1991).

Even where the research focus is on the null hypothesis as inspired by the literature on language as a specialised cognitive faculty, theories that do not share this assumption can be relevant. This would be where research uncovers areas of language that fall outside this specialised cognitive domain, i.e. areas where learners of a given type (first or second) apparently need negative evidence to stop them clinging on to a false hypothesis about the target system. Any subsequent research would then, as already suggested, contribute to the development the more general cognitive theory.

9.4   Conclusion

There is, then, much research to done, both fundamental and applied, before authoritative statements can be made about the effectiveness of different methods and techniques based on current research findings. One suggestion promoted in this book was that, as regards grammatical competence of the intuitive kind, there is, at the moment, more hope for the facilitation of control via intervention than for the manipulation of competence development. However, this leaves vast stretches of lexical and pragmatic knowledge open to forms of intervention more direct than supplying salient, relevant input when the learner is perceived to be ready for it. As people systematically investigate ways of boosting L2 competence and control, their success or failure should be immensely interesting to a whole range of researchers and practitioners. Second language theory certainly involves many different areas of applied and theoretical research and can contribute substantially to our developing understanding of how the human mind actually works.

Questions and topics for discussion

When asked for definitions, try defining the terms and concepts in your own words and (where possible) give new examples, i.e. examples not mentioned in this book.

Chapter 1

1. Learner errors can be viewed from many different points of view: describe what you think the following are interested in, first and foremost:
   (a) the language learner
   (b) the language teacher
   (c) the second language researcher.
2. Define what you think should be the goals of the following:
   (a) non-applied second language (SLA) research?
   (b) applied second language (SLA) research?
   Do you think it is more useful for these two fields to be kept strictly separate? Give your reason(s). If not, how do you think researchers in these two areas can most effectively interact?
3. Define the term 'interlanguage'. Describe various ways/contexts in which it can be used.
4. What is the difference between 'input' and 'intake'?
5. Give a general term used here to describe words like 'word', 'adjective' other than 'terminology'.
6. Why is 'development' a more theoretically neutral term than 'learning'.
7. What is a 'communicative strategy'. Give an example.
8. 'What you *know* of a language is what you get right, what conforms to the native-speaker's usage': discuss this from the point of view of a second language researcher.
9. How would you define 'a fluent speaker of a second language' using terms and concepts taken from this book?
10. Give two examples of how interlanguage could be 'variable'.

11. What is the term used to describe the idea that we possess separate, relatively independent systems in our minds for dealing with different kinds of information? Explain with examples.
12. You could say that 'LAD' is a very general term.
    (a) What does it stand for?
    (b) What are the advantages of using such a term?
13. How does 'elicitation' differ from standard 'language testing'? (*Hint:* think of goals.) Illustrate your answer with examples.
14. Discuss:
    (a) In language teaching, instruction always helps.
    (b) It is impossible to learn a second language.

Chapter 2

1. What did Corder mean by a 'built-in syllabus'?
2. How does 'I want to know the English' pose a problem for the identification of correct versus incorrect utterances?
3. Give an example of a regular pattern that would show that the learner was operating some sort of 'transitional system'.
4. The output (product) of a language system-builder is a system. What is the output of the system?
5. Using the term 'hypothesis', say how the learner and the scientist are:
    (a) similar
    (b) different.
6. Give two ways in which the ideas of Corder, Nemser and Selinker coincided.
7. When we say that the learner is 'creative', what do we mean?
8. What research did Selinker use to justify his position that first and second language learning were fundamentally different, psychologically speaking?
9. Define 'fossilisation' and discuss its implications for our understanding of second (as opposed to first) language acquisition.
10. Show how a non-native form (interlanguage pattern) can have more than one psychological explanation.
11. Give an example of conscious learning strategy and discuss its usefulness to the language learner.
12. Give an example of a learner's 'simplification'. Explain what is

being simplified, how this is achieved and what you think is the reason for the learner's behaviour.

Chapter 3

1. List as many basic differences between first and second language acquisition as you can.
2. What does it mean to say that child syntax is first determined by meaning (semantic) categories?
3. What research specifically gave Corder the idea of the L2 built-in syllabus?
4. How did Dulay and Burt explain away some L2 forms that looked like incorrect transfers from the mother tongue?
5. What does it mean if you say that a model of development is 'incremental'?
6. Does the term in 5 describe Selinker's approach?
7. Give examples of developmental patterns and their corresponding target forms.
8. In what sense is creative construction more target-oriented than the interlanguage approach?

Chapter 4

1. You want to do some research into second language acquisition (SLA). Assuming, for the moment, that you have no theoretical framework to guide you, what are two useful preliminary steps you might take?
2. Give two reasons why you might not want to collect completely spontaneous data.
3. Give a concrete example to illustrate the Observer's Paradox. Suggest possible solutions.
4. Name two advantages of getting elicitation data by making learners speak spontaneously.
5. Discuss any problems there might be in getting spontaneous written data.
6. Classifying the data that have been obtained from learners can be done in various ways, that is to say, using different kinds of categories. Give two examples each of

    (a) a linguistic category

    (b) a psycholinguistic category.

7. What would be the advantage of collecting spontaneous data on the endings compared with data on the use of passives?

8. Assuming that you have classified and described your data, what do you still have to do?

9. Name two experimental subject variables that might affect the outcome of an experiment.

10. When might you use an acceptability judgement task rather than a production task?

11. Name one problem connected with the use of translation as an elicitation technique.

12. Explain:

    (a) elicited imitation

    (b) act-out.

13. Name two problems that arise when trying to get people to judge sentences for acceptability.

Chapter 5

1. Using your own examples, compare the contrastive analysis model, the interlanguage model and the creative construction model with regard to their approach to

    (a) crosslinguistic influence ('transfer')

    (b) differences between L1 and L2 acquisition

    (c) the role of environment in acquisition.

2. When looking at performance on the functor (morpheme) 'the', what important information was missed out in the creative construction analysis (which followed L1 research)?

3. State the case for arguing that there is no such thing as 'free' variation.

4. Name the crucial factor in determining given interlanguage styles following Labov and Tarone.

5. What would Selinker and Douglas call a IL variety that is produced when learners talk to each other informally about their personal lives? Discuss the value of such an approach to interlanguage theory.

6. Summarise what Huebner discovered in his analysis of Ge's English.

7. What is the function of Krashen's Monitor in learner performance?

8. How is the Monitor developed? Describe the kind of test necessary to find out about the development of a given learner's Monitor.
9. Name one person who claimed that conscious knowledge could affect the development of the learner's implicit grammar, and one who denied this. State your own considered opinion on this issue.
10. Discuss the questions in section 5.3.

Chapter 6

1. Explain how transfer and overgeneralisation could be seen as different manifestations of the same process.
2. Explain how an IL process posited by Selinker could be seen as either a competence phenomenon or a performance phenomenon.
3. What did Selinker mean by 'transfer of training'? How does it differ from his other categories of central process in interlanguage?
4. Dulay and Burt's proposals were presented as being based on a Chomskyan view of acquisition. Does Chomsky's approach underlie the idea of the fixed morpheme orders? Explain your answer.
5. Transfer got a bad name in the 1970s. Why was transfer presented by some as being theoretically trivial?
6. Show how incomprehensible input can trigger further development.
7. Define 'heterogeneous' competence. How does this idea differ from other ideas of competence in linguistics?
8. What is a 'variable rule'? How would you go about working one out for an area of grammar (in your language)?
9. Explain in three different ways why a given learner could vary in her usage of, say, 'if' and 'when' in English.
10. Compare two related examples of knowledge: one that is 'more analysed' and one that is 'less analysed' following Bialystok's model.
11. What is the difference between a 'controlled' and an 'automatic' process? How could you find out whether this distinction is valid for language learning?
12. What is Pienemann's 'teachability hypothesis'? Describe a possible way of testing it out.
13. What kind of principles determine the order of acquisition in the

Pienemann model (following Clahsen)? What objections might be raised to them?

Chapter 7

1. Think of as many different ways as you can of defining the notion 'marked'.
2. What was the hierarchy that Keenan and Comrie proposed and how was this interpreted in SLA research?
3. Define 'cross-categorial harmony', providing examples. What test could you devise to see if it guides the acquisition of grammar?
4. In the statement 'marked means more difficult' what two areas of research are being linked? Explain your answer.
5. In Schumann's model, what is it that induces a learner to move away from a pidginised form of interlanguage?
6. What evidence would show that development proceeds via 'denativisation'?
7. Devoicing final stops (obstruents) is apparently easy for English learners. Learning not to devoice poses problems: it is difficult for German learners of English to learn *not* to devoice. What early model of SLA cannot predict this fact and how does Eckman explain this?
8. In an early version of Chomskyan generative grammar, the child had, for any language, to learn a whole battery of transformational rules specific to that language. This kind of rule-learning has now been discarded. What has replaced it?
9. What is the term generally used for 'evidence for a given grammar that is present in the input'? Comment on the availability of other kinds of evidence that might help the learner build up knowledge of the L2.
10. Some languages have head-final grammars and others have head-initial grammars. Does the child need to know in advance which is the default (unmarked) option? Explain your answer.

Chapter 8

1. Comment on the related terms 'language', 'grammar', 'syntax' with reference to theories of linguistics.
2. What is the 'poverty-of-the-stimulus' argument? In what do you think it obtains for second language acquisition?

3. Why is Universal 'Grammar' a misleading term?
4. What is a structure-independent rule? Illustrate your answer.
5. Explain the 'recreative hypothesis'. Contrast it with rival explanations.
6. What is a wild grammar? How might it arise? How might you check whether wild grammars are temporary phenomena?
7. What would be the three phases of development, assuming successful parameter-resetting, which, where a representation of a given aspect of the target grammar is achieved, would coincide with a native speaker's representation?
8. In what circumstances, in the parameter-setting approach, would the second language learner, logically, need negative evidence
9. Explain the overgeneration problem.
10. What are the subset condition and the subset principle? How could you test to see if the L2 learner was guided by such a principle?
11. Connectionist theory seems to be incompatible with UG-based learning theory. In what type of language learning theory could the two live alongside each other?
12. If L2 learners have no access to L1 acquisitional mechanisms (associated with UG), what principles might then drive acquisition?

Chapter 9

Comment on the following:

1. Just because learners produce non-native forms does not mean they are ignorant.
2. Asking whether a learner 'knows' something in a target language begs the question of what kind of 'knowing' is involved.
3. Trying to increase the learner's knowledge of target forms may sometimes be a waste of time.
4. Explanations directed to the learner of how the target language works may be enormously beneficial in some cases and useless in others.
5. The same goes for actually correcting learner errors.
6. If a given language-teaching method appears to work, the official explanation for its success may be misguided.
7. A 'natural' teaching method that involves simple exposure to the language in communicative or otherwise meaningful situations

may work. This does not preclude the use of more 'artificial' techniques to make it work even better.

8. Detail at least six possible ways in which a second language learner might proceed to acquire a new language system in the light of the options and possibilities discussed in this chapter.

Extended glossary of terms

Give your own definitions for the various terms listed in the Glossary (see pages 195–210), then compare your results with the actual definitions given.

Research resources

1. Imagine that you want to do some research into the acquisition of reflexive pronouns by German learners of Japanese (or some other area that you may choose). Describe precisely the steps you would take to set up your investigation (including details of all resources you would use).

2. Write a short (500-word) research proposal that will convince your supervisor that you are worth taking on as a research student.

3. Write a practical list of do's and don'ts for people trying to set up an investigation into L2 acquisition.

Extended glossary of terms

Acquisition   Unless otherwise specified, synonymous with 'learning' and 'development'. Sometimes used to indicate only subconscious processes (see Dulay *et al.* 1982).

Analysis (see also 'automaticity')   Analysis is used by Bialystok (1990) to indicate the degree to which an area of the target system has been broken down into appropriately fine-grained categories. To take a simple example, if the learner (intuitively or otherwise) perceives 'don't' as a single entity rather than as 'do' + 'not', then that learner's knowledge is relatively unanalysed. The learner has not yet perceived the way the auxiliary and negation system work with respect to 'don't'. The process of analysis typically involves integrating formerly isolated bits of knowledge.

Attainment   A term, associated with 'acquisition', 'development' and 'learning', used by the Chomsky school meaning roughly 'growth from within', the idea being to avoid giving the impression that grammatical development was internalising something that came from outside.

Attrition   Another name for language loss, i.e. when a learner's competence or control in a given L1 or L2 undergoes change which may be seen principally as a reduction of knowledge and/or skill and not just as one process in developing towards the language norms; divergence from the norms of the language when the learner no longer uses the language either receptively or productively (often while acquiring a new language).

Automatic process (see also 'controlled process')   From information-processing theory; opposite of 'controlled process': a mechanism whereby a person can perform some task swiftly, unreflectingly and with minimal processing load. Learning, in this view, typically begins with slower, controlled processes some of which may be transformed into efficient automatic routines.

Automaticity (see also 'automatic process')   Used to denote how swift and spontaneous the use of a given linguistic structure may be. Similar to 'fluent use'.

Cognitive variability   The variation in performance caused by the learner's uncertainty about the nature of a given area of the language. The learner may be in the middle of restructuring the system, going from one rule to another.

Communication strategy (see 'strategy')

Compensatory strategy (see 'strategy')

Competence (see also, 'control', 'metalinguistic awareness', 'performance', 'pragmatic knowledge') In its default sense, the tacit grammatical knowledge that a child acquires apparently without reflection and correction (Chomsky 1965, etc., Brown and Hanlon 1970); by extension, the L2 equivalent of L1 competence as just defined; by further extension, any of the knowledge systems underlying human behaviour and excluding the processing mechanisms that control that competence in actual performance.

Comprehensible input As far as information coming from the outside is concerned, the only real requirement for acquisition to take place for those following Krashen's model (Krashen 1985). Learners do not need to analyse what they are doing, but simply to understand messages in L2. Language addressed to them in the normal course of communication should be aimed at conveying meaning to them such as to maximise their understanding. The acquisitional mechanisms will take care of the rest.

Connectionism (see also 'information processing') An approach to the way we develop, store and process knowledge which is modelled on the way neurons are organised in our physical brain. Contrary to the standard view that the mind has knowledge systems composed of symbols and systems for linking them (e.g. nouns and noun phrases), connectionism reduces knowledge to a vast system of interconnected nodes (on analogy with neurons). Some connections are made stronger than others as we experience the world such that given patterns of behaviour, e.g producing Danish utterances, are reflections of particular patterns of strong connections. Hence, talking about nouns and noun phrases may be convenient ways of describing these patterns but they do not accurately reflect the way knowledge is actually represented in the mind. This model, it may be claimed, resembles earlier, behaviouristic learning models in that a much greater role is ascribed to the environment and to the individual's experience. Through experience, different connections, varying in strength are built up in the learner's mind. There is no room for any such notion as UG or 'learner hypothesising'. Nevertheless, connectionism implies a more complicated picture of the organisation of knowledge than behaviourism allows for. The networks of nodes are many and varied and they are typically activated in parallel, not one after the other, hence the associated notion of 'parallel distributed processing' (PDP) ((Rumelhart and McClelland 1986, Sokolik and Smith 1992, Carroll and Meisel 1990, Gasser 1990, Tomlin 1990; for a critique of connectionism see Fodor and Pylyshyn 1988).

Control (see also 'automaticity') On-line processing control over knowledge; the productive and receptive control possessed by language users over the knowledge they have of various aspects of the linguistic system allowing them to deploy that knowledge with greater or lesser facility (Bialystok and Sharwood Smith 1985). Bialystok sees control as involving, above all, the ability to attend selectively to relevant parts of the language system: to pick and choose properly at high speed, as it were.

Control variability Variation in the degree of control a learner has in a language irrespective of what his or her current underlying knowledge consists of, manifested in the contrast, in actual performance, between what a language user does and what he or she does.

Controlled process (see also 'automatic process') In information-processing theory, processes that are not automatised, that, when used, will use up a large amount of available processing capacity (sometimes involving the user being consciously aware of such processes as in city driving as carried out by a beginner). When such mental operations are converted into rapid, smooth, automatised routines, more processing capacity is made available for other operations.

Creative construction (see also 'crosslinguistic influence', 'developmental pattern') The learner's internal, intuitive organisation of the input: this is reflected in the predictable order in the appearance of specific native ('correct') L2 forms in regular learner IL production; the name of a school of thought which maintained the view that L1 and L2 acquisition were highly similar and were driven by the same subconscious learning mechanisms unaffected by conscious intervention and crosslinguistic influence.

Critical Period Hypothesis (CPH) The idea that there is a time limit for acquiring the mother tongue. Lenneberg (1972) set this at around puberty to coincide with the completion of the specialisation of brain function. He also suggested that the learning of a second language after puberty would be more difficult since the mother tongue learning mechanism would have atrophied by then. This idea is taken to be support for the claim made by such people as Selinker that L1 and L2 acquisition are fundamentally different.

Whether or not this is true, it has to be said that this particular scientific basis for the notion of CPH is not generally accepted.

Crosslinguistic influence Commonly called 'language transfer' (Selinker 1972); the influence of the mother tongue on the learner's performance in and/or development of a given target language; by extension, it also means *the influence of any 'other tongue' known to the learner on that target language*. It may also be used in studies of language loss where a previous learned language (e.g. the L1) is changing under the influence of new language learning (Sharwood Smith 1983a). The favoured term in this book has been 'crosslinguistic influence', which also covers avoidance of transfer due to a (not necessarily correct) perception of L1/L2 difference (Sharwood Smith 1983b, Sharwood Smith and Keller-man 1986).

Developmental pattern A non-native structural pattern (form/con-struction) which deviates from the native equivalent but which is not a random occurrence but forms part of a pattern of development as observed by second language researchers within a given well-defined structural area like negation or *wh*-question formation.

Developmental scenario One of a number of theoretically possible courses that a learner may take, i.e., a theoretically motivated history of development, which may later be empirically confirmed or disconfirmed. Suppose given learners were not controlled by the constraints of UG, then we would expect them to show evidence of hypotheses about L2 that violated UG (Van Buren and Sharwood Smith 1985, Sharwood Smith 1988, 1989). Compare this with developmental patterns that are first observed and for which a theoretical explanation is then sought (Clahsen and Muysken 1986, Pienemann 1984).

Deviant form (see also 'developmental pattern') An interlanguage form which deviates from the native equivalent and which may either be random occurrence or form part of a pattern of development.

Discourse domain Selinker and Douglas (1989) use this term to denote an area of interlanguage with its own particular linguistic characteristics and which is defined with regard to the topic area. Learners talking about the personal life may employ an IL that is linguistically different in a principled way from the IL they use when, for example, talking about some professional topic in which they have expertise. In this view, IL is not one monolithic entity but a cluster of varieties based on different IL discourse domains.

Elicitation   The systematic obtaining of learner data selected according to strict principles made clear in advance. To be compared with 'heuristic' data gathering where the principles governing data collection are not very precise and the general idea is to gather as much as possible without preconditions in the hope that something interesting will turn up.

Embedding problem (see also 'matching problem')   To understand any utterance, we need to have a certain amount of contextual information. An L2 learner, for example, with limited L2 resources will have to rely heavily on contextual information to get messages across. Learning an L2 involves finding out how to relate the system to the context of use. Klein refers to this problem as 'embedding' in (Klein 1986).

Error (see also 'deviant form', 'interlanguage')   An error signifies a deviation from the standard norms, understood to be the learner's target. The negative connotation of the notion of error makes it an undesirable term in IL research but many still use it, as a convenience.

Evidence (see also 'negative evidence', 'positive evidence')   Evidence for the language learner or learning device (see also INPUT) either serves to confirm or disconfirm an assumption already held about L2. Research should show what kinds of evidence are effective in different kinds of learning situation. The idea of evidence assumes a prior hypothesis on the learner's part (or on the part of the learning mechanisms, at least) that is open to being tested (see Chomsky 1975, 1980).

Fossilisation   A term coined by Selinker (1972) for the apparently final stage when development in some area stops not because there is no more exposure to the language but rather despite repeated exposure and attempts to learn. 'Fossilised UG' is the name used in this book for the hypothesis that claims that (all or given) L2 learners have lost their original language-learning ability and as a result have to rely on general learning principles and the example of their mother tongue to build up an L2 system.

Holophrastic (see also 'analysis')   This is when one lexical item is used where others would use a more complex structure, i.e. as a 'holophrase'. For example, L1 acquirers begin with holophrastic utterances like 'Mummy' which are interpreted as being equivalent to adult phrases or sentences like 'Look, there's Mummy!'.

Hypothesis formation   This is most usually mentioned in connection with so-called 'general' learning strategies, that is, strategies that are not peculiar to language learning. The learner, consciously or subconsciously, devises a rule to account for some phenomenon, say question formation. This 'hypothesis' may be confirmed by the evidence provided by the outside world. More importantly, it needs a counter-example for it to be shown up as incorrect.

Information processing   A concept used in artificial intelligence and cognitive psychology allowing the uses of associated terms such as 'input' and 'output'. The learner may be seen as a processing device which takes certain input, transforms it and produces output. By comparing input and output, we may get an idea of what those transforming processes must be. In this case, the mechanisms under investigation are those that drive development and performance in a second language.

Initial template (see also 'parameter setting', 'universal grammar')   Used here to denote the learner's use of L1 as an initial basis for the L2 system, particularly with regard to the way various parameters of universal grammar should be set for L2.

Input (see also 'evidence', 'information processing')   The default definition of 'input' is *language data which the learner is exposed to*. More properly, it is 'observable, potentially processible language data relevant for acquisition'. Input that is actually processed and turned into knowledge is called 'intake'. Input may contain evidence for or against a given assumption held by the learner/ listening device. Alternatively, it may simply contain information about which no previous assumption is held.

Intake (see 'input', 'knowledge')

Interlanguage   The systematic linguistic behaviour of non-native speakers of a given language, normally understood to be what is produced in natural situations of language use where the focus is on conveying meaning and not on the formal correctness of utterances (see Selinker 1972, 1992).

LAD (see also 'developmental strategy', 'UG')   Language Acquisition Device: an umbrella term for language learning mechanisms; the default meaning of LAD is the set of mechanisms that, following UG principles, allows the child to create L1 competence without the need for negative evidence or conscious analysis (meta mode); usable, by extension in second language acquisition, but only with reference to a given theory about how L1 and L2 acquisition relate to each other.

Language transfer (see 'crosslinguistic influence')

Latent psychological structure (se also 'fossilisation', 'LAD')   The psychological mechanisms assumed to drive second rather than first language acquisition in the IL model proposed by Selinker

(1972, 1992). It entailed fossilisation, i.e. failure to attain full native speaker status.

Learner/learning device (see 'LAD')

Learning (see 'acquisition')

Learning mechanisms (see 'LAD')

Learning strategy (see also 'strategy')   A conscious or subconscious attempt to change one's current knowledge of L2. The status of the term 'strategy' varies a lot depending on which model is adopted (see discussion in Bialystok 1990).

Markedness (see also 'Parameters', 'UG')   In phonology, morphology and syntax, certain principles, forms or structures may be seen as 'basic' forms, in some sense, i.e. 'unmarked'. The label 'marked' is used in many ways: for example, it is used to mean forms that have more structure than their unmarked counterpart, or that require more rules or possess more informational content than (unmarked) forms directly associated with them, or which occur less frequently in the world's languages and by virtue of this are less typical (cows versus cow, active versus passive versions of a sentence, full devoicing of final stops before a silence as in German Bad [bad] versus English bad [bæd] , etc.). Markedness is seen in many different ways (Comrie 1981, Eckman 1977, White 1990). In Chomskyan theory, markedness is the property of forms which require evidence in the input for their adoption by the learner (see 'positive evidence'). In the absence of such evidence, the learner automatically assumes that the less marked options hold for the language being learned. The available options are limited in number and are part of a particular parameter along which grammars of natural languages may vary (like the relative order of the head of a phrase and what modifies it, e.g. in the noun phrase, 'white house' [adj. Noun] versus 'house white' [Noun adj.]).

Matching problem   Klein's term for learners' problem of having to notice a discrepancy between their own output and the native-speaker input. They need to match their deviant (IL) forms against equivalent target forms for any development to take place (Klein 1986).

Maturational   Having (here) to do with the mental development of the language learner: at certain points during language acquisition, certain principles may not be available to the child. For example, some claim that UG is not available in its entirety at birth but comes available in stages as the child develops: this means that the child is unable to make use of a particular type of L1 input when not yet maturationally 'ready'. Some claim that L1 and L2 acquisition are fundamentally different because of differences in mental (cognitive) maturity.

Meta mode (see also 'metalanguage', 'metalinguistic awareness') In the meta mode, the language user abstracts away from the meaning of a word or structure and considers its formal properties; carrying out a conscious analysis of language structure; ranges from being (metalingually) 'aware' to applying metalinguistic knowledge.

Metalanguage (see 'metalinguistic awareness', 'rule') 'Metalanguage' and its associated adjective 'metalinguistic' refer to *ways in which language and particularly the language system is seen and exploited as an object.* Hence a linguist or language teacher when drawing attention to the formal properties of a language (or interlanguage), i.e. the sound patterns or graphic patterns or the underlying system, will employ metalanguage, a set of terms to talk about language.

Metalinguistic awareness (see also 'meta mode') The awareness of language as an object: it may appear spontaneously in children who try to exploit it for their amusement (and possible edification) by creating rhymes, and linguistic jokes (word play) and it may be nurtured during formal education and refined by means of analytic activities such as parsing sentences and finding synonyms for words, and so on. In the latter case, a descriptive terminology has to be developed ('synonym' being one example) and, in academic circles, whole theories (see Culioli and Desclés 1981, Klein 1986, Ellis 1991). Formalised awareness allowing the user to talk coherently about language may be termed 'metalinguistic knowledge'.

Metalinguistic knowledge (see 'metalinguistic awareness')

Modularity Breaking down a large system into a number of small (at least) semi-independent systems, possibly working according to different principles. Modularity in Chomsky's, or Fodor's theoretical sense (Chomsky 1980, Fodor 1983) is a theory about how the mind is structured (see also Jackendoff 1987; cf. Rumelhart and McClelland 1986) . The mind may be seen as 'modular' in that different areas of knowledge and ability are qualitatively different from one another and not just special instances of a generalised notion 'knowledge'. The language module is therefore often referred to as a special knowledge/ability area obeying special principles not relevant to, say, mathematical knowledge or ability or to the human vision (see Fodor 1973). Even grammar itself can be seen as modular, as is the case with the current Chomskyan view. That is to say, what is grammatical and what is not grammatical in a given language (or in any natural language) is not determined by a single set of global grammatical principles but rather by a number of quite different 'bodies' of principles each of which takes care of a very specific aspect of the grammar, e.g. the assignment of case. Hence, one modular system of rules can allow a particular structure but that selfsame structure can be ruled out when the principles of another system are applied. Each system is blind to the workings of the other. This is felt to be a much more efficient way of describing the restrictions on natural grammars and accords with the Chomskyan requirement of helping our understanding of how young children acquire language.

Monitor A mechanism whereby language users inspect their own linguistic output during performance to see if it conforms to given rules. It can be seen as a kind of censor that checks and, in certain circumstances, triggers self-corrections (repairs). Krashen used the term in a restricted sense to refer to conscious monitoring using a separate knowledge system built up for this purpose and not the intuitive competence that is involved in the typically subconscious self-monitoring that constantly accompanies normal native-speaker performance.

Naturalistic (see also 'meta mode', 'metalinguistic awareness', 'monitor') Used of learning environments where the learner uses the language to convey and understand messages without much focus on correctness, that is, on the formal properties of the language. Often contrasted with 'formal classroom' situations where the learner is made particularly conscious of being a learner rather than just a user of the L2.

Negative evidence (see also 'evidence', 'metalinguistic awareness', 'overgeneralisation', 'UG') Evidence that some form sanctioned by the IL system is incorrect (non-native): for example, a sentence in L2 actually marked as 'incorrect' would constitute negative evidence. Negative evidence might also come in the form of a teacher's pronouncement, such as 'you may not use the present simple in such and such a situation'. There is also indirect negative evidence, whereby the absence of a form in the input signals to the learner\learning device that the form in question might not be correct. It is an open question how much and where negative evidence helps (Brown and Hanlon 1970).

Output (see also 'input', 'information processing') Output is usually used to refer to the learner's performance. Typically, but not necessarily, this means the production of speech and writing. However, it can also mean the interpretation of speech and writing by the learner (listening and reading). The output of the learning mechanism is a set of knowledges or abilities that underlie performance.

Overgeneralisation (see 'positive evidence', 'negative evidence')   The learner, on the basis of the input, creates new rules that have a wider coverage than is sanctioned on the native L2 norms (Selinker 1972). This is an important issue with regard to the learnability of languages. The learner has to discover the limitations and exceptions to rules. When a learner organises perceived language input into a principle/rule and then applies that principle to create new structures which are not sanctioned by the input, this creates an 'overgeneration problem', i.e. the difficulty of explaining how a learner recovers from such 'errors' without corrective feedback (see Baker 1979). The point here is that the input (positive evidence) may not contain evidence to disconfirm the overgeneralising rule (see Baker 1979, Bowerman 1982, Pinker 1984, 1986, Rutherford 1987b, 1989).

Overgeneration (see 'overgeneralisation')

Parallel Distributed Processing (PDP) (see 'connectionism', 'information processing')

Parameters (see 'markedness', 'metalanguage', 'principles', 'rule', 'UG')   Parameters in linguistics refer to ways in which language systems may vary. For example, there are some languages that have prepositions, e.g. *to* the house, *on* course) and some that do not. Even languages that have prepositions can be said to vary according to whether they allow those prepositions to be separated from the noun phrase. English allows this: '*the house* you went *to*' (correct separation). Standard French does not: '*La maison* que tu es allée *à*' (incorrect separation). This could be called a preposition separation (or 'preposition stranding') parameter. In current Chomskyan linguistics, certain parameters are claimed to be part of universal grammar. This supposedly reduces the learning burden and explains how very young, immature children are able to accomplish the complex feat of L1 acquisition when, logically speaking, the odds are against them. As a language-learning being, the child is equipped with a battery of parameters in advance so the learning task consists simply in (1) establishing whether they are relevant for the mother tongue and, if so, (2) how they should be 'set', i.e. what particular option (setting) is appropriate for the language in question. Theoretical research still has to show if such and such a linguistic parameter (like preposition stranding) is a parameter of UG or not. If not, then the learning task for all kinds of language learners is correspondingly greater. In this way, for many of the fundamental facts of syntax, there is only one human language. In this particular respect, any given 'language' is seen as a variant of the one system. Imagine that you and your friend have two identical computer printers, for example. By changing the switches on your computer's printer to make it type in double-spaced Pica rather than single-spaced Courier, for instance, you are not creating a different type of printer, but the same printer set up in a particular way. If your friend's printer breaks down, he or she will not have to learn much to operate yours.

Parasitic   Used here of a view (on the role of UG in second language acquisition) which claims that learners blindly impose (UG-based) L1 principles on their L2 and thereby give the false impression that their L2 acquisition is controlled directly by UG. It appears that they actively use UG to restrict the form of L2 grammars. In fact, they are capable of developing their L2 further in ways which show they are neither guided nor constrained by UG (see, for example, Schachter 1990).

Performance   (see also 'competence', 'control') Actual instances of linguistic behaviour, demonstrating the fluent and/or faulty use of different knowledge systems, constrained by various capacity limitations (e.g. short-term memory; see, for example, Laver 1970). Performance is what can be observed and/or recorded for analysis. It takes place in real time and implies special mechanisms for producing and interpreting language.

Pidgins and creoles   Pidgins are structurally simple languages which arise out of contact of a highly limited kind between two language communities. They all share some basic characteristics (limited morphology, fixed word order). Pidgins are learned as second languages only. If a pidgin starts to be acquired as a mother tongue, it undergoes considerable complexification since more demands are made on it. It must function as a natural language and not just as a way of conveying simple messages for practical purposes. If pidgins are learned as mother tongues, they become creoles.

Positive evidence   (see 'evidence', 'negative evidence', 'overgeneralisation', 'UG') This is evidence that is actually present in the input and directly disconfirms an assumption held by the learner about the L2. If a learner constructs an overgeneralised version of a native rule, he or she will never encounter evidence in the input to directly disconfirm that overgeneralisation; indirect positive evidence is evidence present in the input that does not directly disconfirm any current learner assumption but, by implication, informs the learner/learning device about the incorrect nature of some other, structurally related aspect of his or her current grammar (Van Buren 1988, Zobl 1989).

Pragmatic knowledge (see also 'competence')   Also called 'pragmatic competence' (Chomsky 1980); the knowledge underlying the appropriate use of language in different contexts of use. Briefly it has to do with knowing which structure (word, grammatical construction, style of speaking, etc.) should be selected from the complete linguistic repertoire available to a language user. This involves, among other things, matching language with specific speaker intentions. The definition of pragmatics, and the width of its scope, is a thorny subject.

Pragmatic mode   The early phases of language learning and in pidgin languages, where syntax is relatively undeveloped. In this way, it is not a syntactic notion like 'subject' or 'object' that determines what comes first or second. The structure of spoken utterances seems to rely more obviously on certain pragmatic principles like 'old information first, new information second'). This has been called using the 'pragmatic' (or 'presyntactic') mode (Givon 1984, Klein 1986).

Prefabricated patterns   Sometimes known as 'unanalysed chunks'; superficially complex linguistic items, which function like much simpler units. Example: 'don't' when used as a single morpheme instead of {do}+{not}. Learners may use what look like complex structures at an early stage of development but their performance in general shows them not to have analysed the item into its component parts. Sometimes such patters may allow a slot which can be filled with a number of alternative items, like 'I'd-like-a . . .'. We would not expect such a learner to produce 'Would you like a' or 'I wouldn't like a'.

Principle (see also 'metalanguage', 'parameters', 'rule', 'UG')   A linguistic principle, unlike a rule, is designed to cover a large area of the language system, or language systems in general. For example, a principle might state that all languages must have a certain feature, or no rule may contain such and such a feature or instruction, or that if a language has one feature, it must of necessity also contain another given feature. A principle of (Chomskyan) Universal Grammar is a principle that children are supposedly born with, or which at least becomes available to them in the course of development. Because it is part of universal grammar, it is there to reduce the learning burden and has the effect of limiting the possible ways in which the child could form a rule based on the evidence provided by the input. There will still be particular morphological, syntactic, semantic and pragmatic rules for particular languages like, for example, the way the past tense is formed in French. These have developed largely through historical accident or according to more general principles that are not directly to do with linguistic structure. They have to be learned in their entirety with each language.

Psycholinguistic variation (see 'control') Variation in performance attributable to the relative degree of control which a learner has over a give area of the language (Bialystok and Sharwood Smith 1985).

Recreation (see also 'parameters',' reorganisation', 'UG') Used here of the view (on the role of UG in second language acquisition) that L1 and L2 learning are essentially identical in that UG is applied exclusively to L2 input and there is no transfer or any other kind of crosslinguistic influence except in areas where UG principles are just irrelevant. Any differences that there might possibly be between L1 and L2 development will have nothing to do with those areas relevant to UG.

Reorganisation (see also 'overgeneralisation', 'parameters', 'recreation', 'UG') Used here of the view (on the role of UG in second language acquisition) that supposes that learners begin with an L2 following L1 in its basic grammatical make-up. They then reorganise the L2 grammar in accordance with L2 input but still actively apply UG restrictions on the new versions of their L2 grammar.

Rule (see also 'metalanguage', 'principle', 'parameters') A rule is an instruction or formula which applies to a specific (grammatical, phonological, etc.) situation and which means the addition, replacement, deletion or movement of some form). Example: 'to form questions add the form "czy" to the beginning of the active declarative sentence'. Note that rules as a type of 'metalanguage' require some technical terms for their formulation, but this can vary in degree according to how formal they are supposed to be. They can also vary in their degree of precision. A language teacher may often have recourse to a rule of thumb (guideline) which is simple, memorable but does not always work. Note that people also talk of rules as being part of a learner's knowledge, i.e. as a psychological entity (mental rules, rules in the head, psycholinguistic rules). Assuming that language users have something equivalent to a set of rules as described above, some rules will relate to mechanisms that drive language performance, other rules may be metalinguistic in character. In other words, some rules may simply be ways of consciously reflecting on, describing and explaining language.

Scenario (see 'developmental scenario')

Second language   Any language other than the first language learned by a given learner or group of learners, irrespective of the type of learning environment (formal or informal) and irrespective of the number of non-native languages possessed by the learner; a 'non-native language'; sometimes 'second' as opposed to 'foreign' and, in this case, a second language means a non-native language that is used regularly in the learner's own community: hence speakers of languages other than German who have immigrated to Germany have to acquire German as a 'second' language in this more specialised sense (see Klein 1986).

Sociolinguistic variation   If a learner wishes to be completely native-like, it is necessary not only to possess the same vocabulary, grammar and pronunciation as a native speaker of the L2 but to be able to choose from his or her repertoire appropriately in various social circumstances. So, when a language exhibits sociolinguistic variation, this means that the choice of words and constructions will vary along sociolinguistic parameters such as class, age, degree of formality, etc. This phenomenon is not exclusive to native-speaker languages. Interlanguages also exhibit sociolinguistic variation (see Tarone 1988).

Strategy   The term 'strategy' should be understood as an organised approach to a task whether or not the language user is aware of applying the strategy in a given context, whether or not that strategy is part of a stable repertoire of strategies possessed by the learner or an ad-hoc invention on the spur of the moment, and whether or not the idea behind the strategy is to facilitate acquisition (in any sense: see above) or simply communication at a given moment in time. Communicative strategies that serve to make up for perceived gaps in the learner's knowledge or other obstacles that may occur during communication are sometimes called compensatory strategies. The task of defining a strategy is still a matter of great controversy (see Poulisse *et al.* 1984, Tarone 1988, Bialystok 1990).

Subset principle (see also 'positive evidence')   A learning principle (see Wexler and Manzini 1986) which assumes that some grammatical systems (in natural languages) may be seen as forming nested sets, i.e. sets and subsets. The subset is always a more restrictive version of its superset(s). If learners initially assume the subset, evidence in the input can always make them aware that the grammar of the language they are acquiring turns out to be more relaxed, less restrictive: they can then reset to a more relaxed grammar. By contrast, if they assume the more relaxed version, they will never hear anything that directly disconfirms this assumption. The subset principle says that learners always adopt the subset until the evidence informs them otherwise.

Teachability This is the idea that, at a given moment, certain areas of a language may be teachable and others may not. Pienemann's Teachability Hypothesis asserts that, with certain types of construction, learners can only benefit from intervention by teachers if they have already passed through given prerequisite stages. Learners have, independently, to show evidence of arriving at the new stage before the teacher can intervene to speed them through that stage. In this way, teachers have to wait for natural processes of acquisition to take place before they can help the learner (Pienemann 1984).

Transfer (see 'crosslinguistic influence')

Transitional form (see 'developmental pattern')

U-Shapes Developmental curves which begin in Stage 1 with the learner producing appropriate native-like forms then 'advancing' to a second stage which involves a move away from nativeness, where the system has been restructured according to the learner's own rule system (see, for example, 'overgeneralisation'), and returning to nativeness only in a final stage. U-shaped development is seen as a sure sign that learners are creative and reinterpret the input according to their own internal needs and perceptions (see Strauss 1982, Bowerman 1982, Kellerman 1984, Karmiloff-Smith 1986, Sharwood Smith and Kellerman 1989).

Unanalysed chunks (see 'prefabricated patterns')

Uniqueness Various researchers have claimed that L1 learners and/ or L2 learners initially (prefer to) assume that one form fulfils only one function, one form expresses only one meaning: this conservative approach to building a new language system has been dubbed by Pinker as the Uniqueness Principle (see Pinker 1979, 1984, cf. Slobin 1973, Andersen 1983a, Kellerman 1978, 1979, 1984).

Universal grammar (UG) (see also 'evidence', 'fossilisation', 'marked-ness', 'overgeneralisation', 'parameters') A set of principles which are supposed to limit the possible ways in which a learner can build a grammar of the L1 (and possibly L2) on the basis of the evidence in the input (Chomsky 1965, 1980). L1 competence can develop on the basis of positive evidence alone, given the operation of UG constraints; UG is neither a grammar in its own right nor a learning mechanism. It is part of the child's biological endowment and comes into operation when the child is exposed to the appropriate input. It directs the child's hypothesising about the structure of the language along particular lines such that the child will not try out every logical possibility when creating its grammar. Controversy rages around the issue of whether it is available to learners of L2s (see Schachter 1990, White 1990).

Bibliography

Adjemian C 1976 On the nature of interlanguage systems. *Language Learning* **26**: 297–320

Adjemian C 1983 The transferability of lexical properties. In Gass and Selinker 1983

Alatis J (ed.) 1968 *Contrastive linguistics and its implications for language pedagogy. Report on the 19th annual round table meeting.* Monograph Series on Language and Linguistics 21. Georgetown University, Washington, DC

Allen P and Van Buren P 1971 *Chomsky: a book of readings.* Oxford University Press, Oxford

Andersen R 1981a Two perspectives on pidginization as second language acquisition. In Andersen 1981b

Andersen R (ed.) 1981b *New dimensions in second language research.* Newbury House, Rowley, Mass

Andersen R 1983a Transfer to somewhere. In Gass and Selinker 1983

Andersen R 1983b *Pidginization and creolization as language acquisition.* Newbury House, Rowley, Mass.

Andersen R (ed.) 1984 *Second languages: a cross-linguistics perspective.* Newbury House, Rowley, Mass.

Anderson J R 1983 *The architecture of cognition.* Harvard University Press, Cambridge

Anderson J R, Spiro R and Montague W (eds) 1977 *Schooling and the acquisition of knowledge.* Erlbaum, Hillsdale

Anderson J 1978 Order of difficulty in adult second language acquisition. In Ritchie W (ed.) *Second language research issues and implications.* Academic Press, London

Anderson H 1986 L'acquisition et l'emploi des pronoms francais par des apprenants danois. In Giacomi and Véronique 1986

Arabski J 1971 A linguistic analysis of composition errors made by Polish students. *Studia Anglica Posnanensia* **10**: 135-143

Bailey C-J 1973 *Variation and linguistic theory.* Center for Applied Linguistics, Washington, DC

Baker C 1979 Syntactic theory and the projection problem. *Linguistic Inquiry* **10**: 533–81

Bakker C 1983 *The economy principle in the production of sentential verb complements.* Unpublished Master's Thesis, University of Utrecht

Beebe L 1980 Sociolinguistic variation and style shifting in second language acquisition. *Language Learning* 30: 433–47

Bellugi U and Studdert-Kennedy G (eds) 1980 *Signed and spoken language: biological constraints on linguistic form.* Verlag Chemie, Weinheim

Berwick R and Weinberg A 1984 *The grammatical basis of linguistic performance.* MIT Press, Cambridge, Mass.

Bialystok E 1978 A theoretical model of second language learning. *Language Learning* 28: 69–83

Bialystok E 1987 Influences of bilingualism on metalinguistic development. *Second Language Research* 3: 154–66

Bialystok E 1988 A psycholinguistic framework for exploring the basis of second language proficiency. In Rutherford and Sharwood Smith 1988

Bialystok E 1990 *Communicative strategies.* Blackwell, Oxford

Bialystok E and Kellerman E 1987 Communication strategies in the classroom. In Das 1987

Bialystok E and Sharwood Smith M 1985 Interlanguage is not a state of mind: an evaluation of the construct for second language acquisition. *Applied Linguistics* 6: 101–7

Bickerton D 1975 *Dynamics of a creole system.* Cambridge University Press, London and Cambridge

Bickerton D 1981 *The roots of language.* Karoma Publishers, Ann Arbor

Birdsong D 1989 *Metalinguistic competence and interlinguistic competence.* Springer, New York

Bley-Vroman R 1983 The comparative fallacy in interlanguage studies: the case of systematicity. *Language Learning* 33: 1–17

Bley-Vroman R 1986 Hypothesis testing in second language acquisition theory. *Language Learning* 36: 353–76

Bley-Vroman R 1988 The fundamental character of foreign language learning. In Rutherford and Sharwood Smith M 1988

Bley-Vroman R and Masterson D 1991 *Reaction time as a supplement to grammaticality judgements in the investigation of second language learners' competence.* Unpublished manuscript, University of Hawaii

Bloom L 1970 *Language development: form and function in emerging grammars.* MIT Press, Cambridge, Mass

Blum-Kulka S and Olshtain E 1986 Too many words: length of utterance and pragmatic failure. *Studies in Second Language Acquisition* 8: 165–79

Borer H and Wexler K 1986 The maturation of syntax. In Roeper and Williams 1986

Bowerman M 1982 Reorganisational processes in lexical and syntactic development. In Wanner and Gleitman 1982

Bowerman M 1983 How do children avoid constructing an overly general grammar in the absence of feedback about what is not a sentence? *Papers and Reports on Child Language Development,* 22

Braine M 1963 The ontogeny of English phrase structure: the first stage. *Language* **39**: 1–13

Broselow E 1988 Prosodic phonology and the acquisition of a second language. In Flynn and O'Neil 1988

Brown G (ed.) 1986 *Applied Linguistics* **7**, 3 (thematic issue on comprehension)

Brown R 1973 *A first language.* Penguin, Harmondsworth

Brown R and Hanlon C 1970 Derivational complexity and order of acquisition in child speech. In Hayes 1970

Burt M and Dulay H (eds) 1975 *New directions in second language learning, teaching and bilingual education.* TESOL, Washington, DC

Burt M, Dulay M and Hernandez-Chavez M 1975 *Bilingual syntax measure.* Harcourt Brace Jovanovich, New York

Butler C 1985 *Statistics in linguistics.* Blackwell, Oxford

Carpay, J 1974 *Onderwijsleerpsychogie en leergang-ontwikkeling in het moderne vreemdeetalenonderwijs.* Tjeenk Willis, Groningen

Carroll J B 1968 Contrastive analysis and interference theory. In Alatis 1968

Carroll S and Meisel J 1990 Universals and second language acquisition. *Studies in Second Language Acquisition* **12**: 201–8

Carter R and McCarthy M 1988 *Vocabulary and language teaching.* Longman, London

Chafe W 1970 *Meaning and the structure of language* University of Chicago Press, Chicago.

Chaudron C 1983 Research on metalinguistic tasks: a review of methods, theory and results. *Language Learning* **33**: 343–78

Chomsky N 1965 *Aspects of the theory of syntax.* MIT Press, Cambridge, Mass

Chomsky N 1975 *The logical structure of linguistic theory.* Plenum, New York

Chomsky N 1980 *Rules and representations.* Blackwell, Oxford

Chomsky N 1981 *Lectures on government and binding.* Foris, Dordrecht

Clahsen H 1984 The acquisition of German word-order: a test case for cognitive approaches to L2 development. In Andersen 1984

Clahsen H and Muysken P 1986 The availability of universal grammar to adult and child learners. *Second Language Research* **2**: 93–119

Comrie B 1981 *Language.* Universals and Linguistic Typology. Blackwell, Oxford

Cook V J 1985 Universal Grammar and second language learning. *Applied Linguistics* **6**: 2–18

Cook V J 1988 *Chomsky's universal grammar.* Blackwell, Oxford

Cook V J 1993 *Linguistics and second language acquisition.* Macmillan, Basingstoke

Coopmans P 1984 Surface word order typology and Universal Grammar. *Language* **60**: 55–69

Corder S Pit 1967 The significance of learner's errors. *International Review of Applied Linguistics*, **5**: 160–70

Corder S Pit 1973 *Introducing applied linguistics.* Penguin, Harmondsworth

Corder S Pit 1981 *Interlanguage and error analysis*. Oxford University Press, Oxford

Corder S Pit and Roulet E (eds) 1977 *The notions: simplifications, interlanguage and pidgins and their relation to second language pedagogy*. Droz, Geneva

Coulter K 1968 *Linguistic error analysis of the spoken English of two native Russians*. Unpublished MA Thesis, University of Washington

Crookes G 1990 The utterance and other basic units for second language discourse analysis. *Applied Linguistics* 11: 183–99

Crookes G 1991 Second language speech production research: a methodologically oriented review. *Studies in Second Language Acquisition* 13: 113–32

Culioli A and Desclés J P 1981 Systèmes de représentations linguistiques et métalinguistiques. *Collection ERA 642*, numéro spécial. Université de Paris VII

Das B (ed.) 1987 *Communication and learning in the classroom community*. SEAMEO Regional Language Centre, Singapore

Davies A 1991 *The native speaker*. Edinburgh University Press, Edinburgh

Davies A, Criper C and Howatt A (eds) 1984 *Interlanguage*. Edinburgh University Press, Edinburgh

Dechert H and Raupach M (eds) 1989 *Transfer in production*. Ablex, Englewood Cliffs, NJ

Demopolous W and Marras A (eds) 1986 *Language learning and concept acquisition*. Ablex, Norwood, NJ

De Villiers J and de Villiers P 1973 A cross-sectional study of the acquisition of grammatical morphemes in child speech. *Journal of Psycholinguistics* 2: 267–78

Dickerson W 1975 Interlanguage as a system of variable rules. *TESOL Quarterly* 9: 401–7

Dittmar N (ed.) 1992 Grammaticalisation in second language acquisition. Special issue, *Studies in Second Language Acquisition* 14, 3

Dulay H and Burt M 1974 Natural sequences in child second language acquisition. *Language Learning* 25: 37–53

Dulay H and Burt M 1975 Creative construction in second language learning and teaching. In Burt and Dulay 1975

Dulay H, Burt M, and Krashen S 1982 *Language two*. Oxford University Press, Oxford.

Duplessis J, Solin D and White L 1987 UG or not UG, that is the question: a reply to Clahsen and Muysken. *Second Language Research*, 6: 56–75

Dušková L 1969 Sources of error in foreign language learning. *International Review of Applied Linguistics* 7: 11–36

Eckman F 1977 Markedness and the contrastive analysis hypothesis. *Language Learning* 27: 315–30

Ellis R 1984 Can syntax be taught?: a study of the effects of formal instruction on the acquisition of WH-questions by children. *Applied Linguistics* 52: 138–55

Ellis R 1985 *Understanding second language acquisition*. Oxford University Press, Oxford

Ellis R 1987 *Second language acquisition in context*. Prentice-Hall, London

Ellis R 1988 The effects of linguistic environment on the second language acquisition of grammatical rules. *Applied Linguistics* 9: 257–74

Ellis R 1989 Sources of intra-learner variability in language use and their relationship to second language acquisition. In Gass *et al.* 1989a

Ellis R 1990 *Instructed Second Language Acquisition*. Blackwell, Oxford

Ellis R 1991 Grammaticality judgements and second language acquisition. *Studies in Second Language Acquisition* 13: 161–86

Ellis R 1991 *Second language acquisition and language pedagogy*. Multilingual Matters, Clevedon

Emonds J E 1976 *A transformational approach to English syntax, root, structure-preserving and local transformations*. Academic Press, New York

Eubank L (ed.) 1991 *Point counterpoint*. Benjamins, Amsterdam

Faerch C and Kasper G 1986 The cognitive dimension of language transfer. In Kellerman and Sharwood Smith 1986

Felix S 1981 The effect of formal instruction on second language acquisition. *Language Learning*, 31: 87–112

Felix S 1984 Maturational aspects of Universal Grammar. In Davies *et al.* 1984

Felix S 1985 More evidence on competing cognitive systems. *Second Language Research* 1: 47–72

Felix S and de Hahn A 1985 Natural processes in classroom second language learning. *Applied Linguistics* 6: 223–38

Felix S and Wode H (eds) 1983 *Language acquisition at the crossroads*. Narr, Tübingen

Ferguson C and Slobin D (eds) 1973 *Studies of child language development*. Holt, Rinehart and Winston, New York

Fisiak J (ed.) 1985 *Contrastive Linguistics: Prospects and Problems*. Mouton, The Hague, pp. 409–18

Fletcher P and Garman M (eds) 1986 *Language Acquisition* (2nd edn). Cambridge University Press, Cambridge

Flynn S 1986 *A parameter-setting model of second language acquisition*. Reidel, Dordrecht

Flynn S and O'Neil W (eds) 1988 *Linguistic theory and second language acquisition*, Reidel, Dordrecht

Fodor J 1983: *Modularity of mind*. MIT Press, Cambridge, Mass

Fodor J and Pylyshyn Z 1988 Connectionism and cognitive architecture: a critical analysis. *Cognition*, 28: 3–71

Foster S 1985 *Taking a modular approach to universals of language acquisition*. Paper presented at SLRF, Los Angeles, February

Frazier L 1986 The mapping between grammar and processor. In Gopnik and Gopnik 1986

Fromkin V A 1973a The non-anomalous nature of anomalous utterances. In Fromkin 1973b

Fromkin V A 1973b *Speech errors as linguistic evidence*. Mouton, The Hague

Gass S 1979 Language transfer and language universals. *Language Learning* 29: 327–44

Gass S 1983 Language transfer and universal grammatical relations. In Gass and Selinker 1983

Gass S (ed.) 1987 *Second language acquisition: a linguistic perspective*. Cambridge University Press, Cambridge

Gass S and Madden C (eds) 1985 *Input in second language acquisition*. Newbury House, Rowley, Mass.

Gass S and Selinker L (eds) 1983 *Language transfer in language learning*. Newbury House, Rowley, Mass.

Gass S, Madden C, Preston D and Selinker L 1989a *Variation in second language acquisition: psycholinguistic issues*. Multilingual Matters, Clevedon

Gass S, Madden C, Preston D and Selinker L 1989b *Variation in second language acquisition: discourse and pragmatics*. Multilingual Matters, Clevedon

Gasser M 1990 Connectionism and universals of SLA. *Studies in Second Language Acquisition* 12: 179–99

Gazdar G, Klein E, Pullum G and Sag I 1985 *Generalized phrase structure grammar*. Harvard, Cambridge, Mass.

George HV 1972 *Common errors in language learning*. Newbury House, Rowley, Mass.

Giacomi A and Véronique D 1986 *Acquisition d'une language étrangère: perspectives et recherches*. Université de Provence, Aix-en-Provence

Givon T 1979 From discourse to syntax: grammar as a processing strategy. In T. Givon (ed.) *Discourse and Syntax*. Academic Press, New York, pp. 81–111

Givon T 1984 Universals of discourse structure and second language acquisition. In Rutherford 1984

Goodluck H 1986 Language acquisition and linguistic theory. In Fletcher and Garman 1986

Gopnik I and Gopnik M (eds) 1986 *From models to modules*. Ablex Norwood, NJ.

Greenbaum S (ed.) 1977 *Acceptability in linguistics*. Mouton, The Hague

Greenbaum S and Quirk R 1970 *Elicitation experiments in English: linguistic studies in use and attitudes*. Longman, London

Greenberg 1974 *Language universals: a historical and analytic overview*. Mouton, The Hague

Gregg K 1984 Krashen's monitor and Occam's razor. *Applied Linguistics* 5: 79–100

Gregg K 1988 Epistemology without knowledge: Schwartz on Chomsky, Fodor and Krashen. *Second Language Research* 4: 66–80

Gregg K 1990 The variable competence model of second language acquisition and why it isn't. *Applied Linguistics*, 11: 364–83

Grimshaw J B 1979 Complement and the lexicon. *Linguistic Inquiry* **10**: 279–329

Hakuta K 1974 Prefabricated patterns and the emergence of structure in second language acquisition *Language Learning* **24**: 287–98

Hakuta K 1976 A case study of a Japanese child learning English as a second language. *Language Learning* **26**: 325–51

Halliday M A K 1975 *Learning how to mean: explorations in the development of language.* Arnold, London

Halliday M A K 1978 *Language as a social semiotic.* Arnold, London

Hammarberg B 1988 *Studien zur phonologie des zweisprachenerwerbs.* Almquist and Wiksell, Stockholm

Hatch E (ed.) 1978 *Second language acquisition: a book of readings.* Newbury House, Rowley, Mass.

Hatch E 1979 Apply with caution. *Studies in Second Language Acquisition* **2**: 123–43

Hatch E and Farhady H 1982 *Research design and statistics for applied linguistics.* Newbury House, Rowley, Mass.

Hatch E and Lazaraton A 1991 *Design and statistics for applied linguistics.* Newbury House, Rowley, Mass.

Hawkins J 1983 *Word order universals.* Academic Press, New York

Hawkins J 1987 Implicational universals as predictors of change. *Linguistics* **25**: 453–73

Hayes J R (ed.) 1970 *Cognition and the development of language.* Wiley, New York

Hilles S 1986 Interlanguage and the pro-drop parameter. *Second Language Research* **2**: 33–52

Hornstein N and Lightfoot D (eds) 1982a *Explanations in linguistics: the logical problem of language acquisition.* Longman, London

Hornstein N and Lightfoot D 1982b Introduction. In Hornstein and Lightfoot 1982a

Huebner T 1983 *A longitudinal analysis of the acquisition of English.* Karoma Press, Ann Arbor

Huebner T 1985 System and variability in interlanguage syntax. *Language Learning* **35**:141–64

Hulstijn J 1987 Onset and development of grammatical features. Two approaches to acquisition orders. Paper given at Interlanguage Conference, Trobe University, Melbourne

Hulstijn J 1990 A comparison between the information-processing and the analysis/control approaches to language learning. *Applied Linguistics* **11**: 30–45

Hyltenstam K 1977 Implicational patterns in interlanguage syntax variation. *Language Learning* **27**: 383–411

Hyltenstam K and Obler L (eds) 1988 *Bilingualism across the lifespan.* Cambridge University Press, Cambridge

Hyltenstam K and Pienemann M (eds) 1985 *Modelling and assessing second language acquisition.* Multilingual Matters, Clevedon

Hymes D 1972 On communicative competence. In Pride and Holmes 1972
Ingram D 1989 *First language acquisition*. Cambridge University Press, Cambridge
Ioup G and Weinberger S H (eds) 1987 *Interlanguage phonology*. Newbury House, Cambridge, Mass.
Jackendoff R 1987 *Consciousness and the computational mind*. MIT Press, Cambridge, Mass.
Jakobson R 1968 *Child language, aphasia and phonological universals*. Mouton, The Hague
James A 1986 Phonic transfer and phonological expectations: some theoretical and methodological issues. In Kellerman and Sharwood Smith 1986
James A and Leather J (eds) 1986 *Sound patterns in second language acquisition*. Foris, Dordrecht
Johnston M 1987 Second language acquisition research in the Adult Migrant Education Program. In Johnston and Pienemann 1987
Johnston M and Pienemann M (eds) 1987 *Second language acquisition: a classroom perspective*. NSW Adult Migrant Education Service
Jordens P 1977 Rules, grammatical intuitions and strategies in foreign language learning. *Interlanguage Studies Bulletin* 2 : 5–76
Jordens P 1986 Production rules in interlanguage: evidence from case errors in L2 German. In Kellerman and Sharwood Smith 1986
Karmiloff-Smith A 1979 *A functional approach to child language*. Cambridge University Press, Cambridge
Karmiloff-Smith A 1986 Stage/structure versus phase/process in modelling linguistic and cognitive development. In Levin 1986
Kaspar G 1985 Repair in foreign language teaching. *Studies in Second Language Acquisition* 7: 200–15
Kasper G and Dahl M 1991 Research methods in interlanguage pragmatics. *Studies in Second Language Acquisition* 13: 215–48
Kean M-L 1984 On the relation between grammatical markedness and L2 markedness and 'typological approaches'. *Interlanguage Studies Bulletin* 8: 5–23
Kean M-L 1986 Core issues in transfer. In Kellerman and Sharwood Smith 1986
Kean M-L 1989 The relation between linguistic theory and second language acquisition: a biological perspective. In Pankhurst *et al.* 1989
Keenan E and Comrie B 1977 Noun phrase accessibility and universal grammar. *Linguistic Inquiry* 8: 63–99
Kellerman E 1977 Towards a characterization of the strategy of transfer in second language learning. *Interlanguage Studies Bulletin* 2: 58–145
Kellerman E 1978 Transfer and non-transfer: where we are now. *Studies in Second Language Acquisition*. 2: 37–57
Kellerman E 1979 The problem with difficulty. *Interlanguage Studies Bulletin* 4: 27–48

Kellerman E 1984 The empirical evidence for the influence of L1 on interlanguage. In Davies *et al.* 1984

Kellerman E 1985 If at first you do succeed. In Gass and Madden 1985

Kellerman E 1987 *Aspects of transferability in second language acquisition.* Unpublished PhD Dissertation, Catholic University of Nijmegen

Kellerman E and Sharwood Smith M (eds) 1986 *Crosslinguistic influence in second language acquisition.* Pergamon, Oxford

Klein W 1986 *Second language acquisition.* Cambridge University Press, Cambridge

Klima E and Bellugi U 1966 Syntactic regularities in the speech of children. In Lyons and Wales 1966

Kohn K 1982 Beyond output: the analysis of interlanguage output. *Studies in Second Language Acquisition* 4: 137–52

Kohn K 1986 The analysis of transfer. In Kellerman and Sharwood Smith 1986

Krashen S 1976 Formal and informal linguistic environments in language acquisition and language learning. *TESOL Quarterly* 10: 157–68

Krashen S 1982 *Principles and practice in second language learning and acquisition.* Pergamon, Oxford

Krashen S 1983 Newmark's 'Ignorance Hypothesis' and current second language acquisition theory. In Gass and Selinker 1983

Krashen S 1985 *The input hypothesis: issues and implications.* Longman, Londons

Krashen S and Terrell T 1983 *The natural method.* Alemany Press, Hayward, CA.

Krashen S, Butler J, Birnbaum R and Roberston J 1978 Two studies in language acquisition and language learning. *ITL: Review of Applied Linguistics* 39–40: 73–92

Labov W 1970 The study of language in its social context. *Studium Generale* 23: 30–87

Lachman R, Lachman J and Butterfield E 1979 *Cognitive psychology and information processing.* Erlbaum, Hillsdale

Lado R 1967 *Linguistics across cultures.* University of Michigan, Ann Arbor

Lambert W 1966 *Observations on first language acquisition and second language learning.* Mimeo

Laver J 1970 The production of speech. In Lyons 1970

Lawler J and Selinker L 1969 On paradoxes, rules and research in second language learning. *Language Learning* 11: 27–45

Lenneberg E 1972 *Biological foundations of language.* Wiley, New York

Lesser R and Milroy L 1993 *Linguistics and Aphasia.* Longman, London

Levelt W J M 1989 *Speaking.* MIT Press, Cambridge, Mass.

Levenston E 1971 Second language vocabulary acquisition: issues and problems. *Interlanguage Studies Bulletin* 4: 147–80

Levenston E and Blum S 1978 Discourse completion as a technique for studying lexical features of interlanguage. *Working Papers in Bilingualism* **15**: 13–21

Levin I (ed.) 1986 *Stage and structure: reopening the debate.* Ablex, Norwood, NJ

Lewis M M 1936/51 *Infant speech: a study of the beginnings of language.* Harcourt Brace, New York (1st edition published in 1936)

Liceras J 1986 *Linguistic theory and second language acquisition: the Spanish non-native grammar of English speakers.* Narr, Tübingen

Lightbown P 1983 Acquiring L2 English in Quebec classrooms. In Felix and Wode 1983

Lightbown P 1985 Input and acquisition for second language learners in and out of classrooms. *Applied Linguistics* **6**: 263–273

Lightbown P and Spada N 1990 Focus on form and corrective feedback in communicative language teaching: effects on second language learning. *Studies in Second Language Acquisition* **12**, 4: 429–48

Littlewood W 1984 *Foreign and second language learning.* Cambridge University Press, Cambridge

Lococo V M 1976 A comparision of three methods for the collection of L2 data: free composition, translation and picture description. *Working Papers on Bilingualism* **8**: 59–86

Long M 1985 Input and second language acquisition theory. In Gass and Madden 1985

Long M and Larsen-Freeman D 1991 *Second language acquisition research.* Longman, London

Luelsdorff P 1987 The abstractness hypothesis and morphemic spelling. *Second Language Research* **3**: 76–87

Luhan M, Minaya L and Sankoff D 1981 *Implicational universals as predictors of word order acquisition.* Paper given at the Mikwaukee–Wisconsin Conference on Language Contact 1981

Lyons J (ed.) 1970 *New horizons in linguistics.* Penguin, Harmondsworth

Lyons J and Wales R 1966 *Psycholinguistic Papers.* Edinburgh University Press, Edinburgh

Macedo D 1986 The role of core grammar in pidgin development. *Language Learning* **36**: 65–75

Mager RF 1961 On the sequencing of instructional content. *Psychological Reports* 1961: 404–12

Mazurkewich I 1984 The acquisition of the dative alternation by second language learners and linguistic theory. *Language Learning* **34**: 91–110

McClelland J and Rumelhart D (eds) 1986 *Parallel distributed processing: explorations in the microstructure of cognition. Vol. 1: Foundations. Vol. 2: Psychological and biological models.* MIT Press, Cambridge, Mass.

McLaughlin B 1978 The Monitor Model: some methodological considerations. *Language Learning* **28**: 309–32

McLaughlin B 1987 *Theories of second language learning.* Arnold, London

McLaughlin B 1990 Restructuring. *Applied Linguistics* **11**: 13–128

McLaughlin B, Rossman T and McLeod B 1983 Second language learning: an information processing perspective. *Language Learning* **30**: 331–50

McNeill D 1970 *The acquisition of language.* Harper and Row, New York

Meara P 1984 The study of lexis in interlanguage. In Davies *et al.* 1984

Meisel J, Clahsen H and Pienemann M 1981 On determining developmental stages in natural second language. *Studies in Second Language Acquisition* **3**: 104–35

Naiman N 1974 The use of elicited imitation in second language acquisition research. *Working Papers in Bilingualism* **2**: 1–37

Naro A 1978 The study of the origins of pidginization. *Language* **54**: 314–47

Nattinger J R and DeCarrioco J S 1992 *Lexical phrases and language teaching* Oxford University Press, Oxford

Nemser W 1971 Approximative systems of foreign language learners. *International Journal of Applied Linguistics* **92**:115–23

Neufeld G 1980 Towards and theory of language learning ability. *Language Learning* **29**: 227–41

Newmeyer F 1983 *Grammatical theory: its limits and possibilities.* University of Chicago Press, Chicago

Newmeyer F 1987 The current convergence in linguistic theory: some implications for second language research. *Second Language Research* **3**, 1: 1–19

Nunan D 1992 *Research methods in applied linguistics.* Cambridge University Press, Cambridge

Odlin T 1989 *Language transfer.* Cambridge University Press, Cambridge

O'Malley J M and Chamot A U 1989 *Learning strategies in second language acquisition.* Cambridge University Press, Cambridge

Olshtain E 1983 Sociocultural competence and language transfer: the case of apology. In Gass and Selinker 1983

Palmer H 1922 *The principles of language study.* Reprinted in 1964, Oxford University Press, Oxford

Pankhurst J, Sharwood Smith M and Van Buren P (eds) 1989 *Learnability and second languages.* Foris, Dordrecht

Parrish B 1987 A new look at methodologies in the story of article acquisition for learners of ESL. *Language Learning* **37**, 361–84

Peck S and Hatch E 1978. In Hatch 1978

Pica T 1985 The selective impact of classroom instruction on second language acquisition. *Applied Linguistics* **6**: 214–22

Pienemann M 1984 Psychological constraints on the teachability of language. *Studies in Second Language Acquisition* **6**: 186–214 (reproduced in Rutherford and Sharwood Smith 1988)

Pienemann M 1985 Learnability and syllabus construction. In Hyltenstam and Pienemann 1985

Pienemann M 1987a *Determining the influence of instruction on L2 speech processing.* Unpublished Ms, University of Sydney

Pienemann M 1987b *Analyzing language acquisition data with a micro-computer: COLLIAN*. Ms, University of Sydney and Universitat Duisburg

Pienemann M 1991 Report: *COALA*, a computational system for interlanguage analysis. *Second Language Research* 8: 59–92

Pienemann M 1992 Paper presented at the Second EUROSLA Conference, University of Jyväskylä

Pinker S 1979 Formal models of language learning. *Cognition* 7: 217–83

Pinker S 1984 *Language learnability and language development*. MIT Press, Cambridge, Mass.

Pinker S 1986 Productivity and conservatism in language acquisition. In Demopolous and Marras 1986

Pollock J-Y 1990 Linguistique, biologie ou psychologie: la linguistique, peut elle se définir comme science cognitive? *Recherches Linguistiques de Vincennes* 19: 107–26

Poulisse N, Bongaerts T and Kellerman E 1984 On the use of compensatory strategies in second language performance. *Interlanguage Studies Bulletin* 2: 58–145

Pride J and Holmes J (eds) 1972 *Sociolinguistics*. Penguin, Harmondsworth

Radford A 1990 *Syntactic theory and the acquisition of child syntax*. Blackwell, Oxford

Ravem R 1974 The development of *wh*-questions in first and second language learners. In Richards 1974

Richards J (ed.) 1974 *Error analysis perspectives on second language acquisition*. Longman, London

Ringbom H 1986 Crosslinguistic influences and the foreign language learning process. In Kellerman and Sharwood Smith 1986

Ritchie W (ed.) 1978 *Second language acquisition research*. Academic Press, New York

Robson C 1973 *Experiment, design and statistics*. Penguin, Harmondsworth

Roeper T and Williams E (eds) 1986 *Parameters and linguistic theory*. Reidel, Dordrecht

Rumelhart D and Ortony 1977 The representation of knowledge in memory. In Anderson *et al.* 1977

Rumelhart D and McClelland J 1986 On learning the past tenses of English verbs. In McClelland and Rumelhart D 1986

Rutherford W (ed.) 1984 *Language universals and second language acquisition*. Benjamins, Amsterdam

Rutherford W 1987a *Second language grammar: learning and teaching*. Longman, London

Rutherford W 1987b *Learnability, SLA and explicit metalinguistic knowledge*. Unpublished Ms, University of Southern California, Los Angeles

Rutherford W 1989 Preemption and the learning of L2 grammars. *Studies in Second Language Acquisition* 11: 441–58

Rutherford W and Sharwood Smith M 1985 Consciousness-raising and universal grammar. *Applied Linguistics* 6: 274–82

Rutherford W and Sharwood Smith M 1988 *Grammar and language teaching.* Newbury House, Rowley, Mass.

Sachs J 1967 Recognition memory for syntactic and semantic aspects of connected discourse. *Perception and Psychophysics* 2: 437–42

Sajavaara K 1981 The nature of first language transfer: English as an L2 in a foreign language setting. Paper presented at the first Eunam workshop on second language acquisition, Lake Arrowhead, CA, August 1981

Sajavaara K 1986 Transfer and second language speech processing. In Kellerman and Sharwood Smith 1986

Schachter J 1976 An error in error analysis. *Language Learning* 24: 205–14

Schachter J 1988 Second language acquisition and its relationship to Universal Grammar. *Applied Linguistics* 9: 219–35

Schachter J 1990 On the issue of incompleteness in second language acquisition. *Second Language Research* 6: 94–124

Schachter J, Tyson A and Diffley F 1976 Learner intuitions of grammaticality. *Language Learning* 26: 67–76

Schachter J and Rutherford W 1979 Discourse function and language transfer *Working Papers on Bilingualism* 19: 3–12

Schmidt R 1977 Sociolinguistic variation and language transfer in phonology. *Working Papers on Bilingualism* 12: 79–75

Schneider W and Shiffrin R 1977 Controlled and automatic processing II: perceptual learning, automatic, attending, and a general theory. *Psychological Review* 84: 127–290

Schumann J 1978 The relationship of pidginization, creolization and decreolization to second language acquisition. *Language Learning* 8: 367–88

Schwartz B 1986 The epistemological status of second language acquisition. *Second Language Research* 2: 120–15

Seliger H 1978 Implications of a multiple critical period hypothesis for second language learning. In Ritchie 1978

Seliger H and Shohamy E 1989 *Second language research methods.* Oxford University Press, Oxford

Selinker L 1969 Language transfer. *General Linguistics* 9: 67–92

Selinker L 1972 Interlanguage. *International Review of Applied Linguistics* 10: 209–30

Selinker L 1992 *Rediscovering Interlanguage.* Longman, London

Selinker L and Douglas D 1989 Research methodology in contextually-based second language research. *Second Language Research* 5: 93–126

Selinker L and Lamendella J 1978 Two perspectives on fossilization in language learning. *Interlanguage Studies Bulletin* 3 :143–91

Selinker L, Swain M and Dumas G 1975 The interlanguage hypothesis extended to children. *Language Learning* 25: 139–53

Sharwood Smith M 1980 Consciousness-raising and the second language learner. *Applied Linguistics* 2: 159–68

Sharwood Smith M 1981 On interpreting language input. Paper presented at

224   Bibliography

the BAAL Seminar on Interpretative Strategies in Language Learning, September 1981, University of Lancaster

Sharwood Smith M 1983a On first language loss in the second language acquirer: problems of transfer. In Gass and Selinker 1983

Sharwood Smith M 1983b Crosslinguistic aspects of second language acquisition. *Applied Linguistics* 4: 192–31

Sharwood Smith M 1985a Preface. *Applied Linguistics* 63: 211–13

Sharwood Smith M 1985b Modularity in muddy waters: linguistic theory and second language developmental grammars. Paper presented at the Working Conference on Second Language Acquisition and Linguistic Theory, at MIT, Boston, October 1985

Sharwood Smith M 1985c Learnability and second language learning. In Fisiak 1985

Sharwood Smith M 1985d From input to intake: on argumentation in second language acquisition. In Gass and Madden 1985

Sharwood Smith M 1986 The competence/control model, crosslinguistic influence and the creation of new grammars. In Kellerman E, Sharwood Smith M (eds), pp. 10–20

Sharwood Smith M 1988 Imperfective versus Progressive. In Rutherford and Sharwood Smith 1988

Sharwood Smith M 1989 L2 acquisition: logical problems and empirical solutions. In Pankhurst *et al.* pp. 9–35

Sharwood Smith M 1989 On the role of linguistic theory in explanations of second language developmental grammars. In Flynn and O'Neil 1988

Sharwood Smith M 1991 Speaking to many minds: on the relevance of different types of language information for the L2 learner. *Second Language Research* 7: 118–32

Sharwood Smith 1992 The death of the Native Speaker. Unpublished paper presented at the EUROSLA Conference at the University of Jyväskylä, 1992

Sharwood Smith M 1993 Input enhancement in instructed second language acquisition: theoretical bases. *Studies in Second Language Acquisition* 15: 165–80

Sharwood Smith M and Kellerman E 1986 Introduction to Kellerman and Sharwood Smith 1986

Sharwood Smith M and Kellerman E 1989 U-shaped learning in second language learning. In Dechert and Raupach 1989

Skehan P 1991 Variability and language testing. In Ellis 1991

Slobin D 1973 Cognitive prerequisites for the development of grammar. In Ferguson and Slobin 1973

Slobin D 1980 The repeated path between transparency and opacity. In Bellugi and Studdert-Kennedy 1980

Sokolik M E and Smith M E 1992 Assignment of gender to French nouns in primary and secondary language: a connectionist model. *Second Language Research* 8: 39–58

Sorace A 1985 Metalinguistic knowledge and language use in acquisition-poor environments. *Applied Linguistics* **6**: 239–54

Sorace A 1986 Linguistic intuitions in interlanguage development: the problem of indeterminacy. In Pankhurst *et al.* 1989

Sorace A 1992 *Lexical conditions on syntactic knowledge: auxiliary selection in native and non-native grammars of Italian.* PhD Dissertation, University of Edinburgh

Sperber D and Wilson D 1986 *Relevance: communication and cognition.* Blackwell, Oxford

Stauble A 1978 The process of decreolization: a model for second language development. *Language Learning* **28**: 29–54

Strauss S (ed.) 1982 *U-shaped behavioral growth.* Academic Press, New York

Tang G 1990 *Second language acquisition of English interrogatives.* Unpublished PhD Dissertation, University of Edinburgh

Tarone E 1979 Interlanguage as chameleon. *Language Learning* **29**: 181–91

Tarone E 1983 On the variability of interlanguage systems. *Applied Linguistics* **4**: 43–163

Tarone E 1985 Variability in interlanguage use: a study of style-shifting in morphology and syntax. *Language Learning* **35**: 373–404

Tarone E 1988 *Variation in interlanguage.* Arnold, London

Taylor B 1975 Adult learning strategies and their pedagogical implications. *TESOL Quarterly* **9**: 391–9

Thomas J 1983 Cross-cultural pragmatic failure. *Applied Linguistics* **4**: 91–122

Tomlin S Russell 1990 Functionalism in second language acquisition. *Studies in Second Language Acquisition* **12**: 155–77

Traugott E 1977 Natural semantax and its role in the study of second language acquisition. In Corder and Roulet 1977

Trévise A 1986 Is it transferable, topicalisation? In Kellerman and Sharwood Smith 1986

Tyack D and Ingram D 1977 Children's production and comprehension of questions. *Journal of Child Language* **4**, 211–24

Van Baalen T 1983 Giving learners rules: a study into the effect of grammatical instruction with varying degrees of explicitness. *Interlanguage Studies Bulletin* **7**: 71–100

Van Buren P 1988 Some remarks on the subset principle in second language acquisition *Second Language Research* **41**: 33–40

Van Buren P and Sharwood Smith M 1985 The acquisition of preposition-stranding by second language learners and parametric variation. *Second Language Research* **1**: 18–46

Van der Sande, W and Opstal, C 1987 *Exploiting Dbase III; First steps towards an Interlanguage Dutch-English Computer Corpus.* Unpublished MA dissertation, Utrecht University, English Dept

Van Riemsdijk H and Williams E 1986 *Introduction to the theory of grammar.* MIT Press, Cambridge, Mass.

Wanner E and Gleitman L 1982 *Language acquisition: the state of the art.* Cambridge University Press, Cambridge

Wells G 1985 *Language development in the pre-school years.* Cambridge University Press, Cambridge

Wexler K and Manzini R 1986 Parameters and learnability in binding theory. In Roeper and Williams 1986

White L 1982 *Grammatical theory and language acquisition.* Foris, Dordrecht.

White L 1985 The pro-drop parameter in second language acquisition. *Language Learning 35*: 47–62

White L 1987 Against comprehensible input: the input hypothesis and the development of second language competence. In *Applied Linguistics* 8, 2: 95–110

White L 1990 *Universal grammar and second language acquisition.* Benjamins, Amsterdam

White L 1991a Adverbial placement in second language acquisition: some effects of positive and negative evidence in the classroom. *Second Language Research* 7: 133–161

White L 1991b Second language competence versus second language performance: UG or processing strategies?. In Eubank 1991

Wode H 1976 Some stages in the acquisition of questions by monolingual children. Reprinted in Wode 1983

Wode H 1978 Developmental sequences in naturalistic L2 acquisition. In Hatch 1978

Wode H (ed.) 1983 *Papers on language acquisition, language learning and language teaching.* Narr, Tübingen.

Zobl H 1978 The formal and developmental selectivity of L1 influence on L2 acquisition. *Language Learning 30*: 43–57

Zobl H 1984 The Wave Model of linguistic change and the naturalness of interlanguage. *Studies in Second Language Acquisition* 6: 160–85

Zobl H 1989 Configurationality and the subset principle: the acquisition of V1 by Japanese learners of English. In Pankhurst *et al.* 1989

Appendix: Standard research resources

There are obviously a number of different reasons for consulting various information resources, one of which would simply be to gain general knowledge of the field of second language acquisition studies. Another would be to find out what has been done in a particular aspect of SLA so that the researcher does not start on a given project in ignorance of work already done in that area. A scan through the last five years of relevant research journals would be a good starting point for either endeavour. General knowledge is best gained from journals by seeking out overview articles which are published from time to time.

Journals

The following journals may be described as mainline IL research resources:

Language Learning. University of Michigan. Ann Arbor, Michigan.
Studies in Second Language Acquisition [SSLA]. Cambridge University Press, Cambridge, United Kingdom
Second Language Research [SLR]. Edward Arnold/Hodder & Stoughton, Sevenoaks, United Kingdom

The first two also contain contributions of a more applied (teaching/classroom-testing) nature. Two further reputable applied journals that also contain some very relevant articles for IL researchers are:

Applied Linguistics. Oxford University Press, Oxford, United Kingdom
TESOL Quarterly. TESOL Publications, 1660 Cameron St, Alexandria, Virginia, United States

The *International Review of Applied Linguistics* (Julius Groos Verlag, Heidelberg, Germany) has occasionally published some important papers specifically on IL (e.g. Selinker 1972).
Language Acquisition (L. Erbaum, Hillsdale, New Jersey, United

States), which has just appeared, contains articles on both first and second language acquisition.

Further valuable sources of IL research at working paper level include three series, which have now stopped but which still represent a useful additional research resource, and an applied linguistics journal, produced by graduate students, which sometimes includes contributions of interest to SLA researchers:

> *Working Papers on Bilingualism* (28 numbers). Ontario Institute for Studies in Education, Toronto, Canada
>
> *Studies in Second Language Acquisition.* University of Indiana Press, Bloomington, Indiana. Forerunner of SSLA
>
> *Interlanguage Studies Bulletin* (8 volumes). English Department, University of Utrecht, The Netherlands. Forerunner of SLR
>
> *Issues in Applied Linguistics.* The Department of TESL and Applied Linguistics at the University of California, Los Angeles, United States.

A researcher into interlanguage should consult at the very least the previous 5 years of publications in the mainline journals mentioned above before embarking on a project. Use of abstract publications is also to be recommended, for example, *Language and Language Behaviour Abstracts* (LLBA) available in most large university libraries.

Finally, associations which include IL research, such as AILA (Association Internationale de la Linguistique Appliquée), or which are more directly concerned with second language research from many points of view but irrespective of practical application, such as EUROSLA (European Second Language Association: contact Vivian Cook, Department of Language and Linguistics, University of Essex, Colchester, United Kingdom) and PacSLRF (Pacific Second Language Research Forum: contact Manfred Pienemann, LARC, University of Sydney, Australia) publish their own bulletins containing notes, details of conferences and research facilities. AILA has its own affiliates in various countries around the world. The current AILA address is: David Singelton, Centre for Language Studies, Trinity College Dublin, Ireland.

Informal exchange

As in other disciplines, the most up-to-date work is circulated between active researchers well in advance of publication, and much of the current debate goes on via personal communications and bulletin-boards like SLART-L via electronic mail (email).

Index